TRAVELLER'S GUIDE TO CENTRAL AND SOUTHERN AFRICA

A complete travel companion to
Angola, Botswana, Burundi,
CAR, Congo, Lesotho, Malawi,
Mozambique, Namibia, Rwanda,
South Africa, Swaziland,
Zaire, Zambia and Zimbabwe

Seventh edition

TRAVELLER'S GUIDE
TO
CENTRAL AND SOUTHERN AFRICA

an IC publication

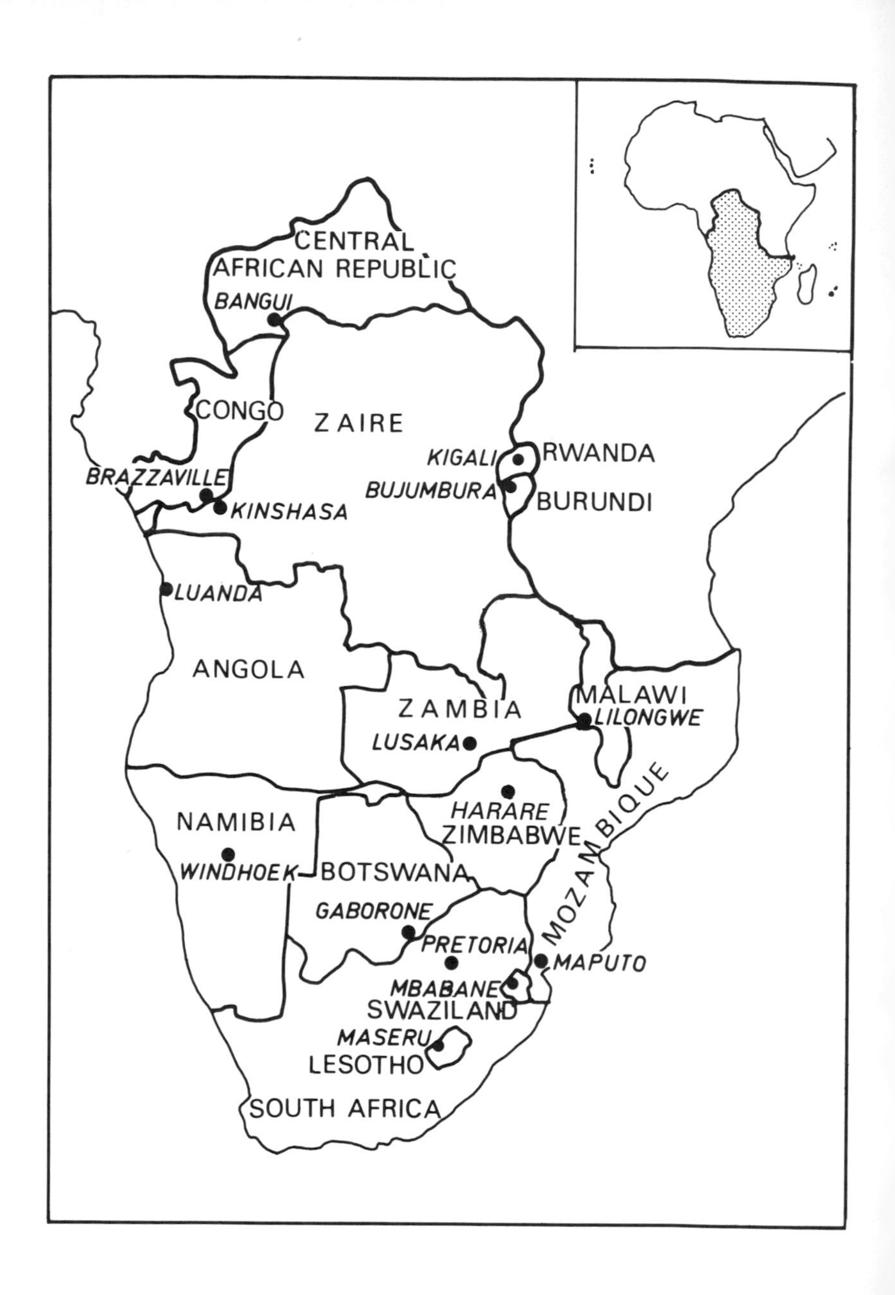
CENTRAL AFRICAN REPUBLIC
BANGUI
CONGO
ZAIRE
KIGALI
RWANDA
BUJUMBURA
BURUNDI
BRAZZAVILLE
KINSHASA
LUANDA
ANGOLA
ZAMBIA
MALAWI
LILONGWE
LUSAKA
MOZAMBIQUE
HARARE
ZIMBABWE
NAMIBIA
WINDHOEK
BOTSWANA
GABORONE
PRETORIA
MAPUTO
MBABANE
SWAZILAND
MASERU
LESOTHO
SOUTH AFRICA

Publisher Ahmed Afif Ben Yedder

Editor Alan Rake

Published by IC Publications Ltd
London Office P.O. Box 261
69 Great Queen Street, London WC2B 5BN
Telephone 01-404 4333
Cables Machrak London WC2
Telex 8811757
US Office. IC Publications Ltd
Room 1121, 122 East 42nd Street
New York, N.Y. 10168
Telephone (212) 867 5159
Telex 425442

US Edition published by Hunter Publishing Inc
300 Raritan Center Parkway
Edison, N.J. 08818

Typeset by RSB Typesetters
Bagshot Road
Worplesdon, Surrey

Printed by Page Bros (Norwich) Ltd.

Cover Photograph Alan Rake

Reprinted 1988
ISBN 0905268-55-5
ISSN 0144-7661
ISBN 1-55650-231-1 (US)
Hunter Publishing Inc US$13.95

Introduction and Acknowledgements

Africa is a volatile continent constantly on the move politically, socially and economically. Despite frequent communications and transport difficulties and escalating economic problems in many parts of Africa, the continent as a whole is receiving more visitors than ever before.

The urge to travel leads people further and further afield in search of exotic and remote destinations, and Africa has enough to offer every brand of traveller – mountains, forests, deserts, unspoilt beaches, abundant wildlife, historic sites, cultural festivals, excellent crafts and the attraction of many sophisticated cities.

The *Traveller's Guide to Central and Southern Africa* has been entirely revised and updated, under the editorial direction of Alan Rake, following the total sell-out of the sixth edition.

The *Traveller's Guide to Central and Southern Africa* is a companion volume to the *Traveller's Guide to East Africa,* the *Traveller's Guide to West Africa,* and the *Traveller's Guide to North Africa.* Readers familiar with the *Traveller's Guides to Africa* will recognise the format of these new regional guides which now provide an expanded coverage of each area in a handy pocket-size volume. The Traveller's Guides provide essential coverage of the history, economy and cultural life of the continent as well as offering a mass of practical up-to-date travel information and a hotel reference guide for each country. Our books are aimed at a wide variety of travellers – holidaymakers, businessmen, students, researchers and the independent traveller in search of adventure. We have included a number of background chapters on different aspects of each region which we hope will be of interest to all these categories.

For those who can find the money, the opportunity and especially the time, we hope this book will be an encouragement to see more of Africa, to explore beyond the beaten tourist tracks, to meet and make contact with the people and to come to some understanding of the rich cultural life that Africa offers.

Our thanks go to the many contributors who have assisted us in providing the latest travel information and especially to Roger Murray, Linda Van Buren, Dr Joseph Hanlon, Norman Sowerby and Trevor Grundy. The editor also wishes to acknowledge Roma Beaumont, Kathryn Hopkirk and Gordon Reynell who prepared all the maps included in this guide.

CONTENTS

Rainfall · Temperature

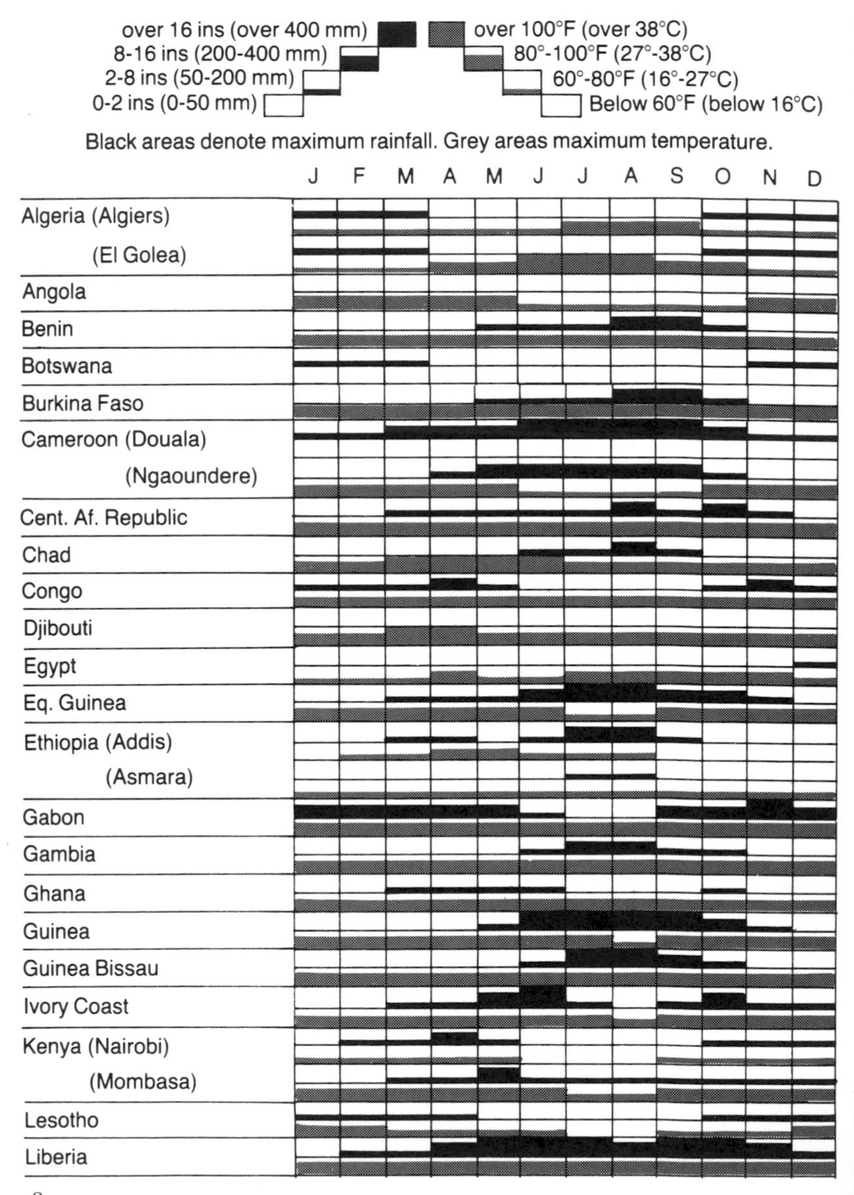

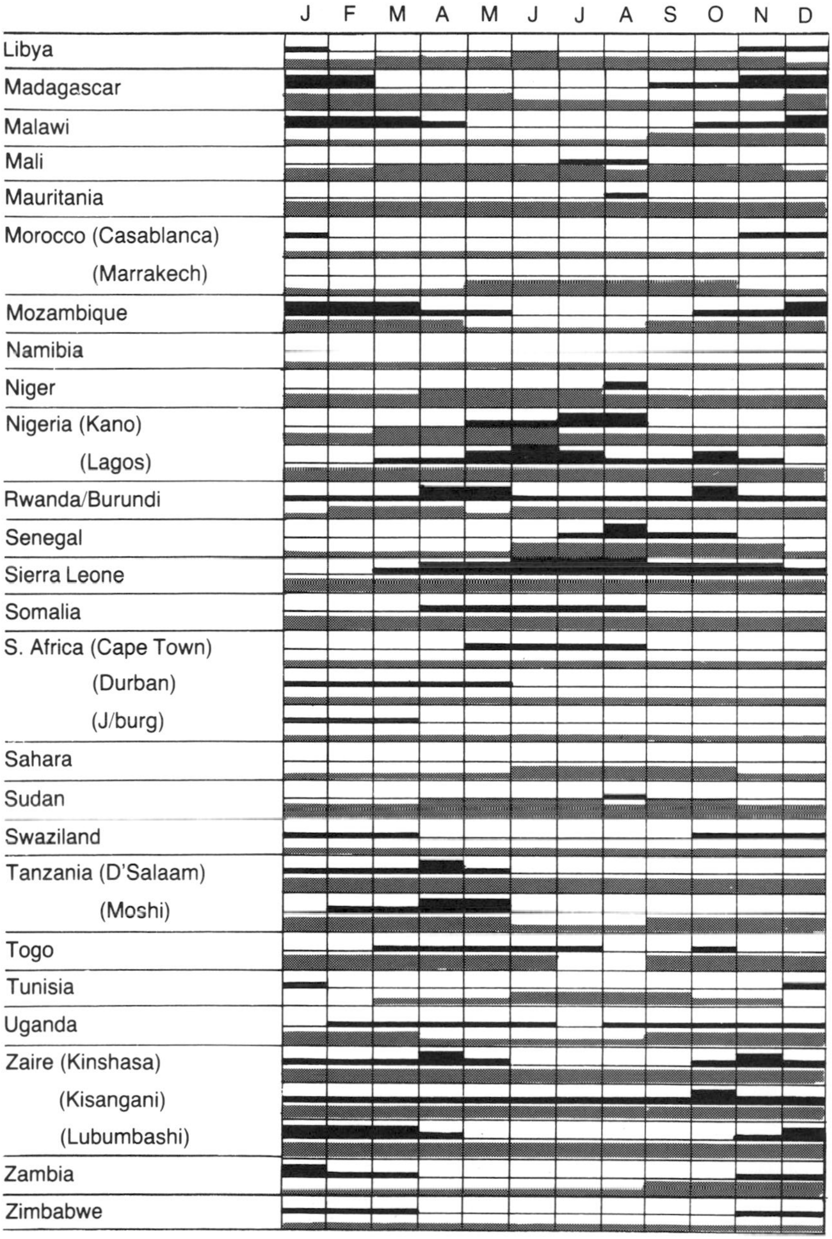

J F M A M J J A S O N D

Libya
Madagascar
Malawi
Mali
Mauritania
Morocco (Casablanca)
(Marrakech)
Mozambique
Namibia
Niger
Nigeria (Kano)
(Lagos)
Rwanda/Burundi
Senegal
Sierra Leone
Somalia
S. Africa (Cape Town)
(Durban)
(J/burg)
Sahara
Sudan
Swaziland
Tanzania (D'Salaam)
(Moshi)
Togo
Tunisia
Uganda
Zaire (Kinshasa)
(Kisangani)
(Lubumbashi)
Zambia
Zimbabwe

Currency Table

COUNTRY	CURRENCY	VALUE TO £1.00	VALUE TO $1.00
Angola	Kwanza	47.56	30.0
Botswana	Pula	3.28	2.07
Burundi	Burundi Franc	255.5	161.5
CAR	CFA Franc	527	337
Congo	CFA Franc	527	337
Lesotho	Maluti	4.3	2.7
Malawi	Kwacha	4.4	2.8
Mozambique	Metical	1150.7	727.6
Namibia	SA Rand	4.3	2.7
Rwanda	Rwanda Franc	131	83.0
South Africa	SA Rand	4.3	2.7
Swaziland	Lilangeni	4.3	2.7
Zaire	Zaire	600	379
Zambia	Kwacha	16.6	10.5
Zimbabwe	Zimbabwean Dollar	3.3	2.1

Exchange rates as of July 1986.

Do's and Don'ts

Whenever you enter or leave a country, you are likely to be required to fill out several forms – memorising your passport number and date of issue helps expedite these formalities. If you do not have a fixed address before you arrive, give the name of one of the big hotels or your embassy. Similarly when completing the 'occupation' section, don't announce yourself as a journalist or television researcher, if you could as easily be something less controversial. Don't get irritated with long bureaucratic procedures – it only makes things worse.

On arrival should your vaccination certificate not be in order, request that any injections required be provided by a qualified medical person.

If you intend travelling from one country to another by car, make sure you have 1) a triptyque or carnet de passage 2) a green card or other proof of insurance cover 3) licence plates with a national symbol 4) an international and/or national driver's licence. If you intend crossing the border in a taxi check that the driver and vehicle have all the proper documents. It is not possible to cross from one country to another in a hired car.

On the Subject of Money

Many countries request that visitors fill in currency declaration forms issued on arrival – it is obligatory to declare how much foreign currency you are bringing into the country and then note each time you exchange money or travellers cheques. The forms are then presented to customs officials on departure. Take this procedure seriously as you do not want to be accused of selling money on the black market. Don't be lured into black market currency deals – you often come off worst and the penalties are severe. On the other hand, on arrival or departure you may be approached by an official who suggests that your documents or baggage are not in order, but that a small cash handout may rectify the situation. Do not be intimidated into paying but ask to see the director of customs or immigration.

Besides banks, it is possible to exchange travellers cheques and currency at most airports and big hotels (although usually at a less favourable rate of exchange). Exchange only what money you think you may need on a daily basis so that you can avoid having to change back into foreign exchange or accumulate worthless notes. If travelling overland try and obtain a little of the currency of each country before you arrive if possible, as at some small border points there is nowhere to change money at all.

Always have your money and passport somewhere close to your body to protect them from pickpockets. A small pouch which you can hang around your neck or wear under your shirt strapped to your body is a good idea. If your passport or travellers cheques are lost or stolen, report this to the local police and to your embassy or consulate.

If you are forced to take a taxi from the airport to town because of lack of airport services, negotiate the price before you leave.

Enjoy Your Stay

Once in Africa it becomes useless to plan the details of your stay closely; throw away your watch and enjoy the unhurried tempo of life: 'African time' is the antithesis of Western clock watching and inflexible planning will only cause frustration. You may want to stay longer in one place or you may be invited to visit the local people in the country or to visit a local festival. Carefully made travel plans are especially bound to go awry. If you're flying from one country to another allow yourself a full day to include the likely chance of delays and lengthy arrival and departure formalities.

Arabic, English and French are probably the three most widely spoken languages in Africa, while Swahili is the first language for many millions in East Africa, but there is no real *lingua franca* in Central and Southern Africa. Wherever you are, the pleasure and response evoked from local people by using a few simple words and phrases in the indigenous language will amply repay the small effort involved. Learn at least how to greet people, to say please, thank you and goodbye.

Try to deviate from the beaten tourist track – you haven't really been to Africa unless you've experienced some rural life. A chance acquaintance with someone you meet, be it a student or taxidriver may bring you in contact with his family in the countryside. Don't miss the opportunity. It is in these areas that you are likely to enounter authentic dance, (rather than the

versions provided by local package tours) hear real traditional drumming and music and see genuine works of African arts and crafts.

If you are lucky enough to be invited into an African family remember that their ideas of correct behaviour may differ markedly from yours. Always show respect to the elders of the community or family; it is disrespectful to call old people by their first names. You should shake hands with everyone in the room when you are introduced even if you do not know them. Most rural Africans are poor, hospitality is of the utmost importance and reciprocity in gifts is part of the code. If you're invited to an African village or home bring along a few small items as gifts. As most of these people live largely outside the money economy, they value things according to their usefulness or novelty. A penknife or a cheap cigarette lighter and a few packs of cigarettes would always be welcome as would bottled drinks and fruit for the children. A polaroid camera is also popular – and overcomes the problem of the promised photographs never sent. Another way to repay hospitality is to do odd practical jobs or engine repairs; offer your services in the best way you can.

CLAUDIO MUNOZ

When you arrive in Africa don't photograph the airport, harbour, soldiers or anything which could be regarded as a military installation. This includes railways and bridges. Be polite and always ask before taking anyone's photograph. Sometimes the donation of an instant polaroid photo can overcome initial reluctance but it is also likely that a small fee will be requested for the privilege. Pay up or don't go ahead!

Be warned that in some countries the authorities do not welcome people who can be labelled 'hippies' and who are considered as Western degenerates. To avoid being harassed it costs little effort to keep one's hair relatively short and appearance tidy. Women or girls travelling alone should be quite safe if they do not wear provocative clothing. In many African countries there are also heavy penalties and strong hostility to the smoking of marijuana.

Don't walk alone after dark in unfrequented places in major cities. As in any big Western city it is dangerous. However, petty thieving from your room or vehicle is more likely than getting mugged, so take sensible precautions.

If you go to South Africa, remember you need a permit to visit areas off designated tourist routes, especially black townships or any of the Homelands. It is still an offence in many cases to use public amenities reserved for a different colour group.

Motoring

If you intend renting a car inspect your car thoroughly before you accept it. Check that it has proper documents, spare tyres (you will be driving on rough roads if you leave the city), tyre changing equipment, and a tool kit. Check the rental contract for responsibility for cost of repairs (especially broken windshields, common from flying stones), breakdown and towing, and accidents. Attempt to get this in writing. Remember that although driving is one of the best ways to see Africa, there are few good roads such as you may be used to, and distances are enormous. Always carry extra petrol in rural areas, petrol stations are few and far between. Drive carefully – there is a high accident rate in Africa. Don't be afraid to use your hooter on bends and in market areas where there are lots of pedestrians and when passing another vehicle. If you do have an accident, especially one involving a pedestrian, it is advisable to go immediately to the nearest police station. If you need repairs done to your vehicle negotiate the price before work begins.

If you are planning a long overland expedition by car – remember that Western commodities are imported and tend to be expensive so take plenty of basic supplies from home.

Desert Travel

Crossing the desert should not be attempted by hitchhikers. A four-wheel drive vehicle in good order is essential. Always carry spare parts, extra water, food and petrol, a first aid kit and a compass. Don't overload the vehicle. Desert travel should be in convoy with other vehicles. In the event of a breakdown or loss of direction, passengers should remain with the vehicle and inside the car during the heat of the day. Anyone seeing a parked car in the desert will stop, assuming you need help. It is advisable to give local authorities a precise route plan before setting out. This makes rescue easier in case of difficulties.

Stay Healthy

Don't swim, wash or even paddle in slow moving water; bilharzia, carried by small water-snails, is endemic throughout the continent. If you contract

CLAUDIO MUNOZ

dysentry make sure you seek treatment immediately; it is debilitating and can cause dehydration if left untreated. If you are far away from any big town, bush hospitals or mission stations will treat you.

More common stomach upsets can have several causes – change of routine, exposure to a different diet or the reaction to a new virus strain. However, attacks are frequently caused by food that has been improperly cooked or that has been cooked in unhygienic circumstances, or by impure water. Avoid foods that have been prepared in advance and left standing. Always use water purifying tablets outside major cities and try to wash fruit and vegetables in purified water. Don't eat salad unless you know it has been carefully washed. Even where fresh milk is available, it is not always advisable to drink it – drink powdered milk instead. Most of these stomach disorders can be cleared up with drugs.

Try and eat in reasonable restaurants when possible, although don't be extreme and be put off trying local foods or risk being impolite by being over-cautious if offered hospitality in some remote village. It would be a great shame to eat only uniform hotel food when there is often interesting African fare to be sampled. Each country has its own specialities.

It is very easy to forget how strong the sun is in Africa. Wear a hat and sunglasses, use a sunscreen (rather than a suntan) lotion or cream, and stay out of the sun during the hottest part of the day. Take time to acclimatise to very hot weather, drink plenty of liquids, take salt tablets and don't undertake any strenuous activities in the middle of the day.

Shopping

Haggling over prices in street markets is normal procedure and also in many shops where prices are not displayed. Bargaining is not bad manners – it is expected and it is a good idea to check prices on items in the shops and expect to do about 25-50% better by bargaining in the market. Your starting price should be about half of what you would be prepared to pay. Don't be rude or aggressive or feel pressed for time. You do not do the trader down, bargaining is a ritual requiring patience and a sense of humour. Get into the spirit of it!

If you do not enjoy haggling in market places, purchasing directly from a craftsman probably ensures the best quality and price. Many shops will arrange to ship things home for you but these will be at a higher price. Some shops allow discount for purchases made with travellers cheques or foreign exchange.

When you buy hides, skin goods and ivory in shops, you should be given Game Department Certificates. Customs require these when you leave – this is to discourage the sale of poached skins. Be cautious when game skins are offered at low prices – they may not have been properly cured. Traditional sculpture survives but you will have difficulty finding genuine 'antiques' and should be prepared to pay the expected price as well as meeting government export licence requirements. When you purchase gold jewellery, ivory or rugs look for government seals or stamps endorsing the quality.

In the Game Parks

Firearms and domestic pets are prohibited in parks. Warning notices must be taken seriously. When notices warn you to stay in your car don't get out because you feel no animals are near; nature camouflages them well. Don't make the mistake of thinking of small, furry looking wild animals as pets. Always travel slowly, otherwise you frighten the animals and see very little. Leave radios behind in the camp and don't blow your horn. If watching animals which are close by, don't talk loudly. Remember that the big cats can be the most dangerous animals because they can see you in the car – all the other animals see only the vehicle. Don't hop out of the car just to get that perfect shot from 10ft nearer! A very powerful telescopic lens is essential for good wild life photography. Carry a good pair of binoculars with you and a good reference book describing the wildlife you are likely to meet.

Taking Photographs

Most modern cameras and film are capable of giving excellent results in countries where the lighting is harsh. Remember to make allowances in your exposure meter readings for bright sand or strongly lit white buildings. Try close-up photographs in the shade and use the bright reflected light from the ground or a wall to give soft lighting.

Suggested films: Kodachrome 64 (slides), Ektachrome II (colour prints), Tri-x (black and white).

Suggested lenses: telephoto, wide-angle (for single lens reflex cameras). A powerful telephoto is essential for photographing wildlife.

Suggested filters: (either gel or glass) polarised against reflected glare, or daylight filter for a cool tone. Both give richer sky colour and cut glare.

It is also very important to remember if you have an automatic electric exposure meter or flash gun to carry spare batteries. **Never** leave a camera or film in bright sunlight for long. Film is stored best over long periods in a cool refrigerator if this is possible, but wait until it has reached room temperature before opening the containers.

Ready, Steady, Go

Planning a trip to Africa can be time consuming and harassing; there seem to be endless travel arrangements to make, documents to put in order, and mental notes of essential items to remember. We have compiled a brief list of ideas and reminders to make all this simpler. The idea of a trip to Africa need not be a daunting one – but taking sensible precautions and opening yourself to experiencing a totally different culture, Africa is probably one of the most exciting and enjoyable places to travel anywhere in the world.

Before You Go

A good introduction for your forthcoming trip to Africa is to read something about the country. An introduction to the history, culture, people, food specialities, wildlife and major places of interest can only make your trip more enjoyable and provide you with a much richer experience.

Novels written by indigenous authors often give added valuable insight into the people and their cultural and social values. Similarly, if you are interested in music, it is also worth listening to some of the many available recordings of traditional and urban African music before you leave. This may help you to choose from the many performances available.

Planning your trip: Even if you do not like an organised schedule when travelling, there are certain things which if thought about beforehand are always an advantage. Book your charter flight well in advance and pay attention to dates when off-season rates go into effect for both hotels and charter flights – a week one way or the other can make all the difference to your budget. It is also worthwhile considering local holidays and festivals which may make travelling or accommodation difficult and expensive. On the other hand, you may like to plan a trip around a major cultural or religious festival of a particular region. Even if you are naturally opposed to dealing with travel agents, using one frequently saves time, aggravation and even money (remember there is no charge for booking and reservation services) as some of the package deals available may incorporate your basic requirements and cost less than individual arrangements. It is worthwhile shopping around for an agent – ask friends or colleagues who have had similar travel needs to recommend one who has done a good job for them.

When planning travel in South and Central Africa, you will find a copy of Thomas Cook Overseas Timetable invaluable. The timetable, which is published every two months, gives schedules and sample fares for all the major rail, bus and ferry services throughout the area. You can get a copy by post from Thomas Cook Ltd., (Dept. TPO/ICH), PO Box 36, Peterborough, England, PE3 6SB for £4.50 and in North America from Forsyth Travel Library, PO. Box 2975, Shawnee Mission KS 66201, USA, for US$14.95.

Make sure you have good maps

Documents: Once you have purchased your ticket check to see that dates, times, and destinations have been filled in correctly. Always telephone to confirm international flights. Ensure that your passport is still valid and that you have all the necessary inoculations (see under Entry Regulations in the General Information section of this guide for the requirements of each individual country). Check that the latter have been correctly noted in your International Certificate of Vaccination. Make sure you obtain visas for countries where these are required well in advance. Although it is possible to get visas while travelling, it is infinitely more time consuming and troublesome.

When ordering traveller's cheques, it is advisable to request small denominations so that you can reduce the quantity of local currencies that you carry around with you. The rates for changing money back into foreign exchange are highly unfavourable, and most African currencies are worthless outside their own borders. For entry into some countries the authorities may demand evidence that you can pay your way out again. Sufficient proof of this is a valid return air ticket, a guarantee from your bank at home, or a guarantee from your national embassy.

If you intend hiring a car it is essential to obtain an International Driving Licence before leaving home. This is valid for one year and is recognised by most African countries. Your national driving licence is also useful for identification if you lose your passport or misplace your international licence. If you belong to an automobile association, your membership card often facilitates service from partner clubs abroad.

Student identity cards allow students special rates on trains and buses, and access to hostels and university dormitories. As a card-carrying member of the YMCA/YWCA, similar facilities would be available.

Check with the embassy, consulate or national airline of the country concerned if there are specific regulations or licences required for special equipment or sporting gear (guns, aqualungs etc) you plan to take with you.

Try to get introductions to family or business friends before you leave for Africa. One introduction usually leads to others and it is only by interacting with the people who live there that you will really get to know a country.

It is always advisable to take out health insurance. There are schemes available which are specifically for travel. Health insurance can also be part of a wider insurance policy which would cover loss of baggage, and insure against flight cancellation. The latter is advisable if flying with a charter organisation, while baggage insurance is essential, as the enormous distances and frequent air traffic confusion increase the chance of baggage loss.

Medical Precautions: Always pack a small supply of medicines to take along (see check list). Although in most big towns medical facilities are available, you may be in a remote area where medical help and drugs are difficult or impossible to obtain. The two main common health problems likely to be incurred in Africa are either some form of stomach upset or gastro-enteritis or sunburn and, even more severely, sunstroke. (See Do's and Dont's for how best to avoid these complaints once you get there). Before you leave ask your doctor to prescribe the correct drug to combat diarrhoea or stomach upsets. Ask for a sulphur based drug.

Besides the other statutory inoculations it is advisable to have a gamma-globulin injection as it helps to prevent hepatitis and other infections. If you intend travelling in any region host to malaria, it is important to remember to begin a course of malaria prophylactics two weeks before you leave, and to continue taking them once you arrive. If you suffer chronic ill-health, contact your doctor before you leave, take an adequate supply of necessary medication and any prescriptions that may need to be made up. It is a good idea to carry a card stating your blood type and any chronic health problems or allergy to drugs which you may have. If your visit is likely to be a long one, have a dental checkup before you leave. Travellers who wear glasses or contact lenses should carry an extra pair and the prescription.

For a small charge, it is possible to secure a booklet listing all participating English-speaking doctors, clinics and hospitals around the world from the International Association of Medical Assistance to Travellers (IAMAT). The booklet includes a climate chart and inoculation information for every country in the world. Write to IAMAT, 350 5th Ave, Room 5620, New York, NY 10001, USA.

What to Pack

Clothing: For African travel you always need far less than you think, and this really depends on what you intend doing rather than where you are going – ie will you be on safari, mountain-climbing, lying on the beach or staying in sophisticated hotels? Rather than be fashionable you should concentrate on good boots for hiking and the other basics not easily obtainable in Africa.

It is easy to rinse out cotton shirts and skirts as they dry very quickly, and always remember that cotton is preferable to synthetic clothing, as the latter combined with the heat can irritate your skin. Even in summer a sweater or jacket is often necessary in the evening. Be able to dress in layers so that with the dramatic temperature changes that frequently occur, clothing can be added or removed as required. Cotton T shirts and light woollen sweaters are ideal for this. Long sleeved cotton shirts and long socks are also useful to keep arms and legs covered while walking in the bush. A widebrimmed hat and sunglasses are essential, while a pair of canvas shoes for walking on coral are also useful. Coral is very sharp and can cause cuts to turn septic.

Consult the Climate and What to Wear sections in the individual country chapters in this guide for more specific advice and for what rules of dress apply for visitors to Muslim countries or countries with conservative outlooks.

Miscellaneous items: If you intend travelling overland at all, or exploring beyond the usual tourist areas, make sure you have good maps with you. These may be easier to obtain before you leave; the most accurate and exhaustive of the available maps of Africa are the Michelin 'red' maps (No. 153 for North and West Africa, 154 for North East Africa and 155 for Central, East and Southern Africa including Madagascar). These maps contain details which include distances, road surfaces, seasonal road conditions, accommodation, rainfall and temperature. If you intend going on a safari or you are particularly interested in wildlife, it is certainly worth investing in a good pair of binoculars and buying a good book on the birds, animals, flora and fauna of Africa.

Wear something suitable for the occasion

CLAUDIO MUNOZ

It is worth carrying as much of your own film with you as possible – colour and black and white film are available in Africa, but both are expensive. A lens hood is a good idea, while an ultraviolet filter cuts down the effects of glare.

Take a few empty plastic bags with you – they may be scarce in out of the way places and are always useful to keep things wet, dry or dustproof, eg to protect your camera lens from sand and dust, or to keep a spare set of clothes dry when hiking etc.

Leave large heavy beach towels at home and buy one of the all purpose strips of local coloured cloth or fabric found all over Africa. This can be used as a beach towel and has the advantage of not collecting grains of sand and of drying very quickly. It also doubles as a wrap around skirt, a picnic cloth and a ground sheet. It is very light and folds away to nothing, and makes an attractive table cloth when you get home!

All countries have their cheap hotels but if you intend staying out of towns, it is best to have rudimentary camping equipment – a lightweight warm sleeping bag should be sufficient, while a small lightweight tent and light mosquito net for the tropics would also be useful.

Checklist

Documents

valid passport
visas where required
international certificate of vaccination
air tickets
extra passport photographs
traveller's cheques
international driving licence
student identification card
youth hostel card
credit cards (Diner's Club, American Express)
card carrying address and telephone number of whom to contact in the case of an emergency
any necessary prescriptions for glasses or medication
insurance certificates

Medical kit

salt tablets
vitamin tablets
sun protection cream
antiseptic cream
plasters
crepe bandage
mosquito repellent
malaria preventives
water sterilising tablets
aspirin
antibiotic ointment
anti-histamine cream/tablets (this relieves allergies to grasses, pollens and dust and gives relief from bites and skin rashes)
an anti-diarrhoeal drug (Sulphur based, if possible)
disposable syringes (for use off the beaten track – re-usable needles not properly disinfected can cause hepatitis)

Miscellaneous items

needle and thread
candles
torch
batteries
penknife
bottle opener
plastic bags
binoculars
maps
reference books
camera
film
sleeping bag
lightweight plastic mac

Southern Africa Holiday

by R. Murray; revised by L. Van Buren

Southern Africa is now well-established on the global tourist map. In addition to South Africa, long-established as a tourist destination for West Europeans, Botswana, Swaziland, Zambia and Zimbabwe have made great strides in developing their tourism industries.

For the average holidaymaker from Europe or North America, a visit to Southern Africa is still likely to be a once-off special treat rather than a regular yearly habit. A large number of package tours are now available, and tour operators will risk running experimental destinations, although by and large South Africa even now remains the Southern African destination with the most packages on offer.

Although the first-time visitor may sometimes be surprised by the all-too-familiar modernity of many of the region's major cities, the region really does provide what the travel brochures claim: majestic, remote scenery; one of the world's finest concentrations of wildlife, which can be enjoyed in the many spectacular national parks; friendly peoples with rich and varied cultures; and generally unspoilt environments, beaches and sun. In the brochures wildlife tends to be stressed at the expense of reference to the indigenous people. But Livingstone, a name frequently invoked by safari operators, undertook his explorations to meet the people of Africa as much as to unravel the continent's geographical mysteries. And many of today's travellers do the same.

Today any style of holiday can be arranged – an independent holiday with a hired car or using public transport, an overland camping holiday by truck or minibus, or the most luxurious package safari catering to the visitor's every need. It is also possible to arrange holidays locally while on business in a capital city such as Lusaka or Harare, by using the resources of the tourist board. Air fares are the highest proportion of the cost for a trip, and this can be reduced by carefully shopping around for the best bargains.

Some young, adventurous travellers with more time than money at their disposal choose to see Africa by taking an overland trip across the continent. These expeditions are operated by several companies and traditionally traverse the entire African continent from north to south in trips taking anywhere from 18 to 33 weeks.

Beginning in 1985, however, these trips have taken on a different pattern. Most operators offer an overland London-Nairobi trip (some going down the Nile, others going via West Africa) with an optional Johannesburg add-on of four to six weeks. This change is because of a marked fall-off in demand for travel into South Africa. Some of the operators offer an optional add-on out of Nairobi that takes in Victoria Falls and ends in Harare.

A typical overland trip consists of 15-25 people below the age of 40 (most

Elephant — one of the region's many wildlife attractions

are in their early 20s) travelling in a self-contained converted Bedford or Mercedes truck. Most companies operate between four and 20 departures a year from London, with about one-third of the trips going beyond Nairobi into Southern Africa. A single trip might go from the UK through France, Spain, Morocco, Algeria, Niger, Burkina Faso, Togo, Nigeria, Cameroon, the Central African Republic, Zaire, Rwanda and Tanzania to Kenya, taking 14-26 weeks. The add-on would then go from Kenya through Tanzania, Zambia (or Malaŵi), Zimbabwe and Botswana and possibly to South Africa, taking another four to six weeks.

The cost varies greatly, and so does the level of service provided, so readers are advised to shop carefully. Quoted prices do not include the one-way air fare back to the point of origin nor the compulsory contribution to a "food kitty"; the company sets a fixed amount for the food-kitty contribution, usually between £12 and £20 per week, and it is payable in advance. A five-month London-Johannesburg trip can cost as little as £995 or as much as £2,445, excluding the kitty and the air fare back. The Nairobi-Johannesburg trip is offered separately by some operators for anywhere from £390 for four weeks to £640 for six weeks.

Needless to say, this type of tourism means little in revenue to the string of host countries.

In 1986, the following UK-based companies operated overland trips to Southern Africa (inclusion in this list does not constitute an endorsement by *Traveller's Guide to Central and Southern Africa*):

Overland operator	Address (all are in the UK)	Telephone number	Telex number
Africa Access Ltd	Hill House The Avenue Lewes East Sussex BN7 1QS	(0273) 471539	878159 AFRICA G
Dragoman	10 Riverside Framlingham Suffolk IP13 9AG	(0728) 724184	987129 SHARET G
Encounter Overland Ltd	267 Old Brompton Rd London SW5	01-370 6845	916654 ENCOLD G
Exodus Expeditions	All Saints' Passage 100 Wandsworth High St London SW18	01-870 0151	8951700 EXODUS G
Guerba Expeditions Ltd	101 Eden Vale Rd Westbury Wiltshire BA13 3QG	(0373) 826611	449831 GUERBA G
Long Haul Expeditions	Tamar Travel Agents Ltd 56 Bohun Grove East Barnet Hertfordshire EN4 8UB	01-440 1582	none
Tracks Africa Ltd	The Flots Brookland Romney Marsh Kent TN29 9TG	(06794) 343	966115 TRACKS G

High Street travel agencies unfortunately are not particularly well acquainted with Africa in general, and few can offer an inquirer much help beyond reaching for a few tour operators' worldwide brochures. The number of agencies specialising in African travel is growing, however, and for readers' convenience, a few are listed below:

AUSTRALIA
Bench International Pty Ltd, 70 Erskine St, Sydney, NSW 2000
Phone 290 2877, Toll free phone (008) 22 1451, Telex 22152

Bench International Travel (Vic) Pty Ltd, 7th Floor, 50 Queen St, Melbourne, Vic 3000
Phone 62 7733, Telex 39694

London Court Travel, Suite 22, London Ct., Perth, W Aus 6000
Phone 325 4830

CANADA

Goway Travel Ltd, 40 Wellington St E, Toronto, Ont M5E IC7
Phone (416) 863 0799, Telex 06219621

Goway Travel Ltd, Suite 716, 402 W Pender St, Vancouver, BC V6B 1T9
Phone (604) 687 4004, Telex 0451170

NETHERLANDS

A Reisen BV, Postbus 100, NL-3640 AC Mijdrecht
Phone 02979-3952, Telex 16083

NEW ZEALAND

The Flight & Travel Centre, 28 Lorne St, PO Box 6232, Auckland
Phone 31-756, Telex 60255

UNITED KINGDOM

Trail Finders Ltd, 42-48 Earl's Court Rd, London W8 6EJ
Phone 01-937 9631, Telex 919670 TRAVEL G

Wexas International, 45 Brompton Rd, London SW3 1DE
Phone 01-589 3315

UNITED STATES

Seven Continents Travel, 1287 First Ave, New York, NY 10032

Safariworld, 1500 Wilson Blvd, Arlington, VA 22209

Creative Travel Concepts, 2572 Lennox Rd, Atlanta, GA 30324

Beverly Hills Travel, 10704 S Western Ave, Chicago, IL 60643

Bryan International Travel Service, Suite 210, 421 Powell St, San Francisco, CA 94102

The Travel Company, 9763 W Pico Blvd, Los Angeles, CA 90035

African Holidays, Inc PO Box 36959, Tucson, AZ 85740

WEST GERMANY

Deutschland Explorer, Hüttenstrasse 17, D-4000 Düsseldorf 1
Phone 0211 379064, Telex 8582930

The following country-by-country survey of holiday possibilities in Southern Africa identifies those destinations and types of holiday that might not immediately come to mind as well as the more popular travel packages operated by the major tour firms.

Botswana

Botswana's major tourist attraction has always been the northern region, where the Okavango and Chobe rivers create one of the most extraordinary wildlife areas in the world. This unique combination of swamp and savannah brings together in a single compact area almost the entire range of Africa's wildlife. Like neighbouring Zambia and Zimbabwe, Botswana offers some of the most exciting safari holidays in Southern Africa.

For the adventurous traveller who enjoys the predictability of African desert travel and is prepared to make adequate preparations, a visit to Botswana is best done independently. However, it is also possible to join an organised expedition from London, Johannesburg or Maun, which is the stopping-off centre for the Okavango Delta. If you intend hiring a vehicle yourself, a four-wheel-drive vehicle or Land Rover is recommended. These can be hired in Gaborone, Maun or Kasane and from the major lodges in the Delta. Petrol, water and spares are scarce and must be carried, while a spade and strips of steel mesh wire will prove useful when bogged down in soft sand. It is important to check the road conditions and fuel availability before you set off. It is possible to hire a driver with local knowledge of the area from the principal lodges in the Delta, although this facility is frequently available only to residents of the lodge where a vehicle is hired. If you intend travelling by public transport, remember that away from main roads, the 'buses' into remote areas are usually 10-ton lorries, sometimes without seating or food. The trip from Francistown to Maun used to take more than 18 hours.

The Okavango Delta, Moremi Wildlife Reserve and Chobe National Park offer a real taste of tropical Africa. This is all the more impressive, even staggering, after the long drive through the sandy wastes of the northern Kalahari desert. There are several lodges and tented camps in and around the Delta. Boats and guides can be hired at most of the river lodges, and it is possible to spend several days camping deep in the swamps. Mosquito netting and repellent are essential.

Keen birdwatchers are advised to visit the many pans in the Delta and in the Moremi Reserve. The best place to watch and photograph birds is at Lake Ngami. When it has water, it is possible to see vast flocks of flamingo, white pelicans, waders and waterfowl. There are no lodges or camping facilities at the lake, but there are camping spots along the Nxhabe River.

The wilderness of Chobe is a must for avid game watchers and those independent travellers who enjoy camping rough in an unspoilt environment. Camping is permitted in prescribed areas; tickets for camping are available at the gate. Some of the roads are passable by an ordinary car, but it is advisable to use a four-wheel-drive vehicle. It is possible to drive through the park from Maun to Kasane, but permission must be obtained from the Department of Wildlife and National Parks in Maun. The best time to visit the Okavango Delta and the Chobe National Park is between June and October.

It is well worthwhile venturing into the steep Tsodilo Hills to visit the remarkable Bushmen paintings there (by air or by Land Rover from Maun). There is a Monuments Officer at the Mbukushu village at the foot of the largest hill, and visitors should report to him. He will organise one of the excellent Bushmen guides to accompany visitors to the paintings.

Hunting in Botswana is carefully controlled, and infringements of the government's Fauna Conservation Act may result in heavy penalties. Visitors to Botswana may hunt only under the auspices of a recognised safari company. Hunting safaris should be booked up to a year in advance. Most companies handle everything including plane charter, immigration and customs clearance, accommodation, provisions, licensed guides, hunting licences and final treatment of game.

Photographic safaris are becoming increasingly popular in Botswana as hunting becomes more difficult. The Okavango Delta and Chobe are the main regions for trips of this nature. There are several safari companies which specialise in photo-safaris combined with game viewing. These can often be individually tailored to the client's requirements. Some operators collect their clients in Johannesburg and drive them from South Africa through Botswana (9-22 days), while others offer short visits (4-9 days) where visitors are flown to a base camp in the bush.

The following companies specialise in photographic safaris: Safari South, PO Box 40, Maun, tel (026) 211, telex 2484 BD; Gametrackers Safaris, Rileys Hotel, PO Box 100, Maun, tel (026) 204, telex 2481 BD; and Holiday Safaris, Private Bag 0016, Gaborone, tel (031) 53970, telex 2433 BD.

It is no longer necessary to go through South Africa to get to Botswana. *Worktown International* (Prince Frederick House, 37 Maddox St, London W1R 9LD, tel 01-629 8319, telex 27887 WORKIN G), which now incorporates *MTS Safaris*, offers a 12-day camping safari flying via Harare for £1,170 fully inclusive, with 14 departures a year. Worktown also offers a ten-day camping, lodge and hotel safari, also via Harare, for £1,230 fully inclusive, with 11 departures a year. *Twickers World* (22 Church St, Twickenham, Middlesex TW1 3NW, tel 01-892 7606, telex 25780 TWICKTRAV G) offers a 20-day Botswana trip that includes Zimbabwe and Zambia, and flying via Lusaka, for £2,470.

Lesotho

Lesotho contrasts strongly with the delicate beauty of Swaziland or the vast sandy plains of Botswana. It is an extremely mountainous country, infertile, but with a stark and vivid beauty of its own. Lesotho draws tourists (mainly South African) to its Royal Casino in Maseru, the capital, but its real attraction is for those who enjoy hiking and pony trekking in the solitude of the mountains. The remote Maluti Mountains provide dramatic scenery, and it is possible to walk for days without meeting another soul.

Those undertaking a long hike into the mountains should be fairly fit and seasoned hikers. The climate is very erratic, changing from blistering sunshine to hail and snowstorms in very short time. Campers need warm clothing and should guard against frost-bite. There are several hikes which can be recommended, some more strenuous than others.

A good ten-day hike is from Mokhotlong across the mountains to Butha-Buthe. There are several very pleasant lodges situated in spectacular mountain scenery along the road. Mokhotlong, 'the place of the bald ibis', is the most remote town in Lesotho. The best way to get there is from South Africa over the Sani Pass, but only four-wheel-drive vehicles will do. The highest mountain in Southern Africa, Thabana Ntlenyana, can be seen from the Black Mountain Pass *en route*. Land Rover, pony or mountaineering excursions to the mountain can be arranged from the Mountaineers Chalet at Sani Top, just inside Lesotho.

Another good hike or pony-trek is to the Maletsunyane Falls, one of the highest falls in Africa. Horses can be hired from Semonkona, 64 km away, or one can fly from Maseru. Accommodation is available at Fraser's Rest Camp. A five-day trip on horseback can also be made to Ketane Falls, in a remote part of the mountains. The falls are accessible from Qaba Lodge just south of Malealea, or from Maletsunyane, a 30 km hike or pony trek away.

There are numerous hikes to attempt in the Qachasnek area, which has lovely mountain scenery and breathtaking views. As there are few roads which are more than tracks, it is possible to be flown to various airstrips deep in the mountains and then to hike out again. Possibly the most beautiful part to explore is the Sehlabathebe National Park, which covers approximately 6,000 ha and lies in the Tsoelike Valley, west of the Drakensburg.

For a list of government rest houses and lodges suitable as bases for hikers and pony trekkers, write to Lesotho Tourism Office, PO Box 527, Maseru.

Apart from being a hiker's paradise, Lesotho also offers excellent fishing, the best trout fishing being at Semonkong, Oxbow and Moyeni. Licences are obtainable at one of the sub-accountancy offices in the district headquarters towns. The trout season is from September 1 until May 31. Fishing for black bass or blue gill is open all year round.

As there is snow on the higher ground for part of the winter, Lesotho is virtually the only place in Southern Africa which boasts a skiing resort. Oxbow Lodge high in the Maluti mountains offers skiing facilities between June and August. Transport is available from Butha-Buthe, but it is advisable to book well in advance. Write to Holiday Inn, Maseru or New Oxbow Lodge, PO Box 14, Leribe.

Lesotho attracts mainly South African visitors, and numerous short package holidays are available from South Africa. The country is regarded as an extension destination from South Africa by most European tour operators. However, if you wish to travel to Lesotho independently, it is easy to catch a connecting flight to Maseru from Johannesburg, from Maputo in Mozambique, or from Manzini in Swaziland, or to make your way there independently from Johannesburg. As well as regular flights to Maseru from

Johannesburg, it is possible to take the train on a branch line of the Bloemfontein-Durban line or to hire a car in South Africa.

Malaŵi

A hilly and compact country, Malaŵi's main attraction is without doubt its unique combination of mountains, lake and altitude which produces an extremely appealing holiday environment. The adventurous visitor can explore the lake by self-hired car, and pleasant accommodation is available at very reasonable prices in the form of government rest houses which dot the country.

One of the best ways to see the whole lake region, especially the extremely beautiful northern end, is to take a round trip on the *m/v Ilala* steamer. This is not a tourist vessel but a working lake steamer, and it is the principal means of transport up and down the lake for the people who live en route. It is "for the intrepid few", cautions *Tempo Travel*, but when the trip is sold to the right market they "absolutely adore it". The trips takes a week and leaves Monkey Bay on a Friday, arriving at Chilumba the following Monday. Trips can be arranged through Tempo Travel Ltd, 337 Bowes Rd, London N11 1BA. 361 1131, telex 298781 TEMPO G.

Although somewhat overshadowed by the major wildlife reserves of East and Southern Africa, Malaŵi has three national parks – one in each of the country's three regions – which are delightfully unspoilt and have a wide variety of game. A few days in the game parks followed by some time spent relaxing on the lakeshore would provide an excellent holiday combination.

For the more energetic there is Mount Mulanje to be climbed. The 3,000m forest massif lies between Blantyre and the Mozambique border and can be approached by car, but the ascent is possible only on foot. Several forestry huts offer accommodation.

Namibia

Despite the unresolved political situation in Namibia, which remains under *de facto* South African political control, the country's breathtaking desert/mountain scenery and abundant wildlife are proving attractive to visitors. Some hotels, restaurants and other facilites in the Namibian capital, Windhoek, have now been designated as multiracial.

The country's only direct air links are via *South Africa Airways*, which does have one direct route to Europe, a Windhoek-Frankfurt flight. Otherwise, travellers can take the airline of their choice to Johannesburg and change.

Tours can be booked through *Abercrombie & Kent, Tempo, Afro Ventures, Springbok Atlas* and others, all operating directly through South Africa.

Pony-trekking in the Eastern Highlands, Zimbabwe

South Africa

South Africa's share of the market among African tourism destinations has been steadily declining, and most of its loss is Kenya's gain. In 1986, most of the global tour operators still handled bookings for South Africa but have focussed on Kenya in the brochures. *Kuoni* Worldwide, for example features nine pages for Kenya and four for South Africa and offers 45 tour types for Kenya to South Africa's 12. More importantly, *Kuoni* alone sends some 6,000 tourists a year to Kenya but scarcely 1,000 to South Africa.

South Africa gears its appeal to the more affluent European tourists seeking beaches and scenery. The diversity of the country's natural attractions is reflected in a comprehensive selection of brochures distributed to travel agents. This includes a detailed accommodation guide, a tourist map, up-to-date general travel information and background information on the history of gold and diamond mining, game tours, steam railway tours and the Cape wine route.

The UK occupies the first place in South Africa's tourist arrivals followed by West Germany. Most tour operators offer very flexible packages including multi-centre and self-drive holidays, taking in Kruger National Park. The following major operators in the UK offer holidays in South Africa: *Kuoni, Musgrove & Watson (Castlemarine Tours), Speedbird, Tempo Travel* and *Tradewinds. Rankin Kuhn* has dropped South Africa and now concentrates on Kenya, Mauritius and the Seychelles as its main African holiday destinations. *Abercrombie & Kent* and *Peltours* offer 2-4 week packages to South Africa as well, often tailor-made to the client's requirements. *Afro-Ventures* runs camping safaris.

Swaziland

Visitors to Swaziland still come primarily from South Africa, attracted by the country's high rolling hills, waterfalls and forests – the country is often referred to as Africa's Switzerland – as well as by the casinos in the Ezulwini valley, the main tourist centre. The unspoilt, ruggedly beautiful countryside makes Swaziland ideal for hiking and camping, while there are fairly good roads and comfortable hotels throughout the country for anyone wishing to explore by car. The Pigg's Peak area, the countryside around Hlatikulu and the Mhlambanyati forest area are recommended for hikers.

Tour operators have traditionally treated Swaziland as a convenient extension destination from South Africa, but it is also possible to fly to the country's international airport, Manzini, directly from Nairobi, Harare, Lusaka, Dar es Salaam, Maputo and Gaborone, thanks to a concerted effort to link the landlocked country to its fellow members of the Southern African Development Co-ordination Conference (SADCC).

Kuoni has a 15-day South African Grand Tour with one night at the Royal Swazi Inn. *Tempo Travel* also offer one night in Swaziland as part of a larger 21-day tour of South Africa.

Many Swaziland packages are operated from Johannesburg and Durban, details of which can be obtained from the Southern Africa Regional Tourism Council in South Africa, or from the South Africa Tourist Corporation overseas.

In 1986, Swaziland had no formal tourist office of its own in Europe and none of the major tour operators outside South Africa have separated tours to Swaziland.

Zambia

Zambia's prolific wildlife, the spectacular Victoria Falls which it shares with Zimbabwe, its generally agreeable climate and its location at the heart of Central Africa are major tourist assets. Although landlocked, direct communications with the outside world are excellent. Zambia retains an indefinable African essence, and its local culture is unspoilt by the effects of tourism.

Tourism has developed more slowly than in Kenya, Malaŵi and Zimbabwe. The Zambian National Tourist Board conducts an energetic campaign to attract more tourists. But the government is aware of the dangers of over-commercialisation, which it rightly feels would destroy much of the country's appeal. Services and accommodation are being continually upgraded.

A number of hotels of international standard have been built in the capital, Lusaka, which frequently plays host to meetings of UN agencies and other international and pan-African bodies, while the national parks, lodges and safari camps are carefully located to blend in with their environment. Zambia's wildlife is amongst the finest in Africa; the attractions include the Luangwa Valley, a vast tree-filled park with over 100 species of animals and 400 species of birds a 75-minute flight away from Lusaka, and the even larger Kafue National Park, extending for 22,500 sq kms and less than an hour's flying time westward from the capital. Sumbu National Park is on the southern tip of Lake Tanganyika, and lakeshore resorts are at Kasamba and Nkamba Bays. Livingstone, on the border with Zimbabwe, provides easy access to Victoria Falls.

Walking safaris to see the wildlife at first hand are amongst the packages offered by *Twickers World*, which has five Zambia tours. A 15-day safari based on the Luangwa Valley costs £1,534, while a 17-day whitewater and wildlife safari combines a seven-day river trip on the Zambezi with five days' big game-viewing in the Luangwa at £1,799. Tours can also be combined with visits to other countries: a Zambia/Zimbabwe safari (15 days) costs £1,690, a 17-day Zambia/Malaŵi tour costs £1,599 and a 20-day tour of Zambia Botswana and Zimbabwe costs £2,470.

Guerba offers a three-week expedition entirely in Zambia using a Zambian four-wheel-drive Bedford expedition truck for £1,020 including the London-Lusaka-London flight or £450 land only in 1986 (£1,070 and £470 respectively after 1 July 1987). *Worktown International* operate a 12-day safari using *Zambia Airways* and taking in Lusaka, Mfuwe and Victoria Falls for £1,580.

An independent holiday could be cheaper than a package if viewing wildlife at close quarters is not the main object for the visit. Reasonably priced safari tours can be booked with the National Tourist Board for several days in either Kafue or Luangwa as well as visits to Livingstone and Victoria Falls. The Maramba Cultural Centre in Livingstone is a place to see traditional dance and costume, while a number of colourful cultural ceremonies are still in Zambia, of which the most famous is the Kuomboka of the Lozi people in the Western province, performed every spring when the Zambezi bursts its banks. Details and information about visiting these ceremonies and brochures on all aspects of visiting the country can be obtained from the Zambia National Tourist Board at 163 Piccadilly, London W1V 9DE, tel. 493 1188.

Zimbabwe

Zimbabwe is a beautiful and unspoilt part of Africa, well-suited to the independent travellers so long as he checks with the authorities to assure that he is not wandering into any areas where his security is at risk. Although six tourists were kidnapped in 1982, no similar incidences have occurred since then.

With a discount or Apex fare to Harare, local travel should not be too expensive once in Zimbabwe (especially if you consider taking a tent). The awe-inspiring sight of Victoria Falls ("Mosi-oa-Tunya", or "Smoke That Thunders") is the country's most famous attraction, but it can be enjoyed away from the hubbub of international tourism. Small fishing chalets or tented accommodation along the Zambezi upstream from the falls can be hired cheaply at the water's edge, providing excellent fishing and game viewing as well as tranquillity.

Hikers, pony trekkers and fishing enthusiasts will find solitude and space to enjoy the quiet beauty of the Eastern Highlands, while a visit to some of the less developed and more remote national parks Gona re Zhou, Kazuma Pan, Chimanimani and Mana Pools) will allow you to experience living truly in the wild. It is well worth writing to the Department of National Parks and Wildlife for a list and description of all the parks that can be visited. The hunting safari industry is rigidly controlled by the department, and only limited quotas of hunters are permitted entry into the country.

Near Masvingo are the unique, well-preserved 700-year-old stone ruins of Great Zimbabwe, built by an African people in the 13th-15th centuries AD. In the museum at the site are ancient green soapstone carvings of birds, one of which appears on the country's flag and coins.

Zimbabwe aims primarily to attract the more affluent visitors from Europe, the UK and the US, although travellers of more modest means are in no sense discouraged. However, the National Tourist Board has rejected mass tourism, and the packages available tend to be of the more expensive variety, although all are of a high quality. The stress is on specialist holidays for the wildlife enthusiast at the upper end of the market.

Twickers World has a 15-day Zimbabwe Overland Safari for £1,875 and an 18-day Zimbabwe Wildlife & Bird Life Safari for £1,395. *Worktown International* has a 14-day tour to Harare, Kariba, Mana Pools and Hwange National Park for £1,395. *Tempo Travel* offers a 17-day tour to Kariba, Bumi Hills, Hwange, Victoria Falls and Chobe (Botswana) for £1,498 and a 17-day tour through the Zambezi gorge and to the Matusadona Mountains, the Chizarira Hills, Victoria Falls and Chobe (Botswana) for £1,522 – £1,569 depending on the season. They also offer a one-day (£109) and a seven-day (£887) rafting trip down the Zambezi.

There are numerous local packages on offer from Harare for visitors who are not planning a package directly from Europe or elsewhere. *Capricorn Trails* operates luxury tented camps in the more remote national parks and will tailor safaris to individual requirements. For more details write to *Capricorn Trails* PO Box 4722, Harare, tel. 791268. And Air Zimbabwe's *Flame Lily Tours* offer the Harare visitor several choices for short excursions to scenic spots in all parts of the country, from Victoria Falls to the Eastern Highlands, at a moderate price. Bookings can be made through *Air Zimbabwe* in London, tel 01-491 0009.

Explorers of Africa

by Caroline Oliver

A map of Africa prepared in Egypt under Ptolomaic patronage in about the second century A.D., shows a long south coast line, not many degrees south of the equator. The southern third of the vast continent was not known to exist. In the tenth century an Arab traveller, Al Masudi of Baghdad, recorded a voyage in the Indian Ocean, and mentioned lands inhabited by Zanj, or black peoples on the East African coast. He also wrote of the busy port of Sofala from which gold and ivory were exported. This was in modern Mozambique. In the fourteenth century another distinguished Arab traveller, Ibn Battuta, reached Kilwa island, off the coast of present-day Tanzania. He also heard of the fame of Sofala, and of its export of gold. This was reputed to come from a great empire in the interior, almost certainly the Monomotapa empire, the capital of which moved about, but was always called Zimbabwe. It was not until half way through the second millennium A.D. that an outline map of the whole of Africa could be drawn with any accuracy.

In the fifteenth century, Prince Henry the Navigator of Portugal set in train a great series of voyages by Portuguese seamen. Year by year they sailed further and further down the coasts of West Africa. At the furthest point of each voyage, a pillar was placed on some conspicuous promontory, in proof of the distance gained. Bartholomew Diaz was the first to see the southernmost tip of Africa, which he named the Cape of Storms in 1487. He landed near modern-day Port Elizabeth before returning to Portugal. Eleven years later, Vasco da Gama placed a pillar at Malindi on the coast of what is now Kenya. A considerable part of his journey had overlapped with those of Arab explorers and merchants, and the outline of the whole African continent could then be drawn on the map of the world. Da Gama went on to India, and during his voyage he gave the Cape of Storms its present name, the Cape of Good Hope.

Though both missionaries and merchants visited the coastal areas over the next three hundred years, there was a little penetration of inland Southern Africa. The Dutch established a settlement at the Cape in 1652, mainly as a revictualling station for ships en route for the East Indies. They did explore the hinterland to some extent, but it was not until the arrival of the great Scottish medical missionary, David Livingstone, in the mid-nineteenth century, that any extensive knowledge of the interior was gained. Based at Kuruman in northern Cape Province, he crossed the Kalahari Desert to Lake Ngami. Hearing of the success of this journey, the Royal Geographical Society offered him financial backing for further exploration. He went northward and westward to the Upper Zambezi valley, crossed Angola, and reached the west coast at Luanda. Then he turned back on his tracks, and crossed the whole continent from west to east, eventually arriving at

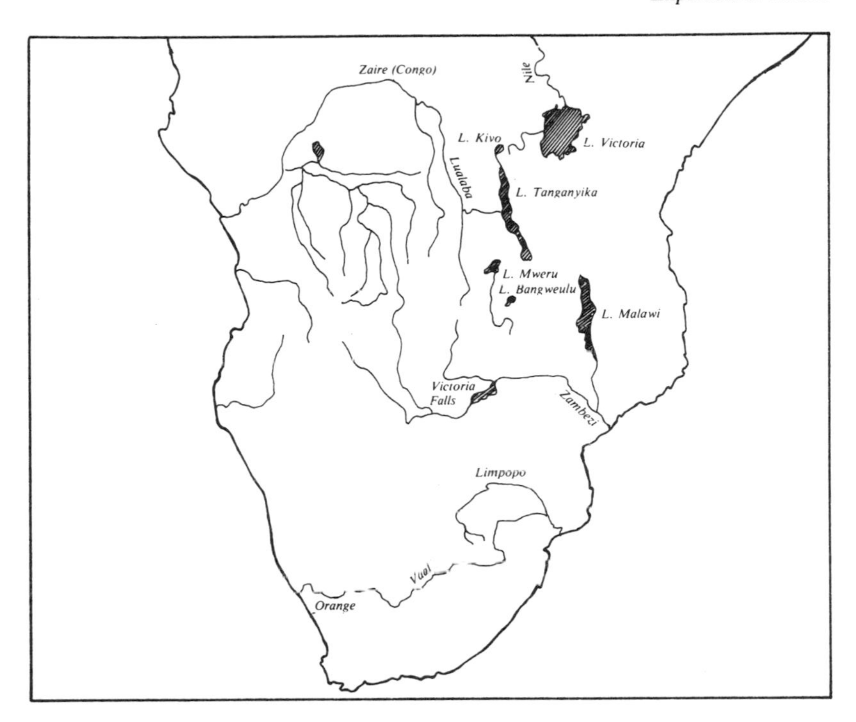

Quilimane on the east coast. For much of the way he descended the Zambezi valley, and he heard of and found the 'Smoke that Thunders'. This was the name given by the local Africans to one of the world's greatest waterfalls; it refers to the clouds of spray that rise up eternally above the cascade. Livingstone named it the Victoria Falls. He was perhaps the greatest of all lone travellers, and his contribution to unknown geography had already been momentous.

In 1861 the Foreign Office combined with the Royal Geographical Society to finance the exploration of the Zambezi by steamer. A large expedition was organised, and it was natural that Livingstone was appointed to lead it. Unfortunately the great lone traveller did not prove as successful in either leadership or organisation. Also, the Zambezi did not prove navigable as Livingstone had thought, because on his crossing of Africa, he had not come upon the formidable rapids at Kabora Bassa, near to the modern Mozambique-Zimbabwe frontier. Still, on this second journey he did turn north up the Shire tributary of the Zambezi, by a trail already known to Portuguese missionaries, thereby discovering the lake now known as Lake Malawi, which he called Lake Nyasa.

While Livingstone had been charting the geography of Southern Africa, farther north there had been great activity in the quest for the still undiscovered sources of the Nile. In 1858, two Indian Army officers, Richard Burton and John Hanning Speke, went westwards up the Arab slave caravan route from the east coast, which led them to Lake Tanganyika. They stayed at the trading port of Ujiji for long enough to make extensive enquiries about the lake shores. They were, however, unable to reach the north of the lake, and so ascertain whether the Rusizi river, of which they had heard tell, flowed into or out of the lake. This was an all-important point in the riddle of the Central African waterways. Speke, who was a fine surveyor of unknown terrain, did not think that Lake Tanganyika could have any connection with the Nile. He subsequently explored the great inland sea to the north-east of Lake Tanganyika, which he named Lake Victoria. It was undoubtedly the Nile's main reservoir. Burton and other experts, including Livingstone and Samuel Baker, continued to think that Lake Tanganyika was its most southerly source.

Livingstone himself then joined in the quest. In 1866 he started inland from Mikindani north of the mouth of the Rovuma. He tried first to investigate the possibility that Lake Malawi was connected to Lake Tanganyika. Going round the south of Lake Malawi, he travelled

Livingstone (left) and Speke

Explorer and bearers

north-eastwards, and realised he was leaving the Zambezi river system and entering another. He reached Lake Bangweulu, which led him on to Lake Mweru and thence to the Lualaba river. With his passionate interest in Holy Writ, he hoped he had found the first beginnings of the Nile, the cradle of Moses. It was in fact the Congo, now known as the Zaire. Short of supplies and literally sickened by slaving atrocities he had witnessed, he turned eastwards to Ujiji, where he confidently expected relief supplies. He found none. His medicine chest had long since been stolen, and his position was desperate. Then one day in 1871 a caravan arrived led by a white man, who held out his hand, and said, 'Doctor Livingstone I presume'. Livingstone gently answered 'Yes'. It was a journalist, Henry Morton Stanley, briefed by the *New York Herald* to find Livingstone, as a journalistic coup. This famous episode was a vital link in the discovery of Africa. They went to the north of Lake Tanganyika together, and settled once and for all that the Rusizi flowed into, and not out of, the lake.

Stanley returned home intending to continue his journalistic career. Livingstone, well refurbished by Stanley, went on with his quest. In 1873, he succumbed to fever near Lake Bangweulu. Just as he had given the first real momentum to Southern African exploration, so by his death, which attracted world publicity, he ensured that it would continue. His dying prayer was that men should come forward to pick up his burden in opening up the dark continent, so cruelly oppressed by the Arab slave trade. First of all came a naval officer, Henry Lovett Cameron, who had set out originally to find Livingstone. He discovered the Lukuja, the inconspicuous outlet of Lake Tanganyika. In some seasons its swampy beginning is scarcely visible, but it drains the lake towards the Lualaba, and thence the Congo and the South

Atlantic. Cameron continued westwards to the Angolan coast, some way south of the Congo. Then Stanley returned. He had come to admire Livingstone greatly during the months they had spent together, and the manner of his death was a challenge; it changed him from a journalist into an explorer. He reached Lake Tanganyika via Lake Victoria, crossed it and continued westwards to the Lualaba. This led him northwards to the mighty Congo. He descended the whole great river to its mouth on the Atlantic. There were, of course, many gaps to fill in, and many fine explorers of various nationalities still to come, notably Savorgnan de Brazza to the north of the Congo. But with Stanley's great crossing of the continent between 1874 and 1877, all the main mysteries of the mountains, lakes and rivers had been solved.

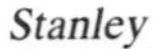

Stanley

Bushmen of the Kalahari

by Roger Murray

The vast Kalahari Desert is the most striking geographical feature of Southern Africa and rarely fails to evoke an awed reaction from the traveller. Covering a broad area of eastern Namibia and western Botswana, it consists of thousands of miles of low sand dunes and huge plains, a harsh environment of heat and thirst and dust. Yet, unlike the Namib desert, the Kalahari is not an entirely arid wasteland of sand; it is a more accurately described as a semi-desert or 'sandveld'. Although there is no surface water, and during the long drought each year from March to December the sun bakes the soil to dust and dry leaves, the area is covered with clumps of low thorn bushes and long grass tufts, amongst which are to be found brown thistles, briers and the dry stalks of spiny weeds. Every so often there is the dramatic sight of a baobab tree, which can be up to 200 feet tall and 30 feet in diameter, dominating the surrounding landscape as effectively as any mountain. Its thick branches, which sprout haphazardly from the great pulpy trunk, bear huge white flowers in the spring, and during the summer, pear-shaped dry fruits which can be eaten.

The key to the ecology of the Kalahari is the three months of rain, often of torrential strength, which begin in December, melting away the heat and drought, turning the grass green at the roots, enabling the plants to bud, flower and fruit quickly. By June all moisture has evaporated leaving only scattered waterholes deep in the soil which in turn dry up by August. The Kalahari supports a variety, if not an abundance, of animal life, including antelope, gemsbok, wildebeest, giraffes and lions, as well as smaller animals such as rabbits, hares and tortoises.

It is in this forbidding but far from lifeless environment that the Bushmen people of Africa have lived for some 25,000 years, since the Middle Stone Age. The Bushmen are believed to have originally inhabited the greater part of south and east Africa; whether they have always lived in the Kalahari or became confined to the area at a later stage is not known for certain. On the evidence of the rock paintings and engravings found throughout the area, such as the renowned White Lady of the Brandberg in the Namib, and the group of paintings in the Tsodilo Hills in Botswana, archaeologists have concluded that the Bushmen are the oldest surviving people of the continent.

The Bushmen are a Khoisan people. Their main physical characteristics are small stature, abnormally large buttocks and yellowish skin pigmentation, with perceptible Central Asian facial features. They speak several complicated 'click' languages, which are not mutually comprehensible. There are five main language groups: the !Kung and the Nharo, the largest groups, the Xu, the Hai//Om and the Xo. Traditionally the Bushmen are nomadic hunter/gatherers without material possessions, and they have always been distinct from the Hottentot pastoralists, who knew

CAMERA PRESS

Two faces of the Kalahari: sand dunes . . .

how to smelt metal and to make clay pottery.

Today, there are an estimated 50,000 Bushmen in all, with 25,000 in Botswana, 20,000 in Namibia, and 2-3,000 each in South Africa's north-eastern Cape area and the south-eastern parts of Angola along the Okavango River. These are the small groups of 'river Bushmen' with a traditional way of life adjusted to a swamp environment. Only some 3,000 Bushmen still exist by hunting and gathering; the !Kung have retained something of the traditional lifestyle in the Omaheke area of north-eastern Namibia, as have the Nharo in central Botswana. The groups of Bushmen who inhabited parts of the Namib until the early 20th century have now completely disappeared. The majority of Bushmen today rely on traditional hunting and gathering for only part of the year, if at all, and are mainly employed on farms and cattle posts owned by the white and black population of Namibia and Botswana. While there has been little integration between Bushmen and the black population in Namibia, partly due to the remoteness of the bushman-inhabited areas and partly to South African colonial policy of emphasising the differences between 'ethnic groups', in Botswana there has been considerable intermarriage between Bushmen and Tswanas. As a result, large numbers of Bushmen have become integrated into Tswana society and many are employed in towns such as Francistown and Gaborone as clerks and messengers, or have learnt shoe-mending and other trades.

Like the Aboriginals of Australia, whose traditional way of life has been similarly shaped by a harsh inland environment, the Bushmen's cultural identity is largely a product of the imperatives of survival in a rigorous terrain. Traditionally Bushmen live in small bands of between 15-30 members. Most members of a group are related by marriage or kinship, but people also join bands out of friendship. The bands are very mobile, always being ready to move on in search of new sources of food, although certain

CAMERA PRESS

. . . and scrubland

areas may be recognised as being associated with a particular band. Marriage generally takes place between families already known to each other. Polygamy is allowed but not often practised, as women have usually been less numerous than men. Many girls are promised even before birth but there is no form of bridal dowry, although traditionally the groom is expected to provide bride-service after marriage by living with the bride's family and hunting for them, during a period long enough for three children to be born. Friendliness, charity and cooperation are regarded as the main social virtues.

Folk tales and myths traditionally play an important role in explaining the world in which the Bushmen live. According to Bushman tradition, long ago, when the first Bushmen inhabited the earth, the sun, moon, rain and animals all lived as one family called the 'Early Race'. The creator deity, Kaang, created all things, but provoked by the disobedience of the first men he made, he sent to the earth both destruction and death while removing his own abode to the sky. Kaang is regarded as the invisible spirit within natural phenomena, but he is especially manifest in the praying mantis or the caterpillar. The adventures and exploits of Kaang form the basic cycle of Bushman mythology. The Bushmen believe the moon was created when Kaang threw an old shoe into the sky.

The principal enemy of the creator deity is Kauha, the trickster God, leader of the spirits of the dead. Though weaker than his rival, Kauha seeks to disrupt Kaang's creation and harass the lives of men and animals. He is central to myths dealing with the relationship between men and women and the act of giving birth. The Greater Bustard, Kauha's servant, was said to have used life-giving fire to create and mark animals with an individual pattern, such as the zebra and the leopard; when his work was completed, people, animals, plants and stars became separate entities in the 'great division'. Humankind is not seen as exceptional, but as needing to co-exist with other parts of nature on equal terms. Human wrong-doing leads to disturbance of the whole natural order, as when the rains are withheld causing drought. Tales are told to the young by the old, at night around the fire, which is also the focus of dancing, still practised even by those Bushmen living on farms and no longer hunter/gatherers. Some dances aim to achieve a trance-like state and contact the supernatural, establishing the human world as part of the greater unknown. The women generally sit around the fire and begin to chant and clap, while the men dance round in a circle, often adopting animal postures, until one of them goes into a trance. In this state it is believed that healing powers can be exercised. Dancing is both a religious ritual and an enjoyable activity. Rhythm is provided by cocoon rattles worn by the women on their ankles. The only musical instrument known is the thumb-piano. This consists of a small wood sounding board about five inches by two inches, to which are attached bone strips (now often recycled metal from cans) of varying lengths which when plucked give off different resonances. The sound is rather similar to the Jew's harp, though less vibratory, and has a pleasing, tinkling tone.

Although hunting with poisoned arrows is the most famous attribute of the Bushmen, the bulk of the diet of the traditional lifestyle comes from wild plants collected by the women. In more favoured areas as many as 80 edible plant species may be used, but only a few form the staple diet, such as the mangetti nut eaten by the !Kung of Namibia, or the tsama melon and other underground tubers which provide a source of both water and food for the bushmen of the central and southern Kalahari in Botswana. Like the Aboriginals, the Bushmen possess the extraordinary skill of locating a source of water in the desert. In the Kalahari, water permeates the surface soil and is trapped deeper down by the underlying rock. The Bushmen dig down three feet or so, fill the hole with grass and insert a hollow reed. The sand is tightly packed around the grass, and a vacuum created in the grass draws the moisture from the surrounding sand. These sip-wells are known to the regular inhabitants of particular areas, and often save life when the large bulbs or tubers cannot be found.

Plants often constitute 90% of the bushman diet, and even in the most favourable times meat rarely exceeds 40% of the total diet. The most sought-after animals are antelope, eland, giraffe, and gemsbok. These are hunted by men with poisoned arrows while the women and children snare smaller animals with twine lassos. Poison for the short, slender arrows is obtained from the *Diamphidia simplex* beetle; the pupae are collected and stored in wooden containers until needed, when they are rolled in the hands until crushed and spread evenly for some four inches behind the arrowhead. The poison has a slow paralysing effect and there is no known antidote. Hunting is by small parties of men, and because the arrows are flimsy, they must stalk their prey until they reach close quarters. This is where the Bushman's phenomenal tracking abilities come into play – the spoor and tracks of each animal can be separately recognised, as well as the age of the particular beast, or whether it is a pregnant female. The numbers of males and females in the herd can be gleaned, as well as their direction and speed of movement. The stalking may involve long periods of watching, in order to select the most vulnerable animal. Arrows are shot from about 50 feet away, and as the herd breaks, the hunters give chase seeking to lodge more arrows. The hunt is resumed the next day, by which time the wounded animal will be semi-paralysed; it is finished off with spears. The meat is shared out according to custom, the hunters and the oldest men distributing the meat to each family group, where it is redistributed in turn to members of the family until all are provided for in a roughly equal measure.

As well as food, animals provide many of the simple materials needed for

Bushman

ALAN HUTCHISON

everyday life, including sinews for bowstrings, ropes and nets; skin, for pouches, clothing and sleeping sacks; and bone for knives, arrowshafts and pipes. Leather aprons, adorned with hundreds of ostrich eggshell beads, also worn in the hair and around the wrists and ankles, comprise the traditional female dress. Wood is the material traditionally used for mortars and pestles, bows, spear-hafts and digging sticks. Huts, which are usually no more than windbreaks, are of branches covered with grass, easily built and vacated. A band may also simply camp under trees or bushes, if the stay is very brief.

The steady expansion of the commercial ranching industry in Botswana has encroached on many traditional hunting grounds, while the restriction of wildlife movements by cordon and foot-and-mouth disease fences has also had an adverse effect, by restricting animal migration. The prospect of permanent water has attracted many to the boreholes of cattle-owners, where they become seasonal labourers. In Botswana the government is formally committed to a resettlement process under the Remote Area Development Programme launched in 1974. The object is to resettle Bushmen from land to which they have no legal title, and which under Botswana's controversial land reform policy is zoned for commercial use by large ranches. Emphasis is placed on teaching English and Setswana, and providing education and health facilities. However, most Bushmen working on farms are exploited, receiving only a minimal wage, while losing their bushcraft and with it their ability to avoid dependence. Some have made a transition to a more settled way of life, for instance around the Nata River in Botswana, where they have built permanent homes, and grow crops and raise cattle.

In Namibia, the traditional Bushmen skills are being put to a military use by the South African army in its war with SWAPO's guerrilla army along the northern Namibian border. As of 1980, some 2,000 Bushmen were serving in the South African Defence Forces stationed in Namibia's operational area, where their superb bushcraft, and their ability as long-distance runners was being used to track infiltrating guerrilla groups.

After independence the fate of the Bushmen of Namibia will probably be similar to those of Botswana, although there may be a substantial legacy of mistrust from the colonial period to overcome.

Although overall the Bushmen population may actually be increasing, their traditional lifestyle appears to be inexorably on the way out. Most are likely to be sucked into the wage sector of the commercial economies of Botswana and Namibia over the next 20 years. This could bring some advantages. Many Bushmen, for example, would benefit from health care: illnesses are rife amongst traditional groups, with very high infant mortality, congenital syphilis, and malnutrition due to protein deficiency, while in times of drought, the old and disabled may be left to die if they cannot keep up. But the immediate prospect is not encouraging. Their traditional culture is almost sure to disappear, and it is unlikely that the new life they are being offered will be an improvement on the old.

Country by Country

ANGOLA

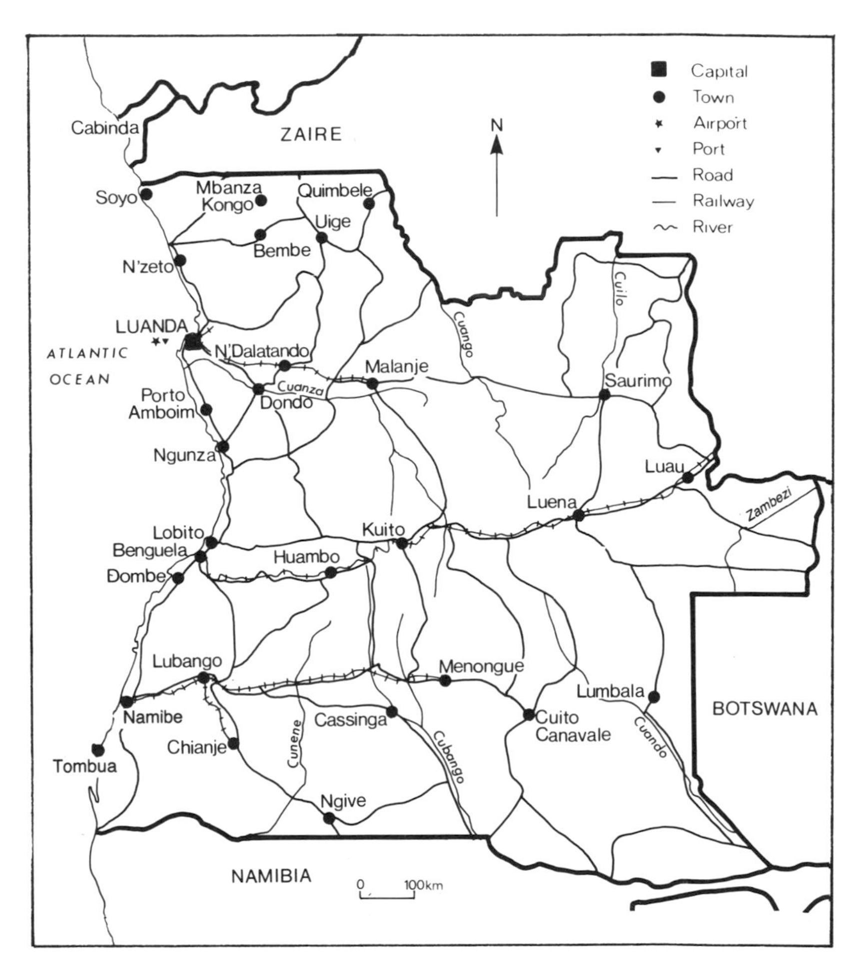

Area: 1,246,000 sq km
Population: 9.31 million (1989 World Bank)
Capital: Luanda

After many years of struggle against Portuguese colonisation, the people of Angola won their independence in November 1975, but there was immediately civil war between the different nationalist movements. The Popular Movement for the Liberation of Angola (MPLA) won this war in 1976 after contending with an armed invasion from South Africa and mercenary forces who backed its enemies, the National Front for the Liberation of Angola (FNLA) and the National Union for the Total Independence of Angola (UNITA).

Since the civil war ended the MPLA has concentrated on consolidating its power, restoring order and rebuilding the damaged economy. This has been hampered in the south by constant South African raids against the SWAPO bases there, and by South Africa's continuing covert assistance to UNITA.

At present, it is not possible for anyone to visit Angola except on Government-approved business, and tourism is unlikely to be allowed for several years.

The Land

From the narrow coastal belt, mountains rise to about 2,000 m, levelling to a plateau of about 1,300m that makes up most of the country. The southern coast borders on the Namib desert, while the northern plateau is thickly vegetated.

There are several large ethnic groups and about 100 tribal sub-groups. Although many Europeans left Angola during 1974-75, there are approximately 30,000 still remaining. There is also a large 'mestiço' population, mainly in the cities.

History

The famous Kongo kingdom was extended over northern Angola by Wene in the 14th century. the empire was still flourishing when Diogo Cao, a Portuguese explorer, reached the mouth of the river first known as Zaire (later Congo) in 1482. The Kongo kings, notably Afonso I (1506-43), were very interested in the foreigners and asked for missionaries and craftsmen to be sent from Europe. They in turn sent their sons to Lisbon for education, and one returned as the first African bishop. By the 17th century, however, the slave trade and unscrupulous traders had undermined the central authority in the kingdom and destroyed any trust between the two countries.

The invasion of the Jaga in 1568 also weakened Kongo. Soon the Ndongo State, ruled by a king known as the Ngola, rose to prominence around the Lucala River. These people became the major target of Portuguese attacks from the coast – 400 settlers had arrived in Luanda in 1575. Throughout the 17th century the settlers drove inland, building first Massangano and then Cambambe forts. They followed the navigable Cuanza River looking for elusive mines.

When defeat at the hands of these settlers was inevitable, Nzinga, queen of Ndonga, moved towards the Cuango River to remain an independent entrepreneur in the lucrative trade between the coast and the interior.

Angola was useful to the Portuguese solely as a source of slaves for Brazil – about one milion were shipped between 1580 and 1680. The strongest tribes joined the slave raiders, and some areas were devastated. The country saw no economic advance. Other Europeans took part in the drive for slaves: the Dutch where they could, the English at Ambriz and the French at Cabinda.

Meanwhile the Portuguese expanded from Benguela to build Caconda fort in 1682. Their Eurafrican agents *(pom-beiros)* travelled far and wide to discover new markets.

The independence of Brazil in 1822 brought the formal abolition of the slave trade (1836); however, it continued for some time thereafter. The loss of Brazil inspired some Portuguese to intensify Angola's colonisation, but the process of conquest and settlement really only accelerated after the Berlin conference of 1884-85 obliged Portugal to show effective occupation of colonial claims. Military campaigns lasted for the next 40 years. Slavery was replaced by its 20th century modification – forced labour in a variety of guises and disguises – through which Angola was exploited until the 1960's

In 1961 a rebellion on the coffee plantations near Carmona, encouraged partly by the new independence of other African countries, was savagely suppressed and 50,000 Africans were slaughtered. The rebellion did, however, awaken the authorities into abolishing forced labour and providing better educational, health and agricultural opportunities for Africans.

The rising of 1961 by supporters of the MPLA and the Union of the Populations of North Angola (UPNA) which became the FNLA in 1962, both brutally countered militarily by the colonial authorities, shifted the anti-colonial struggle to guerrilla warfare in the bush, initially in the north and in Cabinda province, and later in the east of Angola. In 1964, a breakaway group from the FNLA formed UNITA which later engaged in guerrilla operations in a sector of south-east Angola.

Political attitudes within the three groupings varied in the period of guerrilla warfare from 1961 to 1974. The MPLA had a socialist platform aimed at an independent non-racial society and a complete break with the colonial system; the FNLA, with a northern bias, was willing to accept a Portuguese neo-colonial solution, and UNITA's tactics varied between covert co-operation with the Portuguese and a flirtation with the Chinese. When the Portuguese government of Dr Marcello Caetano was overthrown in April 1974, Angola was thrown into confusion as the nationalist movements manoeuvred for power and influence. South Africa entered the fray in 1975 in a bid to crush the MPLA.

The MPLA finally emerged the victor in 1976 after calling in Cuban military support to repulse the South Africans. Under Angola's first President, Dr. Agostinho Neto, much was done to implement the movement's uncompromising Marxist-Leninist policies, despite continuing internal and external opposition. After the death of President Neto in September 1979, Jose Eduardo dos Santos took over as head of state, affirming his commitment to continuing Dr Neto's policies.

At first, UNITA guerrillas led by Dr Jonas Savimbi continued to operate with some success over large areas of the country, with the open support of much of the Ovimbundu population in central Angola, and the covert support of South Africa. By mid-1980 the UNITA guerrilla threat had faded, but at the same time South African military incursions dramatically increased; South Africa actually occupied parts of southern Angola for extended periods. But at the end of 1988, a series of international meetings resulted in a ceasefire, with the withdrawal of South African troops by September and an agreement for the phased withdrawal of Cuban forces from Angola.

Economy

The post-independence social programme of the MPLA represents a nearly total change from the colonial past, with substantial changes in the organisation of industry, agriculture and the channels of commercial distribution. Abandoned enterprises have been taken into State ownership and the State's share has been further increased by confiscation and nationalisation of undertakings that play a significant part in the small industrial and processing sector. Industrial enterprises have been put under the management of workers' committees aided by a large number of technicians from socialist countries e.g. Cuba and North Korea.

The Government has dealt pragmatically with the multinational companies engaged in oil and diamond extraction. American Gulf Oil resumed normal operations in Cabinda in 1976 on the understanding that long-term arrangements would not only include improved royalties accruing to the MPLA, but 51% state participation. The Government also has a controlling interest in diamond production.

Angola's hard currency is earned by oil, coffee and diamond exports. However, the expense of keeping the country at a high stage of mobilisation is deflecting funds which could be available for economic projects. Despite the Marxist orientation of the regime, Angola remains open to investment from the West.

In agriculture, capital-intensive enterprises are run as State economic units, but the main thrust is to encourage the growth of production co-operatives. Production of basic food crops is almost fully restored, but Angola still has to import about half of its food requirements and only survives as a result of external assistance mostly from the Socialist countries. The economy is crippled by its defence expenditure, caused by the war against UNITA, which absorbs 80 per cent of the National budget and 50 per cent of export revenues.

General Information

Government

The head of the single-party State is the President, José Eduardo dos Santos. The government is formed from the Partido do Trabalho (Workers' Party) of the Movimento Popular de Libertaçao de Angola (MPLA).

Languages

Portuguese is the official lanaguage. The main African language groups are U-Mbundu, spoken by the Ovimbundu of the central plateau around Huambo; Ki-Mbundu, spoken by the Mbundu in Luanda and its hinterland; Kongo in the north; Chokwe (Kioko) in the east.

Religion

Christianity and traditional beliefs.

How to Get There

By air: There is an international airport at Luanda, which is served by serveral airlines. TAAG (Angola Airlines) operates external and extensive internal services. It has offices in Belgium, Brazzaville, Havana, Paris, Rome, Moscow, Lisbon, Sao Tome and Cape Verde.

By road: There is a fairly extensive network of well-surfaced roads inside the country, with many more under construction. Border posts with neighbouring countries are not yet open.

By rail: The internal rail network is functioning normally, and the Benguela railway, connecting Angola with Zaire has been reopened despite guerrilla raids.

By sea: The main ports are Luanda and Lobito Bay. There are also ports at Cabinda and Moçamedes.

Currency

Kwanza divided into 100 lwei. (See currency table, Page 10).

Binga water falls

BOTSWANA

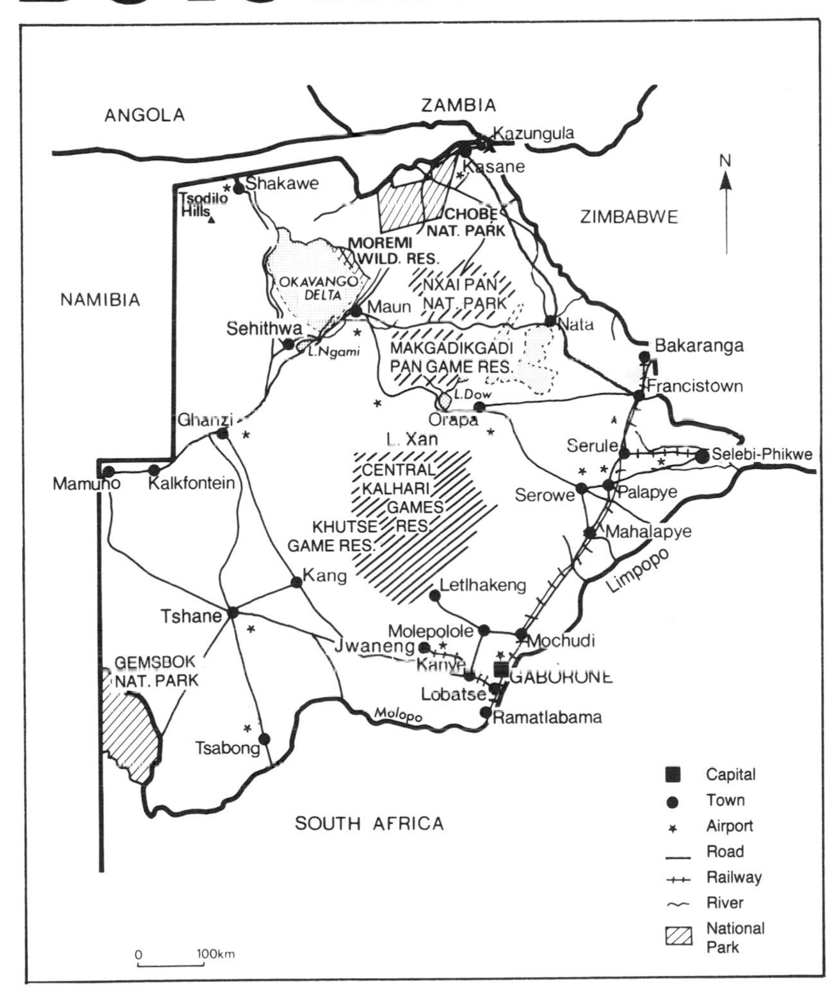

Area: 582,000 sq km
Population: 1.23 million (1989 World Bank)
Capital: Gaborone

The lonely Kalahari Desert covers most of this vast, sparsely-populated country, bounded by South Africa, Namibia and Zimbabwe and touching Zambia. In the north lies the Okavango Delta, alive with birds and game, and potentially a huge source of water in a thirsty land. In the Okavango is the Moremi Wildlife Reserve and nearby the excellent and move accessible Chobe National Park, only one-and-a-half hours' drive from the Victoria Falls. For the truly adventurous visitor the tough journey to the Tsodilo Hills brings a rich reward in a treasure-house of Basarwa (Bushman) cave paintings.

Botswana, formerly known as the Bechuanaland Protectorate, became independent from Britain in 1966 under the leadership of Sir Seretse Khama. After years of neglect and poverty, the country is now experiencing an increase in national wealth from its copper-nickel and diamond mines.

Overland travel in Botswana is not for the 'package tourist'. Distances are long and roads often in bad condition. But for anyone who enjoys the solitude of vast open spaces and game viewing in truly natural surroundings, the real flavour of African travel can be experienced here, both by crossing the flat desert scrublands of the Kalahari and central Botswana, and by exploring the richly tropical Okavango and Chobe areas of the north. Despite the poverty in which many of them live, the local people always provide a warm welcome.

The Land and the People

A land-locked, semi-arid tableland, about the size of France or Texas but with a population of a little over one million, Botswana is a country of great contrasts.

Most of the population live on the eastern rim of the arid Kalahari sandveld which occupies a vast tract of land in central, southern and western Botswana – the 'Thirstland' of the early pioneers. Rainfall averages are very low in this area, about 220 mm per annum in the far south-west, increasing towards the east and the north, and reaching 680 mm per annum in the Chobe district of the north.

As the rainfall varies, so does the aspect of the country. The major part is covered with bush savannah: thorn acacias and mopane trees, low scrub growths beaten down by the sun into the red and brown sandy soils. There are a few low rocky hills scattered in the east. The average altitude is 1,000 m rising to 1,225 m in places. In Ngamiland in the north there is an area of indigenous forest and dense bush, giving way in the north-west to the lush expanses occupied by the Okavango Delta. Here the Okavango River fans out into innumerable water-ways and lagoons, swollen each year by the winter floods from the Angolan high-lands, and extending over 10,400 sq km to create one of the wildest and most beautiful nature reserves in Africa.

80% of Botswana's population is concentrated in the east. 12% of the population live in the traditional towns: Serowe is the capital of the

Bamangwato tribe, Kanye of the Bangwaketse, Molepolole of the Bakwena. A further 10% are in the four 'modern' towns, Gaborone, Lobatse, Francistown, and Selebi-Phikwe. To the west is the Kalahari (locally known as Kgalagadi), whose vast tracts are virtually unpopulated, apart from nomadic groups of Bushmen and some scattered villages clustered around boreholes or seasonally filled pans.

The Bushmen, of which there are estimated to be some 4,000 still living in the Kalahari, are the earliest known inhabitants of Africa. Place names and rock paintings record their presence all over the southern part of the continent. The Kalahari is their last refuge. They live by tracking game and by following seasonal pans of water, moving on as they dry up. However, successive droughts, new game laws and changes in government land policy are gradually eroding the Bushmen's traditional lifestyle and drawing them increasingly into the wage sector.

The majority of the people belong to the eight branches of the Tswana people and still follow a traditional pattern of life. Cattle-rearing is an important feature of the economy. Cattle-ownership is traditionally and symbolically very important to the Tswana, but as a form of real wealth it remains in the hands of only a few. In the 1975 Rural Income Distribution Survey, 45% of rural households in Botswana were said to own no cattle at all. A much larger proportion of the population is wholly or partly dependent on crop-farming – a very vulnerable activity in Botswana's drought-prone environment.

Culture

Perhaps because of the harshness of the climate and the aridity of the land which combine to make subsistence a lifelong pre-occupation, the Batswana have developed few particularly distinctive artistic traditions. Handicraft production has practically died out in the face of competition over the years from cheap imported manufacturers in the local stores. However, fine basketwork is still produced in Ngamiland, and beautiful furs, or karosses, and skin mats are made in the Kalahari. There are still a few people who make magnificent large earthenware pots for cooking and beer-brewing.

Traditional dancing and singing still take place on important occasions, and fine *maboko,* or praise poems, are sung.

The Basarwa Bushmen are well known for their lifelike rock paintings which can be seen at places they used to inhabit, such as Tsodilo Hills.

History

The ancestors of the nomadic Basarwa (Bushmen) who roamed the bush following game and gathering fruit were probably the first inhabitants of Botswana. They engraved and painted pictures of themselves and animals in caves like those in the Tsodilo Hills.

Basotho ancestors of the Batswana came to the Transvaal between the 11th and 14th centuries. Of the Batswana, the Barolong (mostly in the northern Cape) and Bahurutshe (mostly in the Transvaal) are regarded as senior branches. The Bakwena quarrelled with the Bahurutshe, and later, perhaps in the 18th century, some of them came to Botswana.

Early 19th-century travellers were struck by the number of ruins and by places like Dithakong (Old Lattakoo) north of Kuruman with perhaps 3,000 huts partly built of stone. In Botswana there are still some ruins in the south-east but elsewhere no convenient stone is to be found.

Between 1810 and 1830 travellers and missionaries began to penetrate the northern Cape and Botswana from the South. The inhabitants suffered a succession of invasions by Mma Ntatisi, the Ndebele and the Afrikaner Voortrekkers.

Mma Ntatisi was a warrior chieftainess who led her people from the Lesotho area when invaders began pouring over the Drakensberg to escape from the bloodshed of Shaka's Zulu wars. She, in turn, spread chaos among the Tswana but was finally defeated in 1823 by the Batlhaping in the northern Cape.

When the Afrikaners ended their great Trek in the Transvaal they drove the Ndebele to Zimbabwe and caused the flight of many groups of Bamlete, Batlokwa and Bakgatla to Botswana throughout the 19th century. By the 1840's Livingstone and others had set up a mission among the Bakwena at Kolobeng (west of Gaborone). Further north, the son of the Bamangwato Chief went to school and became an ardent Christian. He was Khama the Great, who succeeded to the chieftaincy in 1872. He built up a strong army and united many of the Batswana under him.

Meanwhile the Afrikaners' interest in Botswana was increasing because of gold-finds at Tati (near Francistown). British missionaries, however, were anxious to keep a right of way through to central Africa and encouraged the Chiefs to seek British protection against the Afrikaners. Thus, in 1885, the British Government reluctantly agreed to declare the Bechuanaland Protectorate over Khama's peoples and to annex the other Tswana territory of the northern Cape (British Bechuanaland) as part of the Cape Colony.

Khama's aim in seeking British protection was military. He intended to remain in full control of administration, law and justice in his area. He firmly opposed granting any mining concessions, and successfully resisted proposals that Cecil Rhodes's British South Africa Company, which was ruling in Southern Rhodesia (Zimbabwe) and later in Northern Rhodesia (Zambia), should take over his territory. Later the Chiefs successfully opposed union with South Africa.

In economic terms, the colonial framework in Bechuanaland was disastrous, yet the protectorate was expected to pay its own way from its meagre resources. Botswana became little more than a labour reservoir for the South African mines and farms. It was estimated in the 1940's that almost half of all African cash income derived from such migrant labour. The development of education and health services was by missionaries.

Inequalities deepened within rural society – aristocrats increased their herds, using tribute or serf labour, and invested in new boreholes thereby gaining control of new land. By the time of the run-up to independence, a handful of rich cattle-owners were poised to exploit commercial markets and were already partially independent of tribal controls.

After his return from a six-year exile (1950-56) imposed by the British authorities for daring to marry a white wife, Seretse Khama (nephew of Tshekedi Khama and successor to the Ngwato throne) took the leading part in formulating a republican independence constitution to establish a centralised democratic state. Shortly after independence in September 1966, most of the tribal rights over land were transferred to elected district communities.

In the first general election in 1965 Khama's Botswana Democratic Party (BDP) won 28 of the 31 seats with strong rural support. At independence, Seretse Khama became Botswana's first president. His policies were conservative: a guarantee for the white freehold farmers and open encouragement for foreign investment with a strictly neutral stance towards South Africa and Rhodesia, deriving from expedience rather than principle. Seretse Khama always condemned apartheid and refused to send a representative to Pretoria or to recruit expatriate personnel from there. Botswana's historical links with Britain remained strong, but Seretse Khama worked to extend his links with Zambia and the rest of black-ruled Africa. He played an important role in the efforts to negotiate a settlement in Zimbabwe, and in establishing a Southern African economic grouping whose primary aim is to reduce economic dependence on South Africa.

Botswana has been hit increasingly hard by the repercussions of repression in the white-ruled south. Over 600 Soweto students have remained in the country around Gaborone of the thousands who fled South Africa after the June 1976 riots. Despite meagre resources and with mounting tension on its borders, Botswana was also host to tens of thousands of refugees during the Zimbabwean war. After the ceasefire in Zimbabwe, however, the majority were repatriated to take part in the independence elections in early 1980.

Sir Seretse Khama died in July 1980 and was replaced by Vice-President Dr Quett Masire, who continued Seretse Khama's policies. In a bizarre incident in August 1988 Masire's plane was accidentally shot down over Angola when he was on his way to attend a meeting. He was injured and had to receive treatment in a London clinic.

Economy

The last 15 years have witnessed a sharp acceleration of social transformation in Botswana, mainly in the growth of the urban population, in the expansion of the commercial economy, in cattle-ranching and in diamond and copper mining. Diamonds were exploited only after independence. They are mined at three sites – Orapa, Letlhakane and most recently Jwaneng – and now earn about half of Botswana's foreign exchange. Diamond mining is in the hands of Debswana, which is owned 50% by the Botswana government and 50% by De Beers of South Africa. De Beers has described Jwaneng as "the most important diamond find since Kimberley", in South Africa. Copper and nickel are mined at Selebi-Phikwe by Botswana RST, a joint venture whose main shareholders are Anglo American of South Africa and Amax of the US. Expansion of the mining sector since the 1970s has been phenomenal, but growth has since slowed owing to stagnant world demand for gem-quality diamonds, to debt and to transport problems for copper/nickel matte.

If mining is a foreign enclave, the livestock industry is domestic, and since the devastating drought of 1965/66 which killed off one third of the national herd, there has been a rapid emergence of a small elite of Batswana cattle-ranchers serving the national abattoir at Lobatse. The wealthy ranchers established *de facto* rights over huge tracts of grazing land in the Eastern Kalahari in the post-independence 'land rush'. The state has supported the ranchers by nationalising the abattoir under the Botswana Meat Commission (BMC) and improving producer prices and services as well as negotiating favourable access to the European markets. Botswana is one of only two African countries allowed to export beef to the EEC.

The commercialisation of cattle-raising is an important factor in the wide social cleavage in rural Botswana, and by the early 1970s, 45% of the rural population owned no cattle at all. Land is plentiful, but arable and grazing land is not; this and the glitter of diamond revenue being spent in the towns have drawn Batswana to the urban areas in increasing numbers. But unlike gold-mining in South Africa, diamond and copper mining in Botswana is capital-intensive. In 1983, there were scarcely more than 100,000 formal-sector jobs in Botswana. But the government plans to create 7,600 new jobs per year until 1991, while the projected increase in the labour force is 20,000 per year.

More than 80% of Botswana's imports come from South Africa despite Botswana's membership of the 15-nation Preferential Trade Area for Eastern & Southern Africa and despite the proximity of Zimbabwe with its well-developed manufacturing sector. The nearest alternative transport route is via the Mozambican port of Beira, where the capacity is far too small to handle even Zimbabwe's traffic, let alone Botswana's.

Free education was introduced in 1980, and literacy in Setswana is the main aim of primary education. A scheme called Tirelo Setshaba takes urban Batswana who have earned their "O" level certificates into the rural areas to impart their skills and also to learn about rural problems. English is widely spoken in the towns.

National Parks

The Department of Wildlife, National Parks and Tourism in Gaborone

PETER JOHNSON

White-backed vulture drying its wings.

administers a network of national parks and game reserves protecting wildlife across one-fifth of the total area. Outside the protected areas, the country is divided into 40 hunting blocks, each with a small quota of animals which may be shot annually. Hunting licences are strictly limited.

Chobe National Park: This is open all the year round, but some areas are closed during November-April; the best time to visit is between April and November when lack of rain concentrates the wildlife on the river. Habitats vary from the flood grasslands and thickets by the river to a series of pans. Numerous species of animals and birdlife abound here, from giraffe to elephant, white rhinoceros, lion, leopard, cheetah and the rare Chobe bushbuck, unique to this area. The fishing is superb. There is a good network of roads through the park which make wildlife viewing easy.

Access: There is an airstrip for light aircraft at Kasane, at the entrance to the park. By car from Livingstone (Zambia) take the Mombova road and turn off at the sign to Chobe, crossing the ferry to Kasane at Kazungula. An excellent highway now makes driving to Chobe possible from all Botswana towns, but the distance is 1,040 km from Gaborone.

Accommodation: Chobe Safari Lodge at the park entrance, Kasane, PO Box 10, Kasane, tel: 336; 66 beds in cottages and rondavels, swimming pool, tennis, restaurant, bar and water-skiing facilities. Guided tours are arranged into the park for hunting, photography and wildlife viewing and there are launch trips up the river. The fishing is excellent. Chobe Game Lodge is situated 8 km inside the park. First-class hotel, 100 beds; all amenities plus full air-conditioning. PO Box 32, Kasane, tel: Kasane 26. **Note:** Bookings for many Chobe/Okavango lodges and camps can be made via telex 2482 BD.

Moremi Wildlife Reserve: Situated at the edge of the Okavango Delta where riverine grassland begins, it is bounded by the Khwai, Santantadibe, Gomoti and Mogogelo Rivers. It is perhaps the most spectacular reserve in Southern Africa.

There are only tracks, and a guide is essential; one can be picked up at the entrance on the Maun road. Visitors may go where they like and camp where they like, but a vehicle with four-wheel-drive is advisable. The Reserve is closed during the rainy season, approximately December to April. The wide variety of wildlife ranges from lion, cheetah and leopard to vast herds of zebra, wildebeest, lechwe, kudu and eland, and at least 80 species of birdlife.
Access: Airstrip for light aircraft just outside the Reserve. It is possible to drive as far as Maun in an ordinary vehicle from Francistown, but the road from Maun to Moremi requires four-wheel-drive.
Accommodation: Khwai River Lodge is situated on the banks of the Khwai River just outside the Reserve, PO Box 100, Maun, tel: Maun 48. 32 beds, 16 double units, swimming, water-skiing, fishing trips, launch trips into the Delta. Land-Rover trips into the Reserve for hunting and photography.

Crocodile Camp on the Thamalakane River just outside Maun, PO Box 46, tel: Maun 265. 24 beds, full board. Water-skiing and fishing trips can be arranged into the Delta as far north as Shakawe, which takes 10 days, and into the Reserve.
The Okavango Delta: The Delta consists of 16,000 sq km of waterways caused by the flooding of the Okavango River which flows into Ngamiland from the Angolan highlands. The flood reaches its peak in May, raising the level of the Delta by several feet, and overflows into Lake Ngami and down the Boteti towards the great salt pans of the Makgadikgadi to the south.

Papyrus blocks many of the Delta's waterways in the north, making it impenetrable except by *mekoro*, the dug-out canoes used by the Yei and Mbukushu people who have settled on the periphery of the Delta. Hippo, by breaking their way through the papyrus, keep the channels open.
Accommodation: Crocodile Camp, mentioned above under Moremi Wildlife Reserve, is a good place from which to approach the Delta. There is also Riley's Hotel in Maun itself. Most of the safari companies operating in Botswana are centred on Maun, and sightseeing or hunting trips up the Delta can be arranged through them. Island Safari Lodge: Situated 12 km north of Maun on the Thamalakane River, PO Box 116, Maun, tel: Maun 300. Accommodation is in 14 thatched bungalows with private toilet facilities and hot showers. Meals are inclusive in the tariff, and a licensed bar, popular with both locals and expatriates, adjoins the restaurant. Outboard motor boat and canoe hire is available and self-conducted canoe safaris can be outfitted from the lodge. There is also a spacious camping site. The Lodge is a good starting point for trips into the Delta.

Other accommodation in the Delta includes the Okavango River Lodge, 13 km north-east of Maun, PO Box 32, Maun, tel: Maun 298 (6 chalets) and Xaxaba Camp, PO Box 147, tel: Maun 205, a fairly comfortable 'bush-camp'.

General Information

Government

Presidential democracy. The President and the National Assembly are elected. There are several political parties.

Languages

Setswana is the national language; English is the official language.

Religion

Traditional beliefs and Christianity.

How to get there

By air: Air Botswana operates a regular service Johannesburg-Gaborone-Selebi-Phikwe-Francistown-Maun. Air Botswana and Air Zimbabwe share a regular service to Harare in Zimbabwe. Royal Swazi and Zambia Airways link Gaborone to Mbabane and Lusaka. These services are all heavily used and it is advisable to reserve seats well in advance.

Sir Seretse Khama Airport at Gaborone opened 9 December 1984. It has a 3,000-metre runway and a modern passenger terminal.

Most of the main towns and game reserves have airstrips served by light aircraft operated by charter companies.

By road: Normal car insurance from the country of origin, provided it includes third-party risks, is valid in Botswana. Visitors holding valid driving licences issued in their own countries may drive in Botswana for up to six months. The roads from South Africa and Bulawayo leading to the more developed south-east are either tarred or gravelled and fairly good. A good tarred road links Francistown to the Kazungula ferry on the Zambian border.

By rail: The railway from South Africa to Zimbabwe passes through Botswana offering regular passenger services. Southbound: Departs Bulawayo (Zimbabwe) Tuesday 11.45, Francistown Tuesday 15.51, Gaborone Wednesday 01.30, Lobatse Wednesday 03.25; arrives Mafikeng (South Africa) Wednesday 05.30, Johannesburg Wednesday 12.35, Durban Thursday 08.15. Dining car attached, Bulawayo-Gaborone. Northbound: Departs Durban Wednesday 18.30, Johannesburg Thursday 13.30, Mafikeng Thursday 21.00, Lobatse Thursday 22.40, Gaborone Friday 01.04, Francistown Friday 09.56; arrives Bulawayo Friday 14.10. Dining car attached, Gaborone-Bulawayo. A slow train runs in both directions daily (Bulawayo-Mafikeng 22½ hours). Fridays only, an overnight train runs from Lobatse to Francistown.

Entry Regulations

No visa is required for nationals of all Commonwealth countries, Austria, Belgium, Denmark, Finland, France, Federal Republic of Germany, Greece, Ireland, Italy, Liechtenstein, Luxembourg, Netherlands, Norway, San Marino, South Africa, Sweden, Switzerland, USA and Uruguay. Others must have visas, obtainable from the Immigration Control Officer, Box 942, Gaborone, or a Botswana Diplomatic Mission. Visitors to Botswana are permitted to stay in the country for 30 days without requiring any permits. If they wish to remain longer application should be made in the country from an Immigration Control Officer or police station.

A certificate of vaccination against yellow fever is required for those travelling from infected areas.

Customs Regulations

Between Botswana, South Africa, Lesotho and Swaziland there are in theory no restrictions on the movements of goods, except for liquor, firearms and ammunition, for which permits must be obtained from the relevant Botswana District Commissioner, as well as a general import permit for firearms, obtainable from the Central Arms Registry, Box 516, Gaborone.

Export permits are required for game trophies and skins, and these are obtainable from the offices of the Department of Wildlife, National Parks and Tourism. In certain cases an export fee is payable. From Zimbabwe and Zambia there are customs formalities but personal effects are duty-free, as are new goods for personal use up to P50 in value.

Climate

Most of the country lies in the temperate zone, but the north becomes tropical. Most wildlife parks are open all the year round, but from December to April parts may become impassable and waterlogged. From May to September (the winter) the days are sunny, dry and dusty, with maximum temperatures 22-33°C; early mornings and evenings may be cold and even frosty (minimum 4-14°C). The summer (October to April) is hot, often reaching 38°C in December and January. This is the rainy season, but Botswana has a very low rainfall. October is the hottest month (before the rains cool things down), and Maun and Kasane are the hottest towns.

What to wear: Light-weight summer clothing can be worn during the day throughout most of the year but visitors between May and September should bring sweaters for the sudden drop in temperature, and coats and warmer clothing for the evening.

Health Precautions

As a general rule water outside the main towns should be boiled. Swimming or paddling in stagnant water should be avoided because of bilharzia. In the northern wildlife parks malaria is prevalent and prophylactics must be taken during and after one's stay. In the Moremi Wildlife Reserve, other parts of Ngamiland and western parts of Chobe National Park, tsetse fly, which can cause sleeping sickness, is a danger. The visitor should wear protective clothing, have a fly-spray handy and keep the vehicle's windows shut.

Banks and Currency

Bank of Botswana, PO Box 712, Gaborone (central bank).
Barclays Bank of Botswana Ltd, Commerce House, The Mall, PO Box 478, Gaborone, tel: (031) 52041; telex 2417 BD.
Standard Chartered Bank Botswana Ltd, Standard House, The Mall, PO Box 496, Gaborone, tel: (031) 53111; telex 2422.
Bank of Credit & Commerce (Botswana) Ltd., PO Box 871, Gaborone, tel: (031) 52867; telex 2556 BD.
Currency: Pula divided into 100 Thebe (see currency table, page 10).

Business Hours

Shops: 8.00-13.00 and 14.15-17.30 weekdays; 8.00-10.45 Saturdays.
Government Offices: 7.30-16.30 weekdays.
Banks: 8.15-12.45 weekdays; 8.15-10.45 Saturdays.

Public Holidays

New Year's Day, 1 January
Public Holiday, 2 January
Good Friday, 13 April 1990
Easter Saturday, 15 April 1990
Easter Monday, 16 April 1990
Ascension Day, 24 May 1990
President's Day, 19 July
Botswana Day, 30 September
Public Holiday, 1 October
Christmas Holidays, 25-27 December

Embassies in Gaborone

China: Box 1031; tel: 52209
Denmark: Box 367; tel: 53770
France: Box 1424; tel: 53683
Germany FR: Box 315; tel: 53143
Nigeria: Box 274; tel: 3561-64
Norway: Box 879; tel: 51501
Sweden: Private Bag 0017; tel: 53912-4
UK: Private Bag 0023; tel: 52841
USA: Box 90; tel: 53382
USSR: Box 81; tel: 53389
Zambia: Box 632; tel: 51951
Zimbabwe: Box 1232; tel: 4495-7
Others are represented in Pretoria (South Africa), Lusaka (Zambia) or Dar es Salaam (Tanzania).

Transport

By air: Air Botswana operates a regular flight from Johannesburg to Francistown and Maun via Gaborone and from Harare to Gaborone via Francistown. Its internal services link Francistown, Gaborone, Maun and Selebi-Phikwe. Other airports and airstrips are at Bokspits, Ghanzi, Kanye, Kasane, Lobatse, Machaneng, Mahalapye, Molepolole, Nata, Orapa, Palapye, Rakops, Serowe, Shakawe, Shashe, Tsabong and Tshane.
By Road: Tarred roads link Ramatlabama-Bakaranga, Gaborone-Letlhakeng, Serule-Selebi-Phikwe, Francistown-Kasane, Palapye-Serowe and Lobatse-Jwaneng. Fairly good all-weather roads link Francistown-Orapa and Nata-Maun. The rest of the roads are poor but passable by four-wheel-drive.

All roads from South Africa via the main border posts into eastern Botswana are all-weather roads. Petrol is available at all the towns mentioned. Four-wheel-drive is necessary for minor roads, particularly those through the Kalahari, and for the wildlife reserves. Petrol is available in the Kalahari at Ghanzi, Kalkfontein, Kang and Mamuno and in the north and north-east wildlife area at Sehithwa, Toteng, Kasane, Nata, Orapa, Ramokgwebana, Tsheshebe and Sebina.
Car hire: Trucks and Land-Rovers can be hired from safari companies. Vehicles can also be hired from Avis Rent-a-Car, PO Box 790, Gaborone, tel: 3093, telex: 2723 BD; Cliff Engineering, PO Box 282, Gaborone, tel: 51091; Francistown Toyota, PO Box 338, Francistown, tel: 3856, telex: 2204 BD.
Safari Companies: There are many safari companies for photography and sightseeing in Maun, Gaborone, Francistown and Kasane. Others operate from Johannesburg.

Gaborone

Gaborone was built in 1964 to be the capital of Botswana on independence in 1965. It is divided in half by the main axis, the Mall, a pedestrian shopping area flanked by parking lots and two streets running down from the National Assembly building and Government offices at the top, to the Town Hall at the bottom.

Near Gaborone is an artificial lake ('the dam') lying in a lovely, quiet valley flanked by hills; it is a favourite spot for bird watchers. There are facilities for sailing, water-skiing and fishing at the Yacht Club. However, it is necessary to be a guest of a member. Many stone-age implements were discovered during the construction of the dam and these are exhibited in the National Museum which is a good source of general information on Botswana. There are some worthwhile day trips to be taken from Gaborone: to Manyana where there are Bushmen paintings on a rocky outcrop outside the village, and to the Kolobeng, where there are remains of a mission which was established by Livingstone.
Khutse Wildlife Reserve, 232 km from Gaborone via Molepolole and Letlhakeng, is in the Kalahari sandveld and holds large herds of drought-resistant wildlife, such as kudu, hartebeeste, gemsbok, springbok, lion, leopard, hyena and the bat-eared fox. They move

Hotels

NAME	ADDRESS	TELEPHONE	TELEX
* International class hotels			
GABORONE			
President Hotel*	on the Mall PO Box 200	53631	2434 BD
Gaborone Sun*	near golf course PO Box 0016	51111	2433 BD
Gaborone Hotel	at the station PO Box 5	53991	–
Mphatlalatsane Motel	PO Box 177	52301	–
Oasis Motel	PO Box 20786	56396	2497 BD
FRANCISTOWN			
Thapama Lodge*	PB 31	3872	2662 BD
Marang Motel*	PO Box 807	3991	2264 BD
Tati Hotel	opposite the station PO Box 15	2321	2220 BD
Grand Hotel	PO Box 30	2309	2271 BD
GHANZI			
Kalahari Arms	PO Box 29	Ghanzi 1	–
LOBATSE			
Cumberland Hotel*	PO Box 135	281/2	2323 BD
Lobatse Hotel	PO Box 93	319	–
MAHALÁPYE			
Mahalapye Hotel	PO Box 526	200	–
Broadway Flats	PO Box 55	200	–
MAUN			
Riley's Hotel*	PO Box 1	Maun 204	2481 BD
MOLEPOLOLE			
Mafenya-Tlala Hotel	PO Box 10 Telegrams: MAFHOT	394/5	–

▶

SELEBI-PHIKWE			
Bosele Hotel*	PO Box 177	675/6/7	2201 BD
SEROWE			
Serowe Hotel	PO Box 150	234	–
Tshwaragano Hotel	PO Box 102	377	–

Safari Lodges

CHOBE NATIONAL PARK (KASANE)

Chobe Safari Lodge	PO Box 10, Kasane	Kasane 336	2762 BD
Chobe Game Lodge	PO Box 32, Kasane	Kasane 340	8-6129 SA
Serondella Camp	PO Box 17, Kasane	Kasane 235	–
MOREMI WILDLIFE RESERVE/OKAVANGO			
Crocodile Camp	PO Box 46, Maun Telegrams CROCOCAMP	Kasane 265	2482 BD
Island Safari Lodge	PO Box 116, Maun Telegrams ISLAND	Maun 300	2482 BD
Khwai River Lodge	PO Box 100, Maun	Maun 48	–
Okavango River Lodge	PO Box 32, Maun	Maun 298	2482 BD
OKAVANGO DELTA			
Camp Okavango	PO Box 48, Maun	Maun 205	2482 BD
Xaxaba Camp	PO Box 147, Maun	Maun 205	2482 BD
TULI BLOCK			
Zanzibar Resort Hotel	PO Box 30331, Gaborone	Sherwood Ranch 420	2497 BD
Limpopo Inn Hotel	PO Box 55, Mahalapye	Sherwood Ranch 505	2280 BD
Tuli Lodge	PO Box 882, Gaborone	Gaborone A2RC 76	8-9646 SA
Limpopo Safari Lodge	c/o Pan African Travel, PO Box 2, Gaborone	Gaborone 52321	2521 BD

around a good deal, and numbers depend on conditions in the reserve. Four-wheel-drive vehicles are necessary. Fill up with petrol and water before you leave Gaborone or Molepolole and carry extra supplies of both with you, as well as camping equipment and food, as there is neither accommodation, shopping nor petrol in the Reserve.

Tourist information: The President Hotel and the Gaborone Sun provide airport transfer. They also arrange for the hire of cars and air charter flights.

There is an official tourist office at the east end of The Mall which sells very fine posters.

Maun

The main town of Ngamiland, Maun is interesting for its preservation of some of the customs and commerce established in its earlier days as a trading post and base for white hunters. It is the centre for most of the wildlife viewing and hunting areas of the north-west, and is on an all-weather road from Nata. However, parts of the road are liable to flood during the rains and it is a slow hard day's drive. It is advisable to carry water and petrol. Maun is linked to the road network running into the rest of Botswana, Zambia, Zimbabwe and South Africa. Moremi and the Okavango Delta are accessible from the town (see National Parks), and other trips from Maun include Nxai and Makgadikgadi pans.

Nxai Pan is a fossil lake, lying 32 km north-west of the Nata – Maun road, and is accessible by Land-Rover. There is wildlife during the rainy season (November-April), when large herds of oryx, zebra, springbok and wildebeest congregate there in enormous numbers – it is possible to see up to 5,000 head of game at one time.

Makgadikgadi Pans lie due south of Nxai on the southern side of the Nata – Maun road. The huge salt pans are seasonally filled with water between November and April to a depth of a few inches; then huge flocks of flamingoes visit the pans.

Tsodilo Hills, 400 km from Maun along roads passable by four-wheel-drive vehicles, are the most interesting and spectacular prehistoric site in Botswana. They comprise a micaceous quartzite schist ridge, rising at one end by 400 m and extending for about 18 km, varying in colour from grey to soft yellow, streaked with purple and red. Implements from the middle and late stone ages and iron age, glass and clay beads and pottery can be found there, but the Hills are most famous for their rock paintings, of which there are about 2,000, the majority concentrated on the second, or female, hill. The paintings are attributed to the Bushmen, and Tsodilo is one of the last places where both paintings and Bushmen are still found in the same area.

Most of the paintings are of animals in silhouette, with a few scenes such as an elephant hunt and rhinoceros hunt. Only in one place do pictures overlap, giving some idea of the order of succession of the many different styles found in the paintings. Although their age is uncertain, the style is similar to Transvaal paintings which have been dated back 4,000 years.

Lake Ngami is south-west of Maun on the road to Sehithwa; a four-wheel-drive vehicle is necessary. The amount of water varies in the lake and in some years it is completely dry. When Livingstone saw it, it was 240 km wide. It is a paradise for anglers, and for bird-watchers.

Serowe

The town lies 50 km west of the good road that connects Gaborone and Francistown. It is the chief town of the Bangwato and a fine example of a traditional Tswana village. Huts fan out in ordered patterns from the *kgotla,* or central meeting place, and the hill is where the Chiefly family, the Khamas, are buried.

Besides the Serowe Hotel, the

Tshwaragano Hotel is built in traditional style on a hill overlooking the town. It is less expensive than the Serowe Hotel and runs on a co-operative basis.

Lobatse

Just 76 km south of Gaborone, Lobatse has its own charm and is the seat of a number of craft-related activities. At Tiro ya Diatla, 70 Batswana spin, card and weave karakul wool into carpets, wall-hangings, curtains, bedspreads and even $80 teddy bears (sold for about one-third that price on the spot). At the huge Botswana Meat Commission abattoirs, arguably Africa's best beef is prepared for export to Europe, as well as for local consumption. The High Court is also at Lobatse.

Francistown

Francistown grew from the gold rush to be the first mine discovery in Southern Africa in the 1880's and it still carries many of the trademarks of that period. Today, the town is surrounded by hundreds of old shafts, pit heads and mine dumps. Recent mineral finds in northern Botswana have given new impetus to local industries. Francistown has also become a major staging point for the game parks in north and north-western Botswana.

Places of interest in the town are the Botswana Game Industries' factory and shop, and Lekgaba Centre, about a mile from the main street, where craftwork in wood and ivory is sold. There are ruins north of the town, thought to be contemporary with Great Zimbabwe.

Francistown, on the main road and rail routes across Botswana, is the taking-off point for the great wildlife areas of Ngamiland.

Selebi-Phikwe

This was Botswana's first copper-mining town, built entirely to support the mining community, including a large number of expatriate engineers. The Selebi-Phikwe mine has been beset with difficulties since its inception in 1974, but in the first half of 1985 the company turned an operating profit.

Molepolole

Chief town of the Bakwena and gateway to the Kalahari, it has a good stop-over point in the Mafenya-Tlala Hotel, built in the form of traditional rondavels by the Brigades. All rondavels have hot water and electricity. Molepolole is linked to Gaborone by a good tarred road.

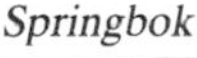
Springbok

BURUNDI

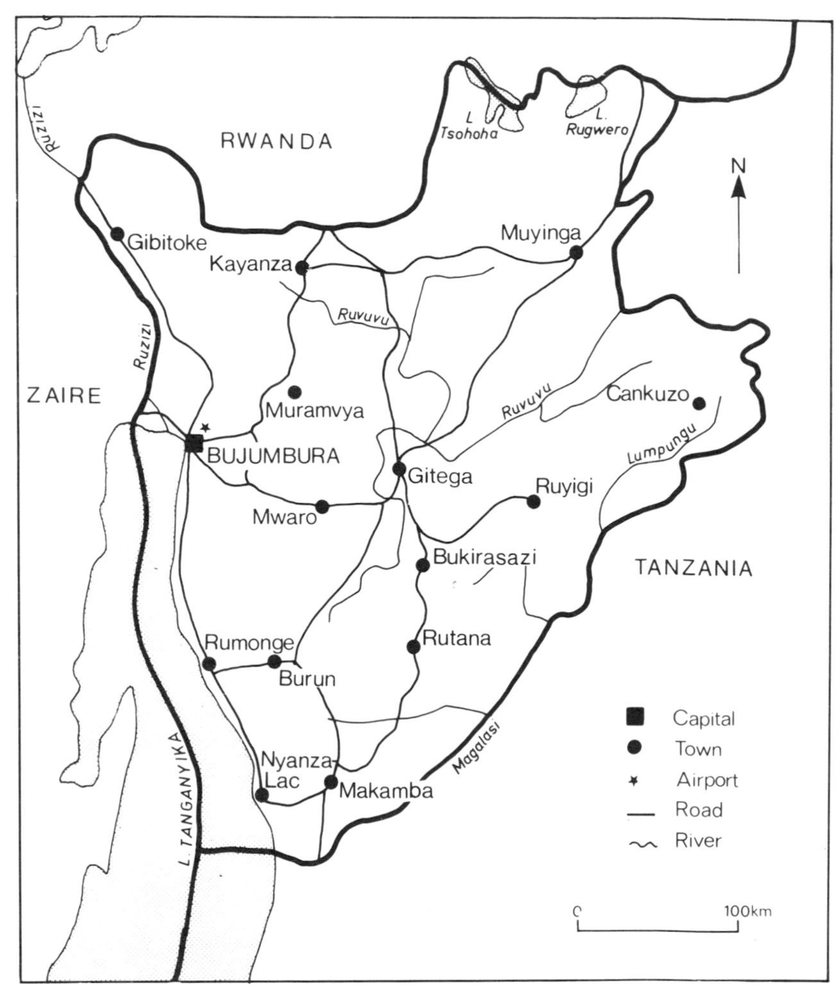

Area: 27,834 sq km
Population: 5.25 million (1989 World Bank)
Capital: Bujumbura

Burundi is a beautifully hilly country nestling at the heart of Africa overlooking the great waterway of Lake Tanganyika. Its recent history has been marked by bloody conflict between the ruling Tutsi and the majority Hutu people and for this reason it is still not considered the tourist paradise it could become.

A Tropical Land

The majestic hills and valleys of Burundi are covered with eucalyptus trees and banana groves, with homesteads scattered among cultivated fields, and with patches of luxuriant pasture. The climate of most of this high, though tropical, country is warm and pleasant. In the east the fertile area gives way to savannah grassland and to the valley of the Ruvubu which receives most of the water from the rivers flowing into the Kagera and Lake Victoria. On the southern frontier the land slopes towards the Malagarasi River which flows into Lake Tanganyika.

Running from north to south is the 2,000-2,500 m high mountain range marking the Nile-Zaire watershed. Little primary forest is left on the ridge, which is now used for cash crops of coffee and tea. Descending steeply on the west it affords extensive views over Lake Tanganyika. A strip along the lake shore dips as low as 774 m and is hot and arid while the mountains behind receive most of the rain (1,500 mm compared with 900 mm by the lake). At the north end of the lake the Ruzizi River enters through a fertile plain where the capital and only large town, Bujumbura, has developed.

The people speak Kirundi but are divided socially by their ancestors' origins: the Hutu (85% of the population) descended from agriculturalists who long ago came from Zaire; and the Tutsi (14%) are tall slender pastoralists who came perhaps from southern Ethiopia. The Tutsi are themselves hierarchically divided and, in fact, the most significant gulf in the past was between the *ganwa* ('princes of the blood') and the rest. The main group are concentrated in the Bu-Tutsi district where they form over 80% of the population, occupying all levels of society.

History

The original inhabitants of Burundi must have been the Twa pygmies, who lived as hunters and gatherers in this region for thousands of years. Among the last survivors of pre-Bantu Africa, they now form only a tiny minority (one per cent) of the population.

The most numerous ethnic group in Burundi, the Hutu (forming 85% of the population), migrated into the region probably at the end of the first millenium AD. But after the 17th century the Hutu peasant farmers gradually came under the economic domination of the cattle-owning Tutsi and Hima who migrated southwards from Ethiopia and Uganda, forming themselves into a semi-aristocracy, through feudal methods of cattle-clientship and land tenure.

The Tutsi ruling structure in Burundi did not develop into the centralised and militarised nation that emerged in neighbouring Rwanda. Although there was a nominal King (*Mwami*), the country was loosely organised and frequently divided by factional rivalries among royal princes (*ganwa*). In each area a chief or *ganwa* could exercise as much control as he liked, but in his disputes with other chiefs he required the support of his kin.

Burundi and Rwanda fell under German control (as Ruanda-Urundi) during the late 19th century 'scramble for Africa'. The colony was scarcely administered at all. During the First World War Belgian forces ousted the Germans and in 1919 the two territories (in close association with the Belgian Congo) were mandated to Belgium by the League of Nations. Belgium continued to rule 'indirectly' through the Tutsi chiefs, and Belgian rule was characterised largely by neglect and lack of social reforms. Colonialism exaggerated rather than reduced the social differences between the Tutsi and Hutu – Tutsi chiefs were given arbitrary powers, while the missions, who were granted a monopoly in education, saw the Tutsi as 'natural rulers'. With the expansion of education and commercial activities even greater social divisions occurred. While in the countryside the peasantry (whether Tutsi or Hutu) saw little improvement, in the towns a modern Tutsi elite became established.

Burundi attained its independence in 1962 without the violence suffered in Rwanda, but in the next four years seven governments unsuccessfully attempted to rule. King Mwambutsa, who ruled between 1962 and 1965, tried to maintain a balance between Hutu and Tutsi but in 1964 he refused to appoint a Hutu Prime Minister after an election in which Hutu candidates were victorious. The Mwami was overthrown in an army coup led by Colonel Michel Micombero and fled to Switzerland. The ruling military clique of Tutsi supremacists began to remove the 'Hutu Threat' – a process that has continued to this day.

Colonel Micombero created a 'Government of Public Safety' in July 1966 and in November 1966, the teenage Prince, Charles Ndizeye, who had succeeded his father, King Mwambutsa, as King Ntare V, was deposed while abroad. Colonel Micombero held the Presidency from 1966 until he was overthrown in 1976. The sporadic purges of Hutu from any government position and systematic killings in Hutu areas sparked off a Hutu rebellion; the fact that the clique around Micombero was severely divided probably further encouraged a Hutu bid for power. The Hutu uprising of April 1972 which coincided with Micombero's dismissal of his government was repressed with extreme violence – the army went on a sustained campaign of selective genocide, killing all Hutu who had received any formal education. Between 80,000 and 200,000 Hutu and Tutsi died in the upheaval. By April 1974 there were 100,000 Hutu refugees abroad, mainly in Tanzania where they remain.

In November 1976 Micombero was overthrown by Colonel Jean Baptiste Bagaza who promised to work towards inter-communal harmony and to revolutionise Burundi society. However, owing to continued Tutsi dominance in government, the Hutu remain without much confidence in the regime which is more military in flavour and has increased the army's corporate power. On 3 September 1987 Major Pierre Buyoya deposed Bagaza and set out to rid his country of tribalism, but not before another wave of killings in August 1988 when hundreds died. Buyoya then set up a Commission for National Unity which formulated proposals for national reconciliation.

Economy

The great mass of the people of Burundi are peasants and they are clearly among the poorest people in Africa. The majority live at subsistence level with very little surplus for selling. Although the majority of the population grow food, widespread malnutrition exists.

Over 80% of export earnings are derived from coffee, and world price fluctuations in the coffee market therefore closely affect Burundi. There has been little economic growth since independence, although there has been a programme of agricultural diversification including cotton and tea production. The new Government has promised co-operatives and villagisation programmes in an attempt to improve the rural economy. Stock is raised but there is competition for space on hillsides where crops are grown.

The industrial sector is very small but finds of valuable minerals such as nickel and uranium are being investigated. The Government has been heavily dependent on foreign aid from the UNDP, OPEC, China and the EEC.

Mountainous landscape

General Information

Government

Military with the sole political party UPRONA determining state policy and supervising the actions of the Government. Head of State: Pierre Buyoya.

Languages

The official languages are French and Kirundi. Swahili is spoken as a commercial language, especially in Bujumbura.

Religion

Half the population follow traditional beliefs and half are Christian (mainly Roman Catholic).

How to Get There

By air: The international airport 15 km from Bujumbura is served by Sabena and Air Zaire flying from Brussels and Kinshasa. A national airline STAB (Société des Transports Aeriens du Burundi) flies between Bukavu (Zaire), Goma (Zaire) and Kigali (Rwanda).
By road: There is a good road from Bukavu (eastern Zaire) and a fair one from Rwanda and thence to East Africa. Land communications with Tanzania are poor. Motoring is difficult in the rainy season.
By lake: Cargo steamers, which also carry some passengers, ply between Kigoma (Tanzania) and Bujumbura, taking one night or one day. There are less frequent services from Kalemi in Zaire (three days via Kigoma).

Entry Regulations

Visitors must have a valid passport and visa and a return or onward ticket. Visas should be obtained well in advance from Burundi embassies, e.g. in Brussels, Paris, Bonn, Kampala (Uganda) or Washington. Passengers arriving without a visa may be put on the next international flight leaving Bujumbura regardless of destination. Travellers intending to visit other countries and to return to Burundi need to hold a visa valid for several journeys, or to obtain a further entry visa in Bujumbura from the Immigration Service.

Visitors must possess valid international certificates of vaccination against yellow fever; inoculation against cholera and typhoid is not compulsory but recommended.

Customs Regulations

All baggage must be declared. Cameras, radios, tape-recorders, etc., are liable to duty, but visitors staying only a few days are usually allowed to take them into the country duty-free. The import of arms without prior customs permission is forbidden.

Visitors must declare all Burundi or foreign currency. There are no restrictions on the amount that may be imported. All exchange transactions must be conducted through one of the main banks or at Bujumbura airport.

Climate

The climate near Lake Tanganyika and in the Ruzizi River plain is equatorial – hot (around 23°C) and humid though often windy on the lake – but in the rest of the country mild and pleasant (average 20°C). The long dry season lasts from June to September while the rains of October to May are interrupted by the short dry season from December to January. The best time for a visit is

June-September or January-February.
What to wear: Lightweight clothing is essential with a cardigan for evenings and a light raincoat in the appropriate season.

Health Precautions

Anti-malarial prophylactics should be taken. Tap water is unsafe for drinking.

Banks and Currency

Commercial banks operate only in Bujumbura.
Banque de la République du Burundi, BP 705, Bujumbura
Banque Belgo-Africaine Burundi, 16 blvd de la Liberté, BP 585, Bujumbura
Banque Commerciale du Burundi, Chaussée Prince-Louis-Rwagasore, BP 990, Bujumbura
Banque de Crédit de Bujumbura, ave Patrice Emmery Lumumba, BP 300, Bujumbura
Currency: The Burundi Franc (FB). (See currency table, page 10).

Business Hours

Banks: Monday-Friday 0800-1200.
Government Offices: Monday-Friday 0800-1200.
Commerce and Shops: Monday-Friday 0800-1200 and 1400-1630. Saturday 0800-1200.

Public Holidays

New Year's Day, 1 January
Easter Monday, 16 April 1990
Labour Day, 1 May
Ascension Day, 24 May 1990
Whit Monday, 4 June 1990
Independence Day, 1 July
Day of Assumption, 15 August
UPRONA Day, 18 September
Rwagasore Day, 13 October
All Saints' Day, 1 November
Christmas Day, 25 December

Embassies in Bujumbura

Belgium: Ave de l'Industrie, BP 1920, tel: 36.76.
China: BP 2550.
France: BP 1790, tel: 31.76.
Federal Republic of Germany: Tel: 32.11.
USSR: BP 1034, tel: 26.98.
USA: BP 1720, tel: 34.54.

Accommodation and Food

Good hotel facilities exist in Bujumbura where meals, although reasonably good, are expensive. Elsewhere in the country there is virtually no accommodation for the visitor.
Tipping: As a rule no service charges are levied, and 10% of the bill is a normal tip at a restaurant.

Hutu pottery at Gitega market

CAMERA PRESS

Hotels

NAME	ADDRESS	TELEPHONE	TELEX
BUJUMBURA			
Aerhôtel Source du Nil	Avenue du Stade, BP 2072	5222 Aernil BD1	Telex 30
Hotel Burundi-Palace	Avenue de l'Uprona	2920	
Hotel Central	Place de l'Independence	2658	
Hotel Grillon	Avenue du Zaire BP 34	2519	
Novotel	Chaussée du Peuple BP 1015		
Hotel Paguidas-Haidemenos	Avenue du Peuple Burundi, BP 2	2251	
Hotel Residence	Avenue de Stanley BP 405	2773	
Hotel Tanganyika	–	4433	

Bujumbura

The capital, a trading and industrial centre as well as a port, was founded in 1899 by the Germans as Costermansville. It is now a bustling cosmopolitan town of over 100,000 inhabitants, attractively located on the shores of Lake Tanganyika with high hills rising behind it. It is well placed for water sports – sailing, skiing and fishing. The public beach lies about 5 km from the town towards the west. Sights in the town include the Postmaster's House, recalling the German period, and the striking modern Parliament Buildings.

The French and Greek restaurants are good and there are several nightclubs. **Sport:** *The Entente Sportive* club offers tourist membership for swimming, tennis, volleyball, basket-ball, golf. It also has a restaurant and bar. For information on water sports contact the Cercle Nautique.
Tourist Office: Office national de Tourisme, BP 902, tel: 20.23/30.84.

Inland

The main road east from Bujumbura climbs over the great Nile-Zaire watershed to Muramvya, which was once the royal city of Burundi. To the south (111 km from Bujumbura) is Gitega, also a former residence of the king and, for a few months after independence, the capital.

About 100 km south of Gitega, near Rutana, is a pyramid marking the source of the Nile. It was set up in 1937 by Burkhart Waldecker. Although the definitive source of the White Nile is much disputed (see RWANDA), this Kigira River is the most southerly of the many rivers running into the Ruvubu, then Kagera and Lake Victoria.

CENTRAL AFRICAN REPUBLIC

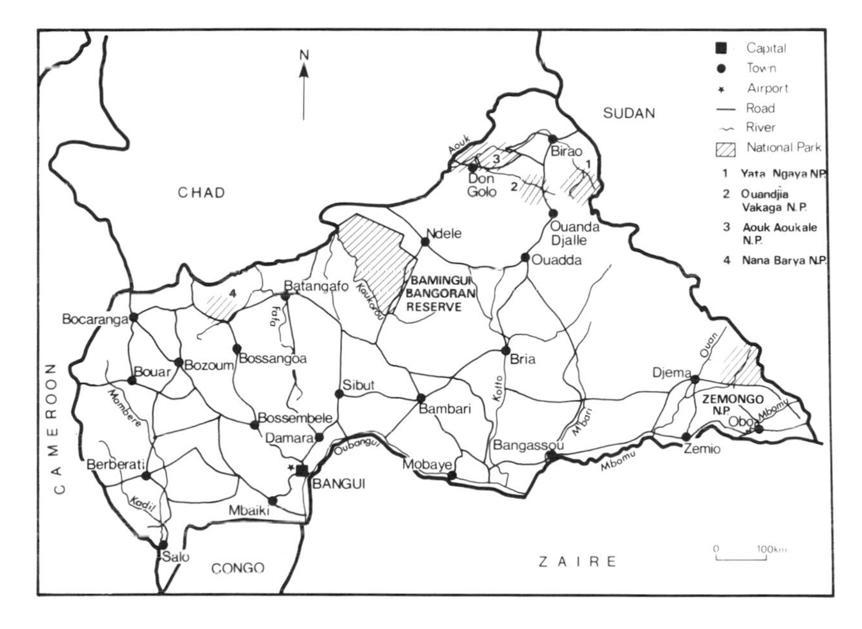

Area: 622,984 sq km
Population: 2.86 million (1989 World Bank)
Capital: Bangui

The Central African Republic is a thinly populated country, rich in natural resources and occupying an important position between Sudan, Zaire, Chad and Cameroon. For 14 years the country suffered the brutal dictatorial rule of Jean-Bedel Bokassa, self-proclaimed 'Emperor' of the 'Central African Empire'. He was replaced by David Dacko, after a French-engineered coup in September 1979, when the Republic was restored. France remains in effective control of the Republic, as it has done ever since independence.

Bangui, the capital city, has an air of cosmopolitan prosperity but it is an enclave within a country where the only commendable developments have been in building some good roads. The majority of villages and towns have inadequate medical or educational facilities and the people live on a poor diet of cassava and other starches, and only occasional meat or fish.

For the traveller to this country, however, the enjoyment is not in Bangui, where life is expensive and the political atmosphere of intrigue and surveillance is oppressive, but in the countryside where there is beautifully varied scenery and the people are universally friendly and welcoming.

An Open Plateauland

A huge territory of largely uninhabited forest and bush, lying between latitudes of 4° and 11°N the CAR has for its southern border the Oubangui River and the M'boumou. The watershed with the Chari River running into Lake Chad cuts through the centre from east to west.

More than half the country lying east of a line joining Bassangassou–Fort Crampel–Batangafo is almost uninhabited and this is where the big game reserves and parks are situated.

The country rises towards Cameroon, with altitudes up to 2,000 m west of Bocaranga in the north-west corner. There is fairly dense tropical rainforest in the south-west, in the inaccessible districts of Haute Sangha and Lobaye towards the Congo border, but most of the country is rolling or flat plateau, at altitudes of about 500 m, covered with dry deciduous forest where this has not been reduced to grass savannah, or completely destroyed by annual bush-fires. To the north-east the country becomes sub-desert, with a Sahelian flora, and very mountainous in places.

The population is probably about three million, but since many people live in the forest out of reach of the administration and others move in and out of neighbouring countries, this figure is approximate. The Baya and Banda peoples make up about half the population. Other prominent groups are the Baka and the Zande. Groups of nomadic Fulani, Chad Arab and Sudanese cattle-peoples move through the country and in and out of neighbouring Cameroon, Chad and Sudan.

The Central African Republic is one of the few African countries with an almost nationally understood language, Sango. It originated as a trading language along the Oubangui River, and is related to Lingala, one of the four main languages of Zaire. Although French is the official language, Sango is widely used in administration, and almost entirely on the radio.

Culture

Each ethnic group has its own lively dancing and characteristic musical instruments. To see these, you have to travel in the bush and hope to happen on one of the frequent village ceremonies. The villagers make for their own use some beautifully simple but practical basketwork and furniture (stools, chairs and beds).

There are quite a number of styles of woodcarving; those from the forest near the Congo border are among the best, but they are not of the high standard found in Zaire. Traders offer a wide variety of animal and snake skins, and also ivory objects. On the pavements in Bangui, Hausa traders offer sandals, belts and other fine leatherwork, much of it from Cameroon.

The Boganda Museum in Bangui is stuffed full with a vast range of traditional implements, drums, religious objects and weapons from all over the country. A morning spent in this museum is more worthwhile than any academic course in African anthropology.

History

Little is known about the people of Central Africa until the 18th century. The Bandia were one of the more powerful groups, giving rise to the Zande nation of the east in the 19th century, but the whole area was subjected to slave-raids from Sudan and Chad. The French called the territory 'Oubangui-Chari' when Equatorial Africa was established in 1910 out of a confusion of territorial claims arising from military penetration since 1886.

The colony was under-administered, except in the plantations where forced labour provoked a series of rebellions that were savagely repressed by the French in the 1930's. With vast expanses of wild uninhabited country, Oubangui-Chari was a favourite big-game hunting ground for French administrators and army officers.

The territory was educationally, economically and administratively unprepared for its political independence in 1960. It was further handicapped by the death in an air-crash in 1959 of Barthelemy Boganda, its outstanding political leader. He was succeeded by David Dacko, whose administration depended almost entirely on French technical assistance, and on a substantial French subsidy. Dacko was overthrown in 1965 in a military coup led by General Jean-Bedel Bokassa. He proved dictatorial, corrupt and eccentric. He ruined the country's economy, while amassing a vast personal fortune. In 1977 he had himself crowned Emperor in a ceremony which attracted worldwide ridicule. While he still enjoyed the support of the French government, Bokassa was able to stay in power, but in 1979 a crisis arose following reports that the Emperor had personally killed some school children during a pupil protest. Deciding that Bokassa could no longer guarantee their interests, in September 1979 the French government flew in the former President, David Dacko, to replace him. Bokassa, who was abroad at the time of the coup, went into exile.

Backed by French troops, Dacko imprisoned opposition leaders and cracked down on trade union and student activities. In early 1980 he established a political party, the *Union Démocratique Centrafricaine*. But on 1 September 1981 he was ousted by General André Kolingba, the Chief of staff of the armed forces, in a military coup.

Economy

By the time of his downfall, 'Emperor' Bokassa had helped reduce the economy to a miserable condition. Dacko inherited a bankrupt treasury, heavy foreign debts and a chaotic administration. Production in most sectors had fallen to below pre-independence levels as a result of poor organisation and the decay of transport and communications facilities. An influx of aid from France and other Western sources has helped the Kolingba government to cope with its immediate problems. However, there is not likely to be any change in a pattern of development that favours a tiny minority of citizens, leaving the mass to a low standard of living with no hope of improvement.

Cotton and coffee are quite widely grown as cash crops for export, but quantities have been declining in recent years as farmers have preferred to grow food crops, or to diversify into growing other cash crops like cocoa, tobacco, or groundnuts.

Rubber is produced in the forests, and timber is a significant export, reaching 700,000 tonnes a year. But the mainstay of the economy is the export of diamonds. This industry was personally controlled by Bokassa and much of the profit from diamond production went to boost his personal fortune, rather than State revenues. There is uranium at Bakouma, which is of interest to French and Swiss mining concerns, although no mining has yet taken place.

Wildlife

Much of this country's rich wildlife is at present preserved because almost two-thirds of the country is uninhabited rather than because of Government policy. Under 'Emperor' Bokassa's rule, the elephant population was reduced from about 40,000 to around 10,000 – a large part of the 'Emperor's' personal fortune was based on the ivory trade. Hunting for food by small groups of villagers with spears, nets and bows and arrows is vigorously carried on, especially in the centre and centre-west regions.

Thousands of hectares of forest are burned each year during hunting, which accelerates the destruction of natural vegetation, and hastens the extermination of many animal species. It was not until the 1950's that seven wildlife reserves, three national parks and one *réserve intégrale* were established.

The number of animals can still compare with that of the East African reserves. All kinds of antelope are represented by big herds: waterbuck, hartebeeste, roan antelope, Buffon's kob, Derby eland and great kudu. There are large numbers of lion, leopard and cheetah as well as elephant, giraffe, hippo and rhino.

The CAR is remarkable for its thousands of brightly-coloured butterflies, many of them unique. They are found all over the country, but especially in the south-west.

National Parks

Zemongo is on the Sudan border in the east of Central Africa. Almost inaccessible except in certain seasons by four-wheel-drive vehicles from Bangassou via Zemio on the road to Obo. Open grass savannah with 'plains game'.

Yata Ngaya is farther north, also on the Sudan border. Contains the **Andre Felix National Park.** Mountainous.

Ouandjia Vakaga – 100 km to the west of the above – and **Aouk Aoukale,** 50 km to the north-west. Between these two reserves is the small **St. Floris National Park.**

The above three reserves and the national parks are accessible from Birao by four-wheel-drive vehicles in certain seasons. Birao can be reached, also by four-wheel-drive vehicles, from Bangui via Bambari and Bria (about three days' drive).

Another group of game reserves is situated near the Chad border and can be reached by road (four-wheel-drive) from Bangui, via Fort Crampel and Ndele.

The game population of these reserves is impressive, and includes large numbers of elephant, buffalo, lion and antelope. The birdlife is very prolific.

There is no possibility of accommodation. All food, water, bedding and petrol should be taken in a very reliable four-wheel-drive vehicle. While it is sometimes said that there are 'resthouses' in Central Africa, and these even appear on maps, you will be lucky if you find a ruined bat-infested building.

The Kembe Falls, near Bangassou

General Information

Government

Military government under General André Kolingba, since 1 September 1981, by the Military Committee for National Recovery (CMRN).

Languages

French is the official language, but Sango is widely used. Each ethnic group has its own tongue, while foreign traders have introduced Arabic in the north, Hausa in many parts and Swahili in the east.

Religion

Traditional, Islam and Roman Catholic.

How to Get There

By air: From Paris: UTA, Air Afrique and ACAV. From Moscow: Aeroflot (via Cairo and Khartoum). From Douala: Air Centrafrique (irregular). From Brazzaville: Air Centrafrique. From Kinshasa: Air Zaire (irregular and unreliable).

By road: The only way across Africa from west to east lies through Bangui. From Ndjamena you can drive south to Bangui through Bossangoa. From Douala you can drive via Yaounde to Bouar and Bangui. The roads are in a reasonable state of repair, although there are stretches that become difficult during the rains. One difficult section is at the entry point to the country from Garoua-Boulai in Cameroon.

From Zaire there are no bridges across the Oubangui River and vehicles must be transported by ferry, either at Bangui, Bangassou or Zemio.

By river: There is transport upriver from Brazzaville to Bangui, and a passenger ferry across the river from Zongo in Zaire.

Entry Regulations

Visas are required by all nationals other than French and Africans from francophone States. Where there is no Central African Embassy, the French Embassy should be able to deliver a tourist visa, but usually for only 48 hours. This has to be renewed after arrival in Bangui.

While immigration controls are normally conducted at Bangui airport, visitors arriving by road should be prepared for the unpredictable at entry points such as Bangassou, or coming from Chad. The Cameroon border controls appear to be normal. The numerous barriers set up on the main roads to control the movement of traffic may be the source of some delay. The worst is kilometre 12 on the road north out of Bangui. Here everyone moving in or out of Bangui is stopped and 'controlled'. Foreigners arriving by road have to present passports and car tryptiques all over again as when arriving at the frontier. Yellow fever and cholera certificates are required.

Customs Regulations

While you can in theory bring in the usual personal goods and belongings, unpredictable behaviour of military personnel at entry points should be expected. Firearms on no account should be brought.

There is no limit on the amount of foreign currency or travellers' cheques which can be taken into the country, although a declaration must be made. Unused foreign currency may be taken out again. Similarly there is no limit on the import or export of French francs or CFA banknotes.

Climate

The climate is generally hot with a marked dry season. Mean annual temperatures are about 25°C in Bangui, but rise to nearly 30°C in the north-east. The rains in the south are from May to October, the season shortening as one approaches Chad and the Sudan. Mean annual rainfall varies from 1,636 mm in Bangui to 2,070 mm in Bangassou. In the north the dusty but cooling harmattan is felt in January and February, but it does not affect Bangui.

Health Precautions

Anti-malarial precautions are essential. Bilharzia is found almost everywhere, so water should be filtered or boiled, even in Bangui. Various kinds of intestinal disorders can be picked up in the bush.

Banks and Currency

Banque des Etats de l'Afrique Centrale: BP 851, Bangui
Banque Nationale Centrafricaine de Dépôt, Place de Republique: BP 801, tel: 61.32.00
Union Bancaire en Afrique Centrale: BP 59, rue de Brazza, Bangui, tel: 61.29.90
Banque Internationale pour l'Afrique Occidentale SA: BP 910, tel: 61.00.42
Currency: CFA Franc divided into 100 centimes
(See currency table, page 10).

Business Hours

Banks: Monday-Saturday 0700-1200
Post Offices: Monday-Friday 0730-1130 and 1430-1630; for stamps and telegrams only, Saturday 1430-1830 and Sundays 0800-1100
Shops: Monday-Saturday 0700-1200 and 1430-1830. Some food shops may be open on Sunday morning.

Public Holidays

New Year's Day, 1 January
Anniversary of the death of Boganda 29 March
Labour Day, 1 May
Mother's Day, 3rd week in May
Liberation of African Continent Day, 25 May
Ascension Day, 24 May 1990
Whit Monday, 4 June 1990
Feast of the Blessed Virgin Mary, 15 August
Proclamation de la République, 28 November
National Day, 1 December
Christmas Day, 25 December

Embassies in Bangui

Cameroon: BP 935
Chad: BP 461
China PR: BP 1430
Congo: BP 1414
Egypt: BP 1422
France: bld. du Général de Gaulle, BP 884
Gabon: BP 1570
Germany FR: avenue G.A. Nasser, BP 901, tel: 61.07.46
Ivory Coast: BP 930
Japan: BP 1367, tel: 61.06.68
Nigeria: BP 1010
Senegal: BP 950
Sudan: BP 1351
USA: Place de la République, BP 924, tel: 61.02.00
Zaire: BP 989

Transport

There are 19,207 km of roads and tracks, including 5,018 km of well-surfaced main roads passable throughout the year. Traffic drives on the right. If driving through the country it is essential to carry the maximum of petrol. There are pumps in many centres but these are very often out of petrol for long periods. Portuguese-owned stores (such as the chains of Moura and Gouveia) can supply quite a good range of supplies, but may be out of items like sugar or oil.

There are very few garages outside Bangui and spare parts for cars are practically unobtainable. When a car has an accident, its owner usually breaks it up and sells the parts at a good profit.

Taxis are available in Bangui. They do not have meters and it is advisable to settle the fare before starting your journey.

Care hire: Self-drive cars are available from Tsiros Location, BP 68, Bangui, tel: 29.86 and Auto Service, BP 13, tel: 22.57.

Accommodation and Food

The only regularly-functioning hotels are in Bangui, where they are mostly very expensive.

The only European-style restaurants are in Bangui but local food is available. There are numerous local bars.

Bangui

The capital takes its name from the rapids on the Oubangui River where it squeezes through a range of low hills. The town is rapidly spreading, with modern blocks and broad avenues, shaded by mango trees and flamboyants. The central

Hotels

NAME	ADDRESS	TELEPHONE
BANGUI		
Minerva	BP 308	26.62
National	BP 823	33.76
New Palace	BP 108	23.77
Rock	BP 569	20.88
Safari	BP 134	30.20
St. Sylvestre	BP 1015	38.00
Sofitel	Scheduled opening early 1986	
BAMBARI		
Hotel des Chasses	–	–
BANGASSOU		
La Palmeraie	–	–

market is a bustling and colourful focus of activity. The Grand Corniche leads to the banks of the Oubangui, where fishermen have their canoes.

Two elegant shops stock fine ivory and ebony art objects, as well as traditional artefacts. Anyone interested in African culture should not miss the Boganda Museum.

The main activity and vitality of Bangui is concentrated in the quarter known a 'Kilometre Cinq'.

The dramatic Boali Falls are 90 km north of Bangui by good road.

Restaurants: Apart from the hotel restaurants there are: **La Banquise, La Portugaise** or the airport restaurant.

Entertainments: In the smart clubs (in the main hotels) drinks are very expensive. Local nightlife is found in the quarter at 'Kilometre 5'.

There are sports at the Rock Club, including swimming, tennis, golf and riding.

Tourist information: Office National du Tourisme, BP 655. Bangui-Tourisme, BP 875, tel: 61.45.66.

Bouar

In a fine position on the edge of the plateau that extends into Cameroon, this dilapidated town has an ancient and mysterious history. The whole area around Bouar is dotted with evidence of a megalithic culture that flourished thousands of years ago before any of the present peoples started to arrive. This ancient civilisation has hardly been investigated but the stone monuments that now stand neglected or overgrown in the rocky landscape seem to point to a link with megalithic cultures elsewhere in the world, perhaps with those of Egypt or western Europe.

No less than 70 individual groups of standing stones in varying arrangements have been found in the Bouar area, which straddles the watershed between the Zaire River and Lake Chad basins. Generally placed at the head of streams, 60% of these granite monuments are on tributaries of the Zaire and 40% are on tributaries of Chad rivers. Several individual stones weigh three or four tonnes and would have had to be transported at least three kilometres to each site. Archaeologists have calculated that the moving of the stones would have required a greater population in the area than is now present. Some of the finest examples of the Bouar megaliths are on the outskirts of the town itself.

Bouar has also featured more recently in world events. It was the Central African headquarters of the free French forces in the World War II under General Leclerc, but now it is completely run down, both as a commercial centre and as a tourist resort. The people in this area are mainly Baya, but there are Hausa and Fulani communities.

Bambari

A typical central African town, once with a semblance of prosperity, now dilapidated, but still pleasant by virtue of its position on the Ouaka River. The people in the area are Banda. The countryside consists of rolling green grassy hills. To the south is some beautiful scenery with neat Banda villages nestling among fields of coffee and food crops. By the rivers the fishing communities have a special lifestyle and vitality.

Bangassou

Another sleepy town but the usual point for overlanders to cross the Oubangui River to or from Zaire. On the road from Bangui are the spectacular Kembe Falls on the Kotto River: a good spot for washing but fatal for anyone attempting to swim.

CONGO

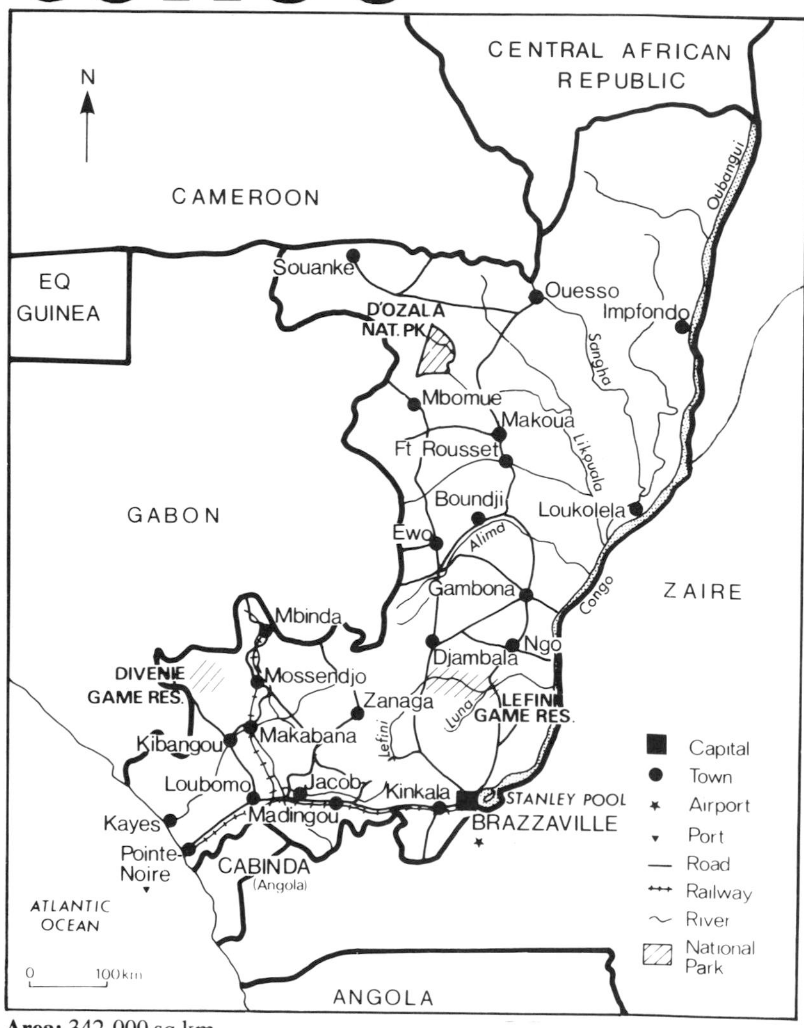

Area: 342,000 sq km
Population: 2.15 million (1989 World Bank)
Capital: Brazzaville

Formerly the French Congo, this country stretching between the Atlantic Ocean and the north banks of the great Congo river used to be confused with the ex-Belgian Congo, now known as Zaire. But its capital city, Brazzaville, was for a long time at the centre of political developments throughout this part of Africa and is still a very important commercial and political centre. The recent growth in the country's oil revenues has led to an upsurge of foreign business and financial interest, despite the government's Marxist-Leninist label.

There are still 25,000 French residents in the Congo, whether as 'technical assistants' or as businessmen and traders. It is an exceptionally friendly country, and the capital is a clean and elegant city. The visitor can also explore some of the country's physical attractions such as the forest areas (which still support rare wildlife species), the rapids of the great river, lovely waterfalls, and beaches around Pointe-Noire. But communications are generally not well developed.

A Country in Transition

Over half the Congo's small population live in the towns, especially Brazzaville. The subsistence life of the forest villages has been increasingly abandoned by each new generation, in favour of wage employment in the towns. Government policies, offering uneconomic prices for agricultural products, have accelerated urbanisation. The Oubangui and Congo (Zaire) rivers are vital means of livelihood as well as transport, both by steamer and the traditional dugout canoe. The Congo river forms a lake-like expanse, 33 km by 25 km, at Stanley Pool before rushing into rapids for most of the remainder of its journey seaward. The two capitals of Brazzaville and Kinshasa (Zaire) were built on opposite banks of the Pool to become the terminal for two railways from the coast. Above the Pool steamers ply upriver as far as Bangui (CAR) and Kisangani (Zaire).

The narrow, sandy, coastal plain broken by lagoons, has low rainfall and grassland vegetation, due to cool sea currents. Behind, the deep forest-clad gorges of the Mayombe Mountains rise abruptly 500 to 800 m until, beyond Loubomo, the landscape dips to the fertile alluvial depression of the Niari valley where the main agricultural crops are grown.

Brazzaville itself lies to the south of the dry, grassy unproductive BaTeke plateau through which rivers cut deep valleys to the Congo. The whole northern half of the country is by contrast swamp and forest of the Congo basin, almost constantly flooded. Three-quarters of the 1.9 million Congolese live in the south, while over one-third of the total population is concentrated in the four large towns: Brazzaville, Pointe-Noire, Loubomo and Kayes. The forests are uninhabited.

The Kongo people, who are also found in Zaire, Angola and the Cabinda enclave, form 45% of the population and live predominantly around Brazzaville. This area was part of the 15th-century Kongo kingdom, with its capital in present-day Angola.

The Vili on the coast were also once united in the Loango kingdom which fell under Kongo and Portuguese domination at that time. The Teke (20% of the population) on the plateau north of Stanley Pool were once loosely knit under the Anzico kingdom, but by the 19th century this had fallen apart, long before Count Savorgnan de Brazza, the explorer, was claiming that his treaty with their chief Makoko conferred rights to the whole plateau. Other ethnic groups are the Boutangui, the Sanga, the Lari (who straddle both banks of Stanley Pool), and the M'Bochi of the far northern Likuala basin. There are also a large number of Gabonese and some 25,000 non-Africans, mainly French.

Culture

Carved wooden masks and figures are the Congo's best-known art form. Similar figures were cut into the soft stone lids of tombs. Kongo art was Christianised early so that, for example, figures of the mythical ancestress of mankind were translated into the Madonna and Child. The M'Bochi made long dancers' staves with a human head for festivals honouring Djo, the Creator, who was envisaged as a snake. Much of the carving was deliberately horrific.

Modern artists have also made a name for Congo – notably the sculptor, Benoit Konongo.

Painting has developed as a new art form. Some of the best modern work can be seen and bought at the Poto Poto arts and crafts centre in Brazzaville. In addition to traditional dance forms, modern song and folklore groups play the popular Congolese style of music.

History

The pygmies were the earliest known inhabitants of the Congo. More recent settlers included the Bateke and the Kongo. The Bateke founded the Makoko Kingdom, which traded in slaves and ivory with the Portuguese and other early European explorers.

Colonised by the French in the late 19th century, Congo became politically independent in 1960. In 1963 the first president was forced to resign following demonstrations and a general strike. In the subsequent election the Mouvement National de la Révolution (MNR) came to power, but in 1968 the army took over under the leadership of Major Marien Ngouabi. The new president replaced the MNR by a single Marxist-Leninist ruling party, the Parti Congolais du Travail (PCT). In 1977 Ngouabi was assassinated, but his assassins were arrested and Col. Yhombi Opango, the chief of staff, became president. However, in early 1979 Opango himself was deposed and the presidency passed to Major Sassou Nguessou. Opango's overthrow marked a resurgence of the party and trade union militants, who demanded the enactment of a whole range of radical, anti-colonial measures, but Nguesso turned out to be a moderate and pragmatic leader.

Economy

The Congo is unusual among African states in that only about 40% of its population is engaged in agriculture. This makes it very difficult to maintain adequate food supplies to the towns. Agricultural output has fallen disastrously over the last ten years, largely as a result of the activities of the state marketing boards, which have offered farmers too low a price for their products.

Traditionally the Congo's major export is timber from its extensive tropical forests, but this has now been far surpassed in importance by petroleum. Oil production reached 6 million tonnes in 1984. Oil revenues then accounted for over 90% of government revenues, but the government has run into serious debt.

Wildlife

Elephant, buffalo, hippo and sitatunga abound in the savannah land of the coast, while the forests support the rare bongo, chimpanzees and gorillas as well as multi-coloured parrots and butterflies. Animals such as buffalo and antelope can be seen near Stanley Pool, but the two main reserves, Lefini and Divenie, are hardly organized to cater for tourists.

The sea and lagoons are full of large species such as tarpon, barracuda, red tuna fish, sword-fish, grouper, horse mackerel, shark and skate. The rivers contain Nile perch and binga, some exceeding 50 kg.

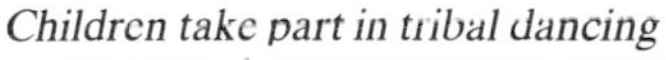

Children take part in tribal dancing

CAMERA PRESS

General Information

Government

The Head of State is the President, Colonel Denis Sassou Nguesso. There is a People's National Assembly and a single party, the *Parti Congolais du Travail* (PCT).

Language

French (official) and African languages of the Bantu group, the main ones being Kongo, Teke and Boutangui.

Religion

The population is divided between Christians, Muslims and those who follow traditional beliefs.

How to Get There

By air: Maya Maya airport is 4 km from Brazzaville. The only transport to town is by taxi. Regular flights are operated from Europe by Air Afrique, UTA and Sabena, from north-east Africa by Aeroflot and Air Algeria, and from West Africa by Air Mali and Air Cameroon. Transgabon flights arrive at Pointe-Noire.

By sea/river: Cargo ships dock at Pointe-Noire. An hourly car ferry operates between Kinshasa and Brazzaville across the Congo River; it takes 20 minutes.

By road: There is a road connection from Lambarene in Gabon to Loubomo and Brazzaville. The surface is not completely tarred. The road from Cameroon is only passable in the long dry season.

Entry Regulations

French and francophone African nationals may enter with a national identity card. Others must produce a valid passport and visa.

Applications for visas may be made to the Congolese Embassy in Paris (37 bis, rue Paul Valéry, Paris 16); allow several weeks for issue. An onward or return ticket or a bank deposit (guaranteeing payment for departure) is necessary.

Yellow fever and cholera vaccination certificates are required.

Customs Regulations

In addition to personal effects, the following may be taken in free of duty, if they are declared: 1,000 cigarettes, two cameras, 10 films, a tape-recorder, one movie camera, a pair of binoculars.

There is no restriction on the amount of foreign currency brought in or taken out, but on arrival visitors must declare all moneys being brought into the country.

Climate

Most of the country has a hot, humid, equatorial climate. The Teke plateau has a longer, cooler dry season and temperatures vary from 21°C-27°C, whereas the Congo basin is more humid with c. 1,600 mm of rain per year and temperatures of 24°C-30°C. The average rainfall is 1,000-1,200 mm per year.

There are four seasons: the long dry season from May to September; short rains October to mid-December; short dry season mid-December to mid-January; long rains mid-January to mid-May. The best time is June to September.

What to wear: Practical lightweight cottons and linens are essential, leather or canvas shoes, and a light raincoat or umbrella in the rainy season.

Health Precautions

Malaria prophylactics must be taken daily a fortnight before, during and a fortnight after the visit. It is not advisable to drink tap water.

Banks and Currency

Banque des Etats de L'Afrique Centrale: BP 126 Brazzaville
Banque Commerciale Congolaise (BCC): BP 79, avenue Amilcar Cabral, Brazzaville
Union Congolaise de Banques (UCB): BP 147, Brazzaville
Currency: CFA franc divided into 100 centimes.
(See currency table, page 10).

Business Hours

Shops: 0700 or 0800-1200 or 1300, 1500-1700 or 1730 Tuesday-Friday, 0700 or 0800-1200 or 1300 Saturday.
Some shops are open on Sunday morning.
Banks: 0630-1130 Monday-Saturday.
Post Offices: 0730-1200, 1430-1730 Monday-Friday. For stamps and telegrams only: 1430-1630 Saturday, 0830-1130 Sunday.
Government offices: 0800-1300 Monday-Saturday, 1430-1700 Monday, Wednesday, Friday.

Public Holidays

New Year's Day, 1 January
Labour Day, 1 May
Readjustment of Revolution, 31 July
'Les Trois Glorieuses', 13-15 August
All Saints Day, 1 November
Children's Day, 25 December
Foundation Day, 31 December

Embassies in Brazzaville

Belgium: BP 255, tel: 81.29.63
Cameroon: BP 2136, tel: 81.34.04
Central African Republic: BP 10
France: rue Alfassa, BP 2089, tel: 81.14.23
Gabon: BP 2033, tel: 81.05.90
Germany FR: BP 2022, tel: 81.29.90
USA: BP 1015, tel: 81.20.70
Zaire: BP 2456, tel: 81.29.38

Transport

By air: The local airline Lina-Congo flies several times daily between Brazzaville and Pointe-Noire and regularly to Loubomo, Owando, Impfondo, Kayes, Loukolela, Makabana, Moanda and Ouesso.
By road: Roads are mostly earth tracks, sandy in the dry season and impassable in the wet, suitable for Land-Rovers only. There are 600 km of tarred road. The main road from Brazzaville to Loubomo is uneven in quality although it is being tarred. It continues to the Gabon border, but the branch to Pointe-Noire is passable only when dry, and even then only with four-wheel drive and plenty of luck.
By river: Inland steamers ply from Brazzaville up the Congo and the Oubangui.
By rail: The Congo-Ocean railway company runs daily service, with dining and sleeping carriages, between Brazzaville and Pointe-Noire and a weekly railcar from Pointe-Noire to Mbinda. The Brazzaville–Pointe-Noire line is at present undergoing extensive repairs.

Accommodation and Food

Accommodation is in short supply, and it is generally well worth booking in advance. There are adequate hotels in Brazzaville, Pointe-Noire and Loubomo; elsewhere there is little accommodation for visitors. Restaurants in these towns provide mostly French cuisine and the coast has excellent fish, giant oysters and shrimps. Some restaurants – those at Nanga Lake and the Grand Hotel in Loubomo – specialize in African dishes such as piri piri chicken (with pepper), Mohambe chicken in palm-oil, palm cabbage salad, cassava leaves or Paka

Hotels

NAME	ADDRESS	TELEPHONE	TELEX
BRAZZAVILLE			
le Beach	BP 65	81.29.58	–
Cosmos	ave du Beach, BP 2459	81.33.81	–
M'Foa	ave du 28 aout 1940, BP 297	–	–
le Mistral	BP 494	81.20.33	–
Olympic Palace	ravin de la mission, BP 728	81.25.02	–
le Petit Logis	BP 318	–	–
Relais-Meridien	Lyautey, BP 588	81.09.10	–
LOUBOMO			
de France	BP 76	20.12	–
Grand	BP 26	21.02	–
POINTE-NOIRE			
Atlantic Palace	BP 939	94.24.34	–
Migitel	BP 1060	94.28.30	–
Novotel	BP 790	94.12.00	8240 KG
Sole et Mare	BP 907	–	–
Victory Palace	BP 939	94.24.49	–

Paka in palm oil.

A 10% tip is customary.

Brazzaville

Set in lush tropical vegetation, the capital city of the Congo has a quiet charm which contrasts sharply with the skyscraper city of Kinshasa on the opposite bank of the Stanley Pool. Brazzaville's clean and pleasant streets are lined with mango and flame trees, which provide a fine display of blossom in November, the country's real springtime. The city's elegance does not exclude popular life: the Poto Poto district (the former African township laid out in 1900) is especially vital and exciting, with its workshops and stalls, all-night bars and restaurants.

There are splendid views over the town and across Stanley Pool to brightly-lit Kinshasa from the cathedral of St. Firmin, built in 1892, and the house occupied by General de Gaulle during World War Two. Other places of interest are: the Basilica of St. Anne du Congo (1943-9), built in a combination of European and African styles; the National Museum of History and Ethnography; the colourful markets; the fascinating arts and crafts centre at Poto Poto, which displays and sells local paintings, masks, carvings, etc.

Restaurants: Le Mistral, tel. 81.23.20; La Pizzeria, tel. 81.11.63; Les Relais, tel. 81.09.10; Olympic, tel. 81.25.02; Armando (Italian), tel. 81.04.88; La Flotille (Lebanese), tel. 81.30.05; Cosmos, tel. 81.33.81; Le Zombi (West Indian), tel. 81.01.55; Charton (Vietnamese), tel 81.07.88; for cheap food: Safari Snack and Les Caimans.

Entertainment: Local groups singing Congolese music are popular and heard everywhere.

Nightclubs in town are Scotch Club (Hotel le Beach), Le Saturne (Hotel Cosmos), Ram Dam (Hotel Relais), Blow-Up (Armando Restaurant), and Chris (Plateau Market). In Poto Poto are the Miki, Cafe Nono, La Fiesta, La Cosette and Angele. In Bacongo are the nightclubs Chez Bibi, Milex, and Chez Tante Jacqueline.

There are two cinemas, Le Vog, tel. 81.28.85; and Le Paris, tel. 81.18.91. All films are shown in French-language versions.

These are also opportunities for sailing, horse riding and golf.

Markets: The main markets are the Plateau, Poto Poto, Moungali, Bacongo and Ouenze. The best time for a visit is in the morning. The Avenue Foch is crowded with street vendors. For those interested in curios, there is the Poto Poto centre and the artisan school on the bank of the Congo.

Car Hire: Holders of French or international driving licences can hire cars from: Auto-Location, rue du Sergeant-Malamine, BP 23.92, tel. 81.16.11; Auto-Service, Ave. Amilcar Cabral, BP 706, tel. 81.21.48.

Tourist information: Office National Congolais du Tourisme, Plateau, BP 456, tel: 81.27.13. Syndicat d'Initiative, Ave. du 28 Aout 1940, BP 173, tel: 81.31.78.

Travel agencies: Congo Voyages, Ave Foch, BP 91, tel: 81.29.99/24.90. SOAEM, Pl du Central Bar, BP 284, tel: 81.48.48.

Excursions from Brazzaville

M'Pila (3 km) is a fishing village, with potteries and an open air market among baobabs overlooking Stanley Pool. Boat trips on Stanley Pool from M'Pila pass the M'Bamou island where huts are built on poles. The Rapids are 10 km away by tarred road. Foulakari Falls (58 km by earth road) is a good picnic spot. There is a motel (10 rooms). Makana is a village of basketworkers on the main Kinkala road. From there one can drive to the panoramic Trou de Dieu, probably formed by a meteorite (60 km).

Pointe-Noire

The main port, commercial and industrial centre, Pointe-Noire is now an oil boom town, enjoying rapidly expanding activity. Its name derives from the black rock of the headland. The Pointe-Noire area is of particular interest to anglers; the lagoons along the coast abound in tarpon, barracuda, tuna, swordfish and skate, while the rivers hold Nile perch and binga.

The Plage Mondaine is a protected beach resort, with water-skiing and yachting. The lagoons of Gounkouati offer excellent fishing and shooting. Lake Nanga (9 km) provides good angling and has an excellent restaurant. To the north,

Loango was the capital of the old Vili kingdom and site of the first Catholic mission (1883). The red gorges of Diosso (31 km) form a semi-circle of cliffs facing the sea. Lake Cayo is 25 km from the town. At Djeno, 21 km to the south, one can fish from the beach. Farther away (150 km) – accessible only in the dry season though also visible from the train – are the abysses, canyons and sombre forests and characteristic flora of the Mayombe Mountains.

Restaurants: Le Dauphin, Sea Club, L'Arpède, Chez Paulette.

Entertainments: Nightclubs include the Sea Club, La Licorne and Le Mikado.

Car hire: Afric-Car, BP75, tel. 94.17.20; Taxis Fregate, BP 361, tel. 94.03.59.

Tourist information: Syndicat d'Initiative, opposite the Post Office.

Ferry on the Congo river

LESOTHO

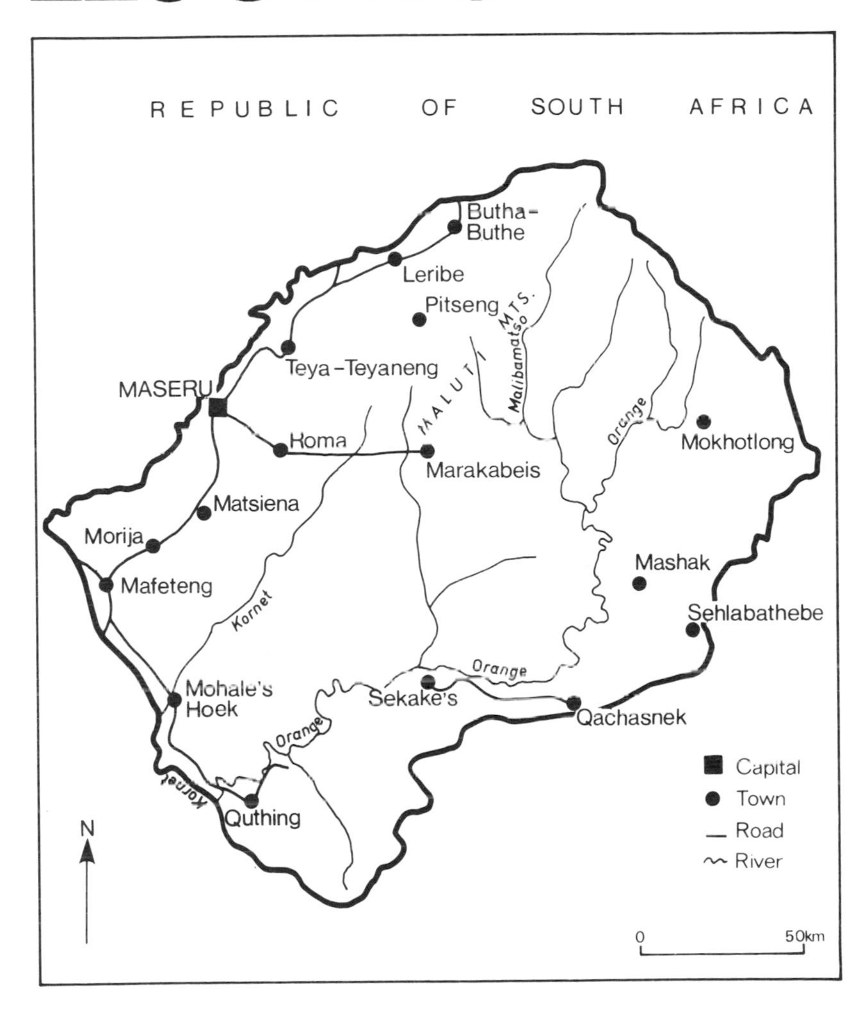

Area: 30,355 sq km
Population: 1.72 million (1989 World Bank)
Capital: Maseru

Lesotho is a mountain kingdom entirely surrounded by South Africa. Situated at the highest part of the Drakensberg escarpment on the eastern rim of the South African plateau, its mountainous terrain, cut by countless valleys and ravines, makes it a country of great natural beauty. Three large rivers have their sources in the mountains so there are numerous trout fishing streams as well as rock paintings by the aboriginal San people who survived in the mountain fortresses of the Drakensberg until late in the 19th century. The country can be explored on foot, but for the more adventurous, an excursion on horseback will provide some of the most breathtaking views Southern Africa has to offer.

Lesotho's geographical location makes it almost totally dependent upon South Africa for its imports, communications and tourists, who are an important source of revenue. The gambling casino at the Holiday Inns complex in the capital is one of the most popular resorts for the many tourists attracted from South Africa. Several major projects are underway to develop communications by road and air which are expected to open up the remoter parts of Lesotho, hitherto largely unexploited, for tourism.

A Mountainous Land

About two-thirds of Lesotho is very mountainous. Elevations in the eastern half of the country are mostly above 2500 metres and in the north-east exceed 3300 metres. Westward the land descends through a foothill zone of rolling country to a belt along the border, the main lowland area where some two-thirds of the population are concentrated. The lowland is a more temperate zone than the rugged eastern region, with an annual rainfall of about 700 mm. Unfortunately the light sandy soils of the west compare unfavourably with the rich black basalt soils of the uplands, so that only about 16% of the land is potentially arable. This has led to serious soil erosion in the western region.

Three large rivers, the Orange, the Caledon and the Tugela (known respectively in the Sesotho language as the Senqu, the Mohokare and the Lethuela) arise in the Lesotho mountains, where the rainfall is about 1900 mm. Lesotho is thus adequately supplied with water, a significant fact since locally-generated income stems overwhelmingly from peasant agriculture. However, Lesotho has insufficient cultivable land to supports its population, so that at any one time, as many as 200,000 Basotho are working in South Africa. Under South Africa's discriminatory controls, the great majority, including the 100,000 on the mimes, are single men, making up 40% of the male labour force. Women are thus extensively engaged in peasant farming and a large proportion of them endure lives of great hardship, separated from the male members of the family and have to undertake arduous manual labour. (A note on nomenclature: the country is called Lesotho; the people are the Basotho; a single person is a Masotho; and the language is Sesotho.)

Culture

The Basotho have a strong literary tradition. They continue to have an active oral tradition and they are also writers of prose, poetry and drama, both in the vernacular and in English. This is partly a result of the strong missionary influence which developed in the 19th century. At the turn of the century a Catholic mission printing press at Morija was producing books. At the same time, Lesotho is still a peasant society, so that much of the traditional culture is maintained. Weaving and pottery are the major activities, and one of the hallmarks of the Basotho is the conical straw hat and colourful blanket.

Since independence, the Lesotho National Development Corporation has established a number of home industries such as carpet and tapestry-weaving, pottery and handicrafts. There are several excellent craft outlets in Maseru. Basotho woven carpets are exported the world over.

History

Lesotho has a remarkable history. Several centuries prior to colonisation, the area was populated by Sotho-speaking clans who mingled with the aboriginal San. Amidst the chaos of the 'difaqane', the 'wars of calamity' of the 1820's, caused by Shaka the Zulu king's bid for absolute power, there arose a leader of extraordinary diplomatic and military skill, Moshoeshoe I, who welded the various clans and the many refugees from the wars into a unified and powerful kingdom which reached its zenith in the 1850's. By 1850 Lesotho had a single language, a unified army and a central government which allowed some measure of democratic consultation through the *pitso*, or assembly, which existed at local and national level. Moshoeshoe was able to keep at bay the armies of Shaka, the Zulu king, and the Boer trekkers, whilst encouraging the advent of missionaries, mostly French and British Catholics. As a result, by 1960 Lesotho had an 80% literacy rate, by far the highest for the Africans in the subcontinent.

By 1868, hard-pressed by the Boer commandos from the Orange Free State, Moshoeshoe sought British protection and as the price, was forced to accept the loss of the kingdom's best land, west of the Caledon River. Britain annexed the country as part of the Cape Colony but later, continuing internal unrest led Britain to make the territory a colony. The protectorates of Bechuanaland (Botswana), Swaziland and Basutoland formed the High Commission Territories, administered separately from South Africa. The territory remained under British rule until its independence in 1965. However, to this day, the loss of land is still bitterly resented by the Basotho. As a result of the latter, Lesotho's territory rapidly became overpopulated, and under-development proceeded at an alarming rate. From being the granary of the highveld between the 1850's and 1870's, Lesotho at the turn of the century was fast declining into a labour reserve for the mines and farms of South Africa. In 1904 alone over 86,000 passes were issued to migrants to

South Africa from a population of 349,000. (All migrant workers in South Africa need a pass.)

Nationalist politics began early in Lesotho. While an expanding and increasingly conservative chieftancy maintained its power through the allocation of land, political associations were growing amongst the Basotho. By 1950 there was a wide range of trade unions, trade and professional associations, co-operatives and semi-political societies. The Basutoland African Congress, later the Congress Party (BCP), was founded in 1952, and in 1955, it launched a militant campaign for self rule under the leadership of Ntsu Mokhele. In the late 1950's the Marema-Tlou Party and the Basutoland National Party (BNP) under Chief Jonathan were formed and by 1960 the first general elections were held and the basis for a constitution was drawn up. By 1966 full independence was granted and Lesotho became a monarchy under Moshoeshoe II, with Chief Jonathan's conservative BNP winning a majority of seats in the 1965 elections, but closely challenged by the more radical BCP.

Afterwards there was widespread and sometimes turbulent resistance to Chief Jonathan's rule. By 1970 the BCP was winning a clear majority of the popular vote when in January 1970 Chief Jonathan, with the help of the paramilitary police mobile unit, staged a coup d'etat, suspended the constitution, banned all opposition parties and arrested their leaders. The king went into exile, and rule by decree was instituted. By 1972 all opponents to Chief Jonathan's rule were released and in 1973 a new National Assembly was established to draw up a new constitution. In January 1974, owing to Mokhele and BCP opposition to the Assembly, political tension erupted and 20 people were killed. The situation then became more stable. The king returned to his country and assumed a purely ceremonial role. However, sporadic acts of violence were still perpetrated by the BCP and its associated Lesotho Liberation Army. Mokhele claims to have up to 1,000 men in the Lesotho mountains.

Since the early days of nationalism, relations with South Africa have been a central issue in Lesotho politics. The freedom of action of any government in Lesotho is severely limited by its hostage status. In recent years, in order to align himself with popular feeling and in order to increase Western economic and political support, Chief Jonathan tried with some success to exploit growing hostility towards South Africa. Lesotho provided a haven to exiles from South Africa of the African National Congress. Jonathan refused to recognise the 'independence' of the Transkei in October 1976, causing new South African restrictions and harassment to be imposed on Basotho crossing into the Transkei. Lesotho took the issue to the Security Council amidst much publicity. In March 1977, a UN mission, endorsed by the Security Council, subsequently recommended that Lesotho be given large grants for emergency aid and accelerated development. In February 1977, Jonathan renewed the claim for large tracts of Orange Free State land which had been compulsorily ceded to Britain in 1869. In December 1982 South African troops raided Maseru on the excuse that Lesotho was harbouring the exiles of the banned African National Congress. In January 1986 South Africa blockaded Lesotho and created the conditions which led to the deposition of Chief Jonathan in a military coup. The army chief, Major General Justinus Lekhanya then assumed power.

Economy

Lesotho is not richly endowed with natural resources. The soil is of poor quality, so that even with modern farming methods, it would not yield sufficient to feed its population. Agriculture nevertheless employs about 85% of the resident workforce and accounts for about 45% of the Gross Domestic Product. The principal crops are maize and wheat and the mountain slopes provide summer grazing for cattle and more generally sheep and goats, whose wool and mohair accounted for over one third of exports in 1981.

Known mineral reserves are sparse. The diamond mine 3,000 metres up in the Drakensberg (Dragon Mountain) at Letseng-la-Terai was closed down in 1982.

Another important source of revenue comes from wages sent home from migrant workers in South Africa. With the rising wage rates in South Africa, these remittances are sufficient to double the Gross Domestic Product.

Manufacturing is in its infancy, and contributes a negligible amount to the Gross Domestic Product. As a member of the Southern African customs union, and a virtual hostage of South Africa, it is all but impossible to establish any industry in Lesotho since it must complete against cheaper producers in South Africa.

Tourism, capitalising on the severe South African gambling and racial restrictions, continues to be significant. The Holiday Inn complex with its casino is a very popular resort, and a Hilton hotel has recently been completed near Maseru.

Rural scene in Lesotho

ALAN HUTCHINSON

General Information

Government

Lesotho is a monarchy ruled by King Moshoeshoe II, but real executive power, since January 1986, lies with the military government under Maj. Gen. Justinus Lekhanya.

Languages

English and Sesotho.

Religion

70% of the population is Catholic. The rest are divided amongst the various protestant denominations and traditional beliefs.

How to Get There

By air: There are regular services every day of the week from Johannesburg to Maseru operated jointly by Lesotho National Airways and South African Airways. There are also direct flights from Maseru to Harare, Gaberone, Maputo and other African capitals.
By road: Several main, tarred roads lead into the west and south of Lesotho from South Africa.
By rail: The South African railway system links up with the capital, Maseru.

Entry Regulations

Visas are no longer required by tourists wanting to visit Lesotho for less than 30 days. Valid passports required.

Since it is impossible to enter Lesotho without going through South Africa, one must conform to South African health regulations.

Customs regulations

Lesotho is a member of the Southern African Customs Union so that there are no extra customs formalities at its borders. Similarly there are no exchange controls.

Climate

This is a land of extremes. In the summer (November-February) the temperature rises to 32 degrees C in the lowlands (less in the mountains) and the rain can turn to hail. Most of the rain falls in short storms between October and April. No month is completely free of rain but the low total and uneven distribution makes drought a common hazard.

In the winter (May-September) the temperatures can drop to −7 degrees C even in the lowlands, and below −18 degrees C in the snowcapped mountains, with frost throughout the country.
What to wear: In summer light cotton clothes are needed during the day, but it can be chilly in the evening. In winter plenty of warm wollen clothing is needed.

Banks and Currency

Barclays Bank International Ltd, PO Box 115, Maseru
Lesotho Bank-National Development Bank, PO Box MS999, Maseru
Standard Bank Ltd, PO Box MS1001, Maseru
Currency: Lesotho Maluti divided into 100 cents. The value of the Maluti is linked to the South African rand. (See p.10 for exchange rates.)

Business Hours

Government offices: Monday-Friday 0800-1245, 1400-1630.

Offices: Monday-Friday 0800-1300, 1400-1700; Saturday 0800-1300.
Banks: Monday-Friday 0900-1300; Saturday 0900-1100.

Public Holidays

New Year's Day, 1 January
Moshoeshoe's Day, 12 March
Arbor Day, 21 March
Good Friday, 13 April 1990
Easter Monday, 16 April 1990
King's birthday, 2 May
Ascension Day, 24 May 1990
Family Day, 6 July
Independence Day, 4 October
National Sports Day, 5 October
Christmas Day, 25 December
Boxing Day, 26 December

Embassies in Maseru

Denmark: tel. 22879
Ireland: tel. 24068
Germany FR: tel. 22750
Swaziland: Maseru
UK: PO Box 521, tel. 23961
USA: tel. 23892

Transport

By air: Considerable use is made of the airstrips at main centres for charter tourist and mail flights.
By road: The system is rudimentary, most of the country being covered only by bridle paths – horses and ponies are the chief mode of transport in the country – but the main road through the towns along the western and southern borders is tarred for over 100 km of its length and a good scenic route leads into the mountains from Maseru. This road can be very dangerous in the wet.

Accommodation and Food

The Maseru Holiday Inn belongs to the international hotel chain of The Holiday Inns group. There are several other hotels of varying quality, and mountain lodges from which Lesotho's rugged scenery can be explored. New hotels have been built at Leribe, and Maseru.

Hotels

NAME	ADDRESS	TELEPHONE
MASERU		
Lesotho Sun	PB A68	(050) 313111
Lancers Inn	PB A84	(050) 322114
Lakeside Hotel	Box 602 – on the shores of Meametalana dam	(050) 313646
Maseru Sun Cabanas	PB A85	(050) 312434
Victoria Hotel	PO Box 212	(050) 312002
Airport Hotel	PO Box 212	(050) 322081

[Hotels]

NORTHERN HOTELS		
Crocodile Inn	PO Box 72, Butha-Buthe	(050) 46223
Moteng Lodge	PO Box 326, Butha-Buthe	(050) 46316
New Oxbow Lodge*	PO Box 43, Maputsoe	09563-3434
Leribe Hotel	PO Box 14, Leribe	(050) 40242
Blue Mountain Inn*	PO Box 7, Teya-Teyaneng	(050) 50231/50362
CENTRAL HOTELS		
Mantsonyane Hotel	PO Box 3, Maseru	(050) 323226
Marakabei Lodge*	PO Box 5, Maseru	(050) 312601
Molimo Nthuse Lodge*	PO Box 212, Maseru	(050) 312002
Semokong Lodge*	PO Box 5, Maseru	(050) 322601
SOUTHERN HOTELS		
Hotel Mafeteng	PO Box 109, Mafeteng	(050) 70236
Hotel Mount Maluti	PO Box 10, Mohale's Hoek	(050) 85224
Orange River Hotel	PO Box 37, Quthing	(050) 80228
Qaba Lodge*	PO Box 5, Maseru	(050) 322601
Qacha's Nek Lodge*	PO Box 20, Qacha's Nek	Qacha's Nek X012
Nthatua Hotel	PO Box 13, Qacha's Nek	(050) 95260
MALUTI AREA		
Bafana Adner Koma Hotel	PO Mokhotlong	
Maleala Lodge	PO Box 922, Makhakhe	(050) 308901
Molumong Hotel*	c/o Boiketlo Trading Store, Mokhotlong	

[Hotels]

Sehlaba-Thebe Lodge*	PO Sehlaba-Thebe, Qacha's Nek	(050) 323600

* All these establishments offer beautiful scenery, hiking, pony trekking, fishing and climbing.

Maseru

Despite its increasing population, Maseru still has the peaceful atmosphere of a village on the banks of the Mohokare (Caledon) river, the frontier with South Africa.

Entertainments: The Royal Casino, within the Holiday Inn complex which caters principally to white South African tourists offers a comprehensive range of table games, including French and American roulette.

Sports: The Holiday Inn has a swimming pool and visitors are allowed to use the bowling greens, tennis courts, and golf course at the nearby Maseru Country Club. Horses may be hired at an hourly rate through the hotel.

Shopping: 'The Basuto Hat' is the official shop of the National Development Corporation. Pottery, basketware, rugs and blankets are on sale here.

Tourist Offices: The Government Information Office in the main street provides details of tours, places of interest, etc. The Lesotho Tourist Corporation runs an information office in the Hotel Victoria complex.

Excursions from Maseru: There are several day excursions from Maseru (which can also be arranged through the Holiday Inn). These include trips up Lesotho's **Mountain Road** an 80 km journey which offers breathtaking views of the Maluti (Drakensberg) escarpment, and a visit to San rock paintings. This should not be attempted in wet weather as the road is both very steep and very slippery. Visits to local weaving and pottery centres are also possible; the weaving centre is particularly interesting as indigenous designs are used.

A 40-minute trip to **Thabo Bosio** – The Mountain at Night – is both scenically and historically interesting. This flat-topped mountain scaleable by a single route only, was the fortress retreat of the Basotho from which they repelled the Boers and kept the Zulu at bay.

The royal capital is **Matsiena,** but a stop is recommended rather at **Morija,** the early missionary settlement with its old printing establishment and a craft centre.

Southern Region

Mountain Lodges: The Government runs two small lodges – one near Sehlabathebe in the east of the country and one at Makone's near Quthing (dry weather only); they provide accommodation but not food.

The Fraser Group has recently built three lodges offering bungalow accommodation with bathrooms and cooking facilities. Although access is difficult, they are situated in some of the most beautiful parts of the country. **Qaba Lodge** (for 12) is 80 km from Maseru. **Semonkong Lodge** (for 8) is only accessible by air from Maseru, **Marakabei Lodge** (102 km from Maseru). Booking office; The Manager, Fraser Lodge System, PO Box 5, Maseru, tel: 2601.

For the more adventurous who want to get right into the mountains the Holiday Inn runs the Maluti chalet camp at Oxbow which can only be reached by four-wheel-drive vehicle but provides accommodation and food, fishing, horse riding, swimming and even skiing.

MALAWI

The Republic of Malawi (formerly Nyasaland) is a country of great beauty, with towering mountains, high plateaux, vast plains and the inland sea of Lake Malawi with its sandy beaches, tideless, sparkling waters and lakeside resorts.

There are several versions of how Malawi came to its name. Its meaning is roughly 'the lake where the sun-haze is reflected in the water like fire'. The early people were known as the Maravi – 'the people of the flames'. When David Livingstone came to the country in the middle 1850s he asked the name of the great stretch of inland water not of the Chewa people who lived by the lake but of the Yao who come from what is now Tanzania, and they told him it was 'nyassa' which literally means 'lake'. Hence the lake came to be known as Lake Nyasa (Lake Lake!) and the country Nyasaland. When Malawi became independent in 1964 the new Republic chose the name of Malawi.

Although the lake is undoubtedly Malawi's dominant tourist feature, its majestic wooded mountains, vast plains and tropical forests give this relatively unspoilt country a tremendous attraction for sightseers and holidaymakers.

Lake, Mountains, Forests

The surface area of Lake Malawi covers nearly 24,000 sq km, about one-fifth of the total territory. The lake lies 473 m above sea level in the deep, trough-like rift valley which stretches the length of the country. High plateaux rise on either side of the trough with wide, rolling, grassy plains with an elevation of around 1,000 m to the west rising as high as 2,600 m in the Nyika Uplands in the north. In the south there is the rugged 3,000 m Mount Mulanje, set in the heart of emerald-green tea plantations, and Zomba Mountain, with the old capital city of Zomba nestling in its foothills.

Almost completely devoted to agriculture, with some of the most fertile soil in South-Central Africa, Malawi is the home of six major ethnic groups.

Malawi is one of the more densely populated countries in Africa with an average of 51 people per sq km, although one is hardly aware of this density when travelling through the countryside, particularly in the Northern Region, which has only 12% of the population. The Southern Region, by contrast, is the most developed and carries 52%. The great majority of the African population are rural dwellers. Along the roadside the travellers will come across the village markets displaying the fruits of their labours – mounds of maize and groundnuts, tropical fruits, beautifully woven baskets

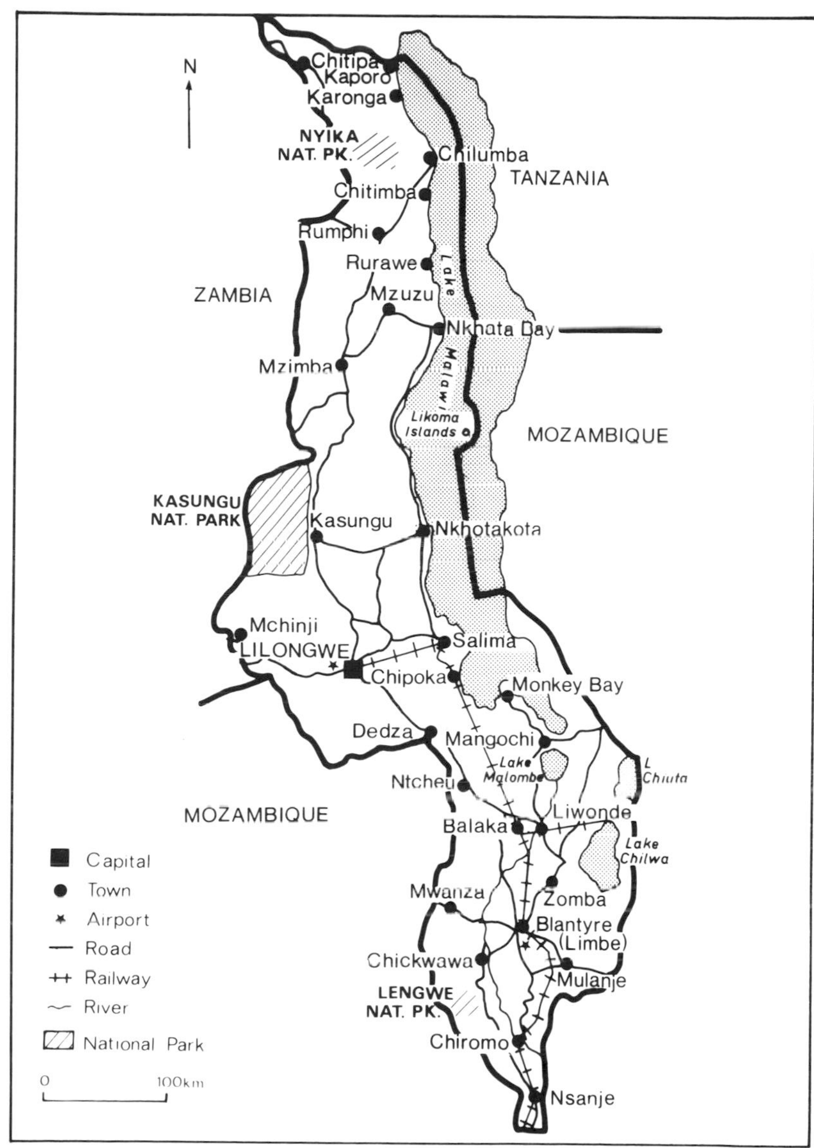

Area: 94,080 sq km (including 24,000 sq km of water)
Population: 8.14 million (1989 World Bank)
Capital: Lilongwe

and mats, wood carvings and beadwork. However, the growth of large tobacco estates has made it increasingly difficult for many peasants to find enough land possible to cultivate.

Along the southern lakeshore, in the Mangochi district, the Yao culture groups predominate. These are mostly followers of Islam, speaking ChiYao, and are also found in considerable numbers at Salima, Dedza and Nkhotakota in the Central Region.

Predominating along the lakeshore, are the Chewa, the country's largest single ethnic group. They speak ChiChewa, the national language.

Around Ntakataka in the Central Region are the Ngoni of Chief Kachindamoto. They are descendants of one of several Zulu warrior groups who broke away from Shaka's iron control and trekked north to Central and East Africa. The *ingoma* is their spectacular war dance.

The Tonga live mainly in the Northern Region as far as Usisya and speak ChiTonga. They have no connection with people of the same name who live in adjacent territories.

The Tumbuka-Henga live mostly between Nkhata Bay and Karonga, and speak ChiTumbuka, a tongue somewhat different from the national language. From Karonga northwards the predominant people are the Ngonde. Mostly Christian, they have their own language, Kingonde.

Cultural Interest

The Malawians are a friendly, colourful people who stem from a number of ethnic stocks and whose culture is marked by a wide range of dance forms.

Dance plays a part in most ceremonies in Malawi including rites of passage such as puberty, marriage, death and initiation ceremonies, and many of the dances have been handed down through the generations. Some are unaccompanied by either vocal accompaniment or music (eg the *Masewe* dance of the Yao) while others have vocal accompaniment by a chorus and musical accompaniment of drums and whistles (eg south and central regions – *Chindidi* women's dance).

One of the most important dances in Malawi is performed by the Chewa and Mang'anja of the southern region; it is called the *Gule Wamkulu* and was originally performed at funerals of chiefs and at weddings. It was later condemned by missionaries for being associated with death and witchcraft, and this forced the men to form a secret organisation in order to perform the dance. Heavily carved masks are worn and the arms and legs of the dancers are bedecked with feathers and paint. The *Gule Wamkulu* has religious and emotional connotations and is recognised for its role in traditional education. The Ngoni people in the northern region perform traditional dances with vocal accompaniment many of which are war dances and a reminder of the past before the Ngoni fled from the wrath of the Zulu chief Shaka in the 19th century. Many of the songs accompanying these dances, in the original Zulu, are staged at annual celebrations, in July.

History

The tribes migrating to the Nyasa region in early times were those belonging to the pre-Luba Malawi group whom the Portuguese called Maravi. Coming down either the east or west side of Lake Tanganyika from the northern lakes, they reached the Nyasa-Tanganyika plateau and settled towards the end of the 15th century. Later in the 19th century came invasions from the south and the east by the warlike Ngoni and Yao who conquered groups of the settled agricultural peoples and began to exploit their labour as well as selling them into slavery.

In the wake of the arrival of David Livingstone in 1859, bands of Scottish missionaries began to establish themselves in the 1870's. They brought with them both Christianity and commerce.

By this time the European scramble for Africa was in full swing. The Germans were busy in the north and east; Portugal was intent on joining Mozambique with Angola and on annexing the intervening territory; Cecil Rhodes was pushing upwards from the south. Alarmed at the Portuguese claims of sovereignty over the Shire Highlands the missionaries in 1880 appealed to the Foreign Office for protection. This was ignored until 1890 when the Foreign Office sent Portugal an ultimatum to withdraw. The British declared a protectorate over the country they called Nyasaland in 1891, and from then on colonial policy concentrated on the agricultural interests of the small settler economy.

Colonial domination and the growth of the settler economy continued unchallenged until the late 1940's. As the early coffee plantations grew the pressure on land increased. Thousands of Malawians (especially from the north) were forced to become migrant workers in search of wage labour. By the 1950's 150,000 had left the country in search of work.

In 1953 the formal launching of the Federation of Rhodesia and Nyasaland caused enormous popular resentment, as it threatened to bring to Nyasaland conditions similar to those of migrants working in the south and in Rhodesia. At the same time, the colonial administration decided that colonial agricultural regulations concerning the usage of land and the limitation of stock should be enforced throughout the country; this caused bitter reaction among the peasants. Although there was therefore widespread opposition to colonialism, the newly formed nationalist party, the Nyasaland African Congress, felt they lacked effective local leadership. They believed that in order to unite the people in their struggle for independence, a charismatic and politically respected leader was necessary, and in July 1958 they invited Dr Hastings Kamuzu Banda to return to Nyasaland after 40 years abroad in South Africa, Britain and the United States, to assume the leadership of Congress.

Banda denounced the Federation, rallied the Nyasaland African Congress and promised to bring his country to independence. In March 1959 the authorities declared a state of emergency, banned Congress and threw Banda and its other leaders into prison. However to avoid further violence the Colonial Office then released Banda and took him to London for a constitutional conference. In 1963 Federation was dissolved and Malawi became independent under Banda's earlier formed Malawi Congress Party in July 1964, six years to the day after his return to the country.

Political differences soon emerged between Banda and a group of his new ministers. Banda took criticism of his policies as personal, and many of his opponents were forced into hiding or exile in Tanzania, Zambia and Mozambique. Banda spent much of the first decade after independence consolidating his power. In 1978 the first general election in 17 years was held. Banda himself, however, became 'President for Life'.

Besides transforming his country into a profitable agricultural society, Banda's other priority has been to maintain cordial relations with his white-ruled neighbours, especially South Africa. South Africa in turn has been generally very willing to respond to Dr Banda's political generosity in financial terms. It funded the Nacala rail link and is a major source of Malawian imports. Banda was the first black president ever to visit South Africa, while many white South Africans visit Malawi for their holidays.

Dr Banda was closely involved with pre-coup Portugal, although he publicly welcomed the advent of Mozambique's independence. During the struggle for black majority rule in Zimbabwe, the President also demonstrated open hostility to the Patriotic Front Alliance. However, since Zimbabwean independence, diplomatic relations have been established with the new government.

Dr Banda's political stubbornness over opposition to white minority rule further south, added to his own dictatorial policies, has created international opposition and has led to the establishment of an active political opposition.

Economy

Under Banda's powerful and paternalistic rule, Malawi has achieved a conservative kind of stability which has encouraged a multitude of development agencies and aid donors to the country. Malawi, with no mineral resources to speak of, has always depended on agriculture as its most important economic activity. More than 90% of the population are directly dependent upon agriculture for their living and agriculture accounts for 95% of export earnings. Maize is the people's chief food crop. Tobacco, tea and sugar are grown on estates, while cotton, groundnuts, cassava, sweet potatoes and rice are grown mostly by smallholders.

The figures for Malawi's economic expansion and increased productivity in the agricultural sector since independence are very impressive. However, these are due mainly to the privately owned tea, tobacco and sugar estates (that together account for over 80% of Malawi's export earnings) rather than an improvement in productivity of the peasant farmer in the smallholder sector (despite extensive foreign aid to smallholder agriculture). The growth and development of private estates reflect Dr Banda's long held conviction that successful development in Malawi must rely on private enterprise. With the emphasis on 'productive' investment, primary education and preventive medicine have both come low in the development budget.

Since independence, the industrial sector of the economy has grown and now accounts for over a quarter of the overall economic activity of the country. Manufacturing and service industries are under a combination of private and government ownership.

Wildlife

Each of Malawi's three regions has its own game park, with a wide variety of animals, but it is not unusual to come across elephant, eland and zebra when motoring through the countryside. Birdlife is particularly prolific, and over 900 species have been recorded.

In the Central Region around Dedza Mountain there are great upland plains. One of the principal attractions is the Kasungu National Park where elephant, buffalo, kudu, sable, lion, oribi, zebra and numerous smaller antelope roam. In the Northern Region the country is less populated and large herds of zebra and eland move freely in the rolling plains. The best time to see this area is between August and November when the wild flowers are at their best and the wildlife is more easily spotted. Most of the 880 sq km Nyika National Park lies at an altitude of 2,300 m with occasional peaks rising to over 2,600 m. It comprises ridge after ridge of undulating grassland with deep valley and patches of evergreen forests.

Lake Malawi, its tributaries and fringing swamps contain over 240 varieties of fish. Over 220 species are to be found in the lake itself and the majority of these are not found anywhere else in the world. Nearly all make good eating when freshly cooked. The main lake types are varieties of catfish, perch and carp.

National Parks

National Park animals are not tame, and drivers should therefore exercise caution when approaching game, particularly potentially dangerous animals such as elephant. There is no camping in any of the National Parks and accommodation must be reserved in rest camps. It is advisable to take your own food which will be cooked for you. Visitors should arrive before dark and should return to camp before dark each day during their stay. Fires of any description are forbidden in the parks outside the game camps and great care should be taken in the disposal of cigarette ends and matches. Firearms, dogs and other pets are not allowed inside the parks.

Camp accommodation in each park can be booked through local agents (see details below). Besides the accommodation charges, a park entrance fee is levied on each vehicle.

Nyika National Park
This park is situated in the northern part of the Northern Region and is open to visitors throughout the year. It covers 3,100 sq km and lies at an altitude of 2,100 m with occasional peaks rising to over 2,400 m. The rolling grassland is broken by deep valleys and patches of evergreen forest. Large herds of eland and zebra roam the plains and groups of roan antelope may be seen, together with the smaller species such as reedbuck, bushbuck, duiker and klipspringer. Warthog are relatively common, and lion and leopard may also be seen. The three dams near Chilinda Game Camp offer find bird-watching.

Accommodation at Chilinda Game Camp is provided for 18 persons in four self-contained chalets and, in addition, 12 people can be accommodated in a block of six double bedrooms adjacent to the central lounge/dining room. Sole booking for the Chilinda Game Camp is at present through the Chief Game Warden, PO Box 30131, Lilongwe, tel: 731322.

Kasungu National Park
The park is situated in the north-west corner of the Central Region and is usually open from 1 May to 31 December. The range of game to be seen is the most extensive in Malawi. Elephant occur in some numbers, together with an occasional rhinoceros. There are buffalo, zebra and many species of antelope, including the stately kudu, sable and roan. Lion, leopard and cheetah may be sighted from time to time.

Lifupa Game Camp has its own swimming pool and electricity supply. Up to 27 persons can be accommodated in the camp's nine chalets. There is a centrally situated lounge, dining room and bar.

The sole booking agent for Lifupa Game Camp is at present Central Reservations, Malawi Hotels Limited, PO Box 284, Blantyre, tel: 635588.

Lengwe National Park
Situated in the south-west corner of the Southern Region, it is only 130 sq km in extent. The park is unique in that it is the farthest place north where the rare, shy nyala antelope is found. The beautiful animal may be seen, often in large numbers, together with bushbuck, kudu, hartebeest, impala and duiker. Other rarities are the Blue or Samango Monkey and Livingstone's Suni. Birdlife is varied and interesting. Visitors may view game at very close quarters from carefully concealed, shaded hides. The best viewing time at these hides is generally early in the morning.

Accommodation at Lengwe Game Camp is provided for eight persons. There is a fully equipped kitchen and the services of a cook are available, but visitors must bring their own food. No provisions or petrol are available at the camp, but soft drinks are on sale.

The sole booking agent is the United Touring Company, PO Box 30193, Chichiri, Blantyre, tel: 634972.

BRIAN MOSER

Hunters with cane rabbit traps.

General Information

Government

National Assembly of 87 elected members and 15 nominated by the President. One political party, the Malawi Congress Party (MCP). Republican status. Member of the Commonwealth.

Languages

ChiChewa (national); English (official). Other African languages are spoken.

Religion

Christianity (50%) and Islam (30%).

How to Get There

By air: From the United Kingdom: British Airways. From France: UTA.

From the United States: direct flight to Nairobi in Kenya to connect with stop-over flights.

From southern Africa: Air Malawi, South African Airways, Deta Mozambique Airways, Royal Swazi Air, Zambia Airways and Air Zimbabwe.

Flights also operate to and from Dar es Salaam, Lusaka, Mauritius, Nicosia, Nairobi and Beira.

Chileka International Airport is 17 km from Blantyre; buses and taxis operate. A new international airport was opened at Lilongwe in 1982, when international services were switched from Blantyre.

By road: Malawi is connected to Zimbabwe by a road running from Blantyre through Tete in Mozambique to Mtoko; to Zambia by a road linking Lilongwe and Chipata; to Tanzania by a road linking Chitipa and Mbeya (via Nakonde in Zambia). Malawi is connected to the Mozambique coast by a road running from Mulanje to Quelimane but recent reports say the road is now impassable. All border posts are open from 0600-1800 Monday-Friday and from 0600-1200 on Saturdays.

Driving licences issued in most countries of the world are valid in Malawi. Visitors are nevertheless advised to obtain a valid International Driving Permit. Motor vehicles, caravans and trailers may be imported temporarily by tourists visiting or in transit through Malawi provided they are currently licensed in their home countries and bear appropriate registration and nationality plates. A vehicle so imported requires a triptyque or a carnet de passage. If neither can be obtained a temporary importation permit, valid initially for up to four months, will be issued at the border.

By rail: The cities of Blantyre and Beira in Mozambique are connected by rail. Passenger services are no longer regular on this service, but there are still odd passenger coaches on the freight trains to Beira. These are emptied at the border however.

Entry Regulations

Nationals of the following countries do not need visas: Britain, Commonwealth countries, Denmark, Eire, Finland, Federal Republic of Germany, Iceland, Luxembourg, Madagascar, Netherlands, Norway, Portugal, San Marino, South Africa, Sweden and the US. All others must have visas but can obtain transit visas covering a period of five days' travel in the country.

Visas can be obtained from Malawi embassies or honorary consuls. In Commonwealth countries with no Malawi mission, visas can be obtained from local immigration authorities. In all other countries visitors should apply to the British diplomatic mission. Travellers must be prepared to show they have adequate funds to support themselves during their stay and the means to leave the country.

Vaccination certificates required for cholera – and yellow fever if arriving from endemic areas.

Customs Regulations

Duty is not normally charged on visitors personal effects, when they are definitely intended for re-export. Visitors may not import firearms without a valid Tourist Firearms Permit, which should be obtained well in advance from the Registrar of firearms, PO Box 41, Zomba. Such permits are issued only in respect of sporting rifles (including air rifles) and shotguns; revolvers and pistols are specifically excluded.

There is no limit to the amount of foreign currency brought into Malawi, but visitors are required to obtain a receipt from the customs officer at the point of entry as they will be asked to declare the balance on departure. Visitors may not import or export Malawi currency in excess of K20 and are therefore advised to keep the amount of Malawi money they carry to the absolute minimum as it is not convertible abroad.

Travellers' cheques in dollars, sterling and other acceptable currencies are freely convertible. When travelling in the remoter regions travellers' cheques can be cashed at the Treasury Cashier's section of the local District Commissioner's office between the hours of 0730-1200 and 1300-1500, Mondays to Fridays; 0730-1100 on Saturdays. PTC stores and Oilcom petrol stations throughout Malawi, and Kandodo stores at Blantyre, Zomba and Lilongwe usually accept travellers' cheques.

Climate

Malawi's climate varies from the bracing air of the highlands to the relaxing, languorous atmosphere of the beaches of Lake Malawi. The dry winter season lasts from May to October (July: 20°C); nights can be chilly, especially on high ground. The rainy season is from November to March (December: 27°C) though intermittent showers occur during the rest of the year. At any time of the year the *chiperone*, a cold wind from the south-east, may blow up bringing cloud and drizzle, particularly on high ground. The area around the shores of Lake Malawi has a particularly low annual rainfall and the lakeshore is cooled by breezes throughout the year.

What to wear – N.B. Visitors must observe certain conventions pertaining to dress. There is a restriction on wearing dresses and skirts in public that do not fully cover the knee-cap when the wearer is standing upright. Women should not wear shorts and trousers in public. These limitations do not apply at any holiday resort on Lake Malawi, on the mountains of Zomba, Mulanje, Dedze, Vipya and Nyika, in the National Parks at Lengwe, Kasungu and Nyika, and at any hotel, airport or railway station if the visitor or wearer is in direct transit to a Malawi holiday resort or to other destinations outside the country. They also do not apply when the wearer is engaged in any form of sport for which short skirts and dresses or shorts and trousers are customary, or if it is part of a national dress. Men must not wear long hair.

Health Precautions

There is supposedly no bilharzia in Lake Malawi and so bathing is safe, but caution should be exercised. All stagnant or slow-moving waters are, however, infected. Piped water supplies, except where labelled to the contrary, are safe for drinking; otherwise water should be boiled. Hotels supply mosquito nets where required and visitors are advised to take prophylactic drugs against malaria.

Banks and Currency

Commercial Bank of Malawi Ltd, PO Box 1111, Blantyre
National Bank of Malawi, PO Box 945, Henderson Street, Blantyre
Reserve Bank of Malawi, PO Box 565, Blantyre
Currency: Malawi Kwacha divided into 100 tambala. (See currency table, page 10.)

Business Hours

Banks: Mondays, Tuesdays, Thursdays, Fridays 0800-1230, Wednesdays 0800-1130, Saturdays 0800-1030.
Government Offices and Commerce: 0730 or 0800 to 1200 or 1230; 1300 or 1330 to 1630, Monday-Friday, 0730 or 0800 to 1200 or 1230 Saturday.
Restaurants: Open daily 1200-1400 and 1800-2200.

Public Holidays

New Year's Day, 1 January
Martyr's Day, 3 March
Good Friday, 13 April 1990
Easter Saturday, 14 April 1990
Easter Monday, 16 April 1990
Kamuzu Day, 14 May
Republic Day, 6 July
August Holiday, 3 August
Mothers Day, 17 October
Christmas Day, 25 December
Boxing Day, 26 December

Foreign Embassies

China (Taiwan): POB 30221, Lilongwe
France: PO Box 30054, Capital City, Lilongwe 3, tel: Lilongwe 730579
Israel: POB 30319, Lilongwe 3, tel: 731333
Germany F R: PO Box 30046, Lilongwe 3
South Africa: PMB 30138, Mpico Building, Lilongwe 3, tel: Lilongwe 730888
UK: PO Box 30047, Lilongwe, tel: Lilongwe 731544, telex: 4727
USA: PO Box 30166, Capital City, Lilongwe 3, tel: Lilongwe 730166/730396
Zambia: POB 30138, Lilongwe 3
Zimbabwe: POB 30183, Lilongwe 3

Transport

By air: Air Malawi, the national airline, operates between Blantyre and Lilongwe, Mzuzu and Karonga and weekly service to Salima. Air Malawi and two private firms, Capital Air Ltd and Spearhead Air Charter operate charter services to the above and also to the following airfields, Nsanje, Dedza, Ntchisi, Lifupa Camp (Kasungu National Park), Likoma Island, Mzimba, Chilinda, Nyika Plateau and Chitipa. Air Malawi also operates the popular all inclusive 'Skylake' package tours from adjacent territories.

By road: There are over 2,700 km of main road and 2,200 km of secondary road connecting Blantyre with all the places of interest in Malawi. Many of the major roads are tarred and the motorist might experience difficult driving conditions only at the height of the rainy season.

The lakeshore road from Mangochi to Monkey Bay is tarred, together with the access road between Liwonde and Mangochi. Just south of Monkey Bay a new link road has been constructed to join the highway between Balaka and Salima, which provides a more direct route to Mangochi, Monkey Bay, Cape Maclear and Salima lakeshore resorts.

An overall speed limit of 80 kmph is maintained throughout the country while there is an internal speed limit of 48 kmph in urban areas.

Petrol stations are officially closed at weekends, but often allowed to remain open when public celebrations and Presidential tours are taking place.

Car hire: Automotive Products Ltd, PO Box 30068, Chichiri, Blantyre 3, tel: Blantyre 30161. Hall's Garage Ltd, PO Box 368, Blantyre, tel: Blantyre 634833. Mandala Motors Ltd, PO Box 467, Blantyre, tel: 633837. United Touring

ALISTAIR MATHESON

The slopes of Mount Mlanje

Company, Car Hire and Conducted Tours, PO Box 30193, Chichiri, Blantyre 3, tel: 631055. Lotus Car Hire, PO Box 5824, Limbe, tel: Blantyre 650960.

For taxi services in Blantyre telephone: 2604, 8929, 8046, 50025, 30812.

Rail: There are regular services from Blantyre to Lilongwe via Salima, one of Malawi's main lake holiday centres. The line has been extended to Mchingi and will eventually link up with the Zambian rail network.

Useful Chichewa Phrases

Greetings	*Moni*
How are you?	*Muli-bwanji?*
I'm well	*Ndili bwino*
Thank you, excuse me	*Zikomo*
Good, fine, OK	*Chabwino*
Go well (Goodbye)	*Pitani bwino*
Stay well (Goodbye)	*Tsalani bwino*
Yes	*Inde*
No	*Iai*
Please	*Chonde*
I want . . .	*Ndifuna . . .*
I don't want	*Sindifuna*
What's the price?	*Mtengo bwanji?*
I come from . . .	*Ndichokera ku . . .*
Is it far?	*Kodi ndi patali?*

Accommodation and Food

In the main centres there are good hotels. Most hotels require booking deposits. There are several Government rest houses which provide adequate accommodation at reasonable rates. All rest houses have bathrooms and cooking facilities, but guests must provide their own food except at Ngabu, Mzuzu, Kasungu Inn and Chitipa Inn.

Rest houses are sited in the following areas: Central Region – Ntcheu, Dedza, Lilongwe, Kasungu and Nkhotakota,

Northern Region – Mzimba, Nkhata Bay, Mzuzu, Rumphi, Livingstonia, Chitipa and Karonga. Southern Region – Ngabu, Nsanje.

Hotel, rest house and game camp bookings should be made well in advance. All hotels are fully licensed. Camping is permitted in the grounds of most rest houses, and in Zomba, Nkopola, Monkey Bay, Cape Maclear and Salima.

Fresh fish from Lake Malawi is the country's speciality. There are trout from streams on the Zomba, Mulanje and Nyika plateaux. Meat, poultry and dairy produce are plentiful and tropical fruits are abundant in season. The locally brewed beer is very good.

Tipping is not necessary in hotels where a 10% service charge is levied, except for extra attention.

Blantyre

Named by missionaries after Livingstone's birthplace in Scotland, the city of

Hotels

NAME	ADDRESS	TELEPHONE	TELEX
BLANTYRE			
Chisakalime Hotel	PO Box 5249	652266	
Mount Soche Hotel*	PO Box 284	635588	
Ryall's Hotel	PO Box 21	635955	
Shire Highlands Hotel	PO Box 5204, Limbe	650055	
LILONGWE			
Capital Hotel†	PO Box 30018	730444	4892
Lingadzi Inn*†	PO Box 30367	720644	
Lilongwe Hotel*	PO Box 44	721866	
LAKE MALAWI			
Chintheche Inn†	c/o P. Office, Chintheche 11		
Club Makokola	PO Box 59, Mangochi	584228	
Grand Beach Hotel†	PO Box 11, Salima	261339	
Muona Inn*	PO Box 176, Mangochi		
Nkopola Lodge*	PO Box 14, Mangochi	584223	
MUZUZU			
Muzuzu Hotel†	PO Box 231, Mzuzu	332622	4853 ▶

[Hotels]

ZOMBA		
Ku Chawe Inn*	PO Box 71	403
REST CAMPS		
Chilinda Game Camp c/o Chief Game Warden	PO Box 30131 Lilongwe	731322
Lengwe Game Camp c/o United Touring Company	PO Box 30193 Blantyre	634972
Lifupa Game Camp c/o Central Reservations, Malawi Hotels Ltd	PO Box 284 Blantyre	635588

* Advance reservations for all hotels marked with an asterisk can be made through Soche Tours and Travel Limited, Victoria Avenue, PO Box 2225, Blantyre, tel: 635 935, telex: 4452.
† These hotels can be booked through HMI Reservations Service London 01-908 3348, telex: 265473.

Blantyre was established in 1895. It is cradled by impressive hills and mountains, and is the country's main commercial, industrial and communications centre. The city covers an area of 190 sq km and comprises the neighbouring centres of Blantyre (1,098 m above sea level) and Limbe which are 8 km apart. Between them lies the industrial area with its many new factories and enterprises, and the modern complex of Government offices at Chichiri. Nearby are the 50,000-seat Kamuzu Stadium, the Museum of Malawi and the Independence Arch.

Places of interest: St. Michael's Church, an ornate redbrick building on the Chileka Road, is a reminder of the part played by the Scottish Missions in the more recent history of Malawi. Sadly there is some risk of it collapsing and it will be closed to visitors while repairs are undertaken.

Other places of interest are the tobacco auctions in Limbe which generally operate between April and October each year; Independence Arch and the Museum of Malawi at Chichiri. Within easy motoring distance from Blantyre is Mulanje, Malawi's highest mountain, 3,350 m, with tea and coffee plantations spreading for miles across its lower slopes. There is a Mountain Club which maintains huts at various places on the Mulanje plateau, and it is possible to join the climbing party of a member to make use of these. There are spectacular views from the top of Mount Mulanje. It is also worth climbing (you can drive half-way) one of the large hills that surround Blantyre, Ndirande and Michiru in particular give magnificent views of the city and the Lower Shire Valley.

Mwalawolemba (rock of writing) Rock Shelter on Mikolongwe Hill off the Limbe-Midima road is interesting for its rock paintings and for the spectacular views of Mulanje Mountain. Other scenic attractions are the Mpatamanga Gorge on the main Salisbury road, Mfunda Falls (60 km distant at Matope), and Kholombidzo Falls on the Shire River about 16 km from Chileka Airport.

Restaurants: The following are popular restaurants in Blantyre.
Ndirande, Mount Soche Hotel – international cuisine, dancing.
21 Room, Ryall's Hotel – continental cuisine.
Balmoral, Shire Highlands – continental cuisine.
China Bar and Restaurant – Chinese food.
Maxim's – continental cuisine.
Cafe Capri – Portuguese food.
Hong Kong – Chinese food.
Flamingo, on the road to Chileka airport – recently opened.

Entertainments: There are four cinemas as well as a well-equipped drive-in on Chikwawa Road. The climax of Malawi's festival calendar is the annual display of traditional dancing held at Kamuzu Stadium on Republic Day (6 July).

Sports: Trout fishermen can obtain licences from the Treasury cashier in Blantyre. Tiger fish (no licence necessary) can be caught at Chikwawa (50 kms from Blantyre).

Shopping and markets: Victoria Avenue is the main shopping area where there are well-stocked shops as well as street vendors displaying locally made curios. Off Victoria Avenue is the Curio and Handicraft Centre. Malawi Arts and Crafts on Glyn Jones Road is often better and cheaper than the street vendors.

Another feature of the local scene is Limbe Market – a bargaining bustle of brightly dressed people and colourful merchandise. Exotic cotton and skirt lengths in brilliant prints called *chirundu* are popular buys; so also are the mats, baskets and hats woven in swamp reeds and raffia in traditional patterns.

Zomba

On the lower slopes of the Zomba Plateau lies Zomba (970 m), the former capital city of Malawi, now the University centre. In addition to State House, whose foundations were laid in 1901, there is the Old Residency, commissioned in 1886.

Spectacular panoramic views, mountain streams and waterfalls, brilliant birdlife and wild flowers distinguish the beautiful 2,000 m Zomba Plateau, a forest reserve planted with the stately Mulanje Cedar, a unique species of conifer, and with pines and cypresses.

There are different one-way routes to and from the plateau and an extensive network of forest roads on it leading to a number of splendid picnic spots.

There is a good camp site near the Ku Chawe Inn, and a fairly cheap and very friendly District Rest House between the market place and the bus station in the centre of town.

Good trout fishing is available; licences obtainable from Ku Chawe Inn.

Lilongwe

Lilongwe is the second largest town and the new capital of Malawi. There is a new and very sophisticated shopping centre on Capital Hill, which is completely separate from the older town where you will find the Asian stores and the market, the bus station, the rest house, and the prison – on opposite sides of the same road. From Lilongwe the visitor can easily reach the nearby Salima lakeshore which is one of the more popular holiday spots on the lake. North of Lilongwe is Malawi's main tobacco growing area where burley leaf is grown and air-cured on small plots and farms around the villages. 90 km from Lilongwe is Dedza. Scenically this area has few rivals in Africa. Dedza Mountain rises 2,000 m and offers some challenge to the climber. On the lower slopes there are splendid wooded walks and fine views over the lake.

Tourist Information: The Department of Tourism, PO Box 30366, Capital City, Lilongwe 3, tel: 731711.

Lake Malawi

Lake Malawi is the backbone of Malawi and the cradle of its culture. Its shores provide the visitor with a fascinating mixture of scenic beauty, golden beaches, holiday amenities, historic sites and picturesque dwellings. The water is fresh and free from bilharzia in resort areas. There are no tides or currents, and the crocodile has been effectively banished from the resort areas, making the lake one of the safest water sports venues in Africa.

Lake Malawi has a constantly changing character depending on the time of the day, the weather and the season – one moment the water may be as smooth as silk and then suddenly waves seven metres high can thrash the shores. It is generally calmest from March to May, and the year-round temperature never drops below 21°C.

One of the best ways of seeing Lake Malawi is to cruise in the 620-ton *Ilala II*, the lake's mini-liner which starts and finishes at Monkey Bay. The present *Ilala* has accommodation of 10 cabins and leaves every Friday at 0800 am. The ship has an annual refit at Easter, when the service is operated solely by the smaller and less salubrious *Chauncey Maples*. There is a heavy demand for cabins on the *Ilala* during the holiday season and booking for more than two months in advance requires full cash payment. Bookings from: the Commercial Superintendent, Malawi Railways, PO Box 5492, Limbe.

Leaving every Friday, the vessel calls at Chipoka, Nkhotakota, Likoma Island, Nkhata Bay, Usisya, Ruarwe, Mlowe, Chitimba, Chilumba and Kambwe, taking seven days for the 1,000 km round-the-lake voyage. The cruise enables the visitor to sample in comfort some of Africa's finest lake and mountain scenery. It visits several interesting ports and historic sites such as Likoma Island, whose mission station, established in 1885, has a cathedral rivalling Westminster Abbey in size. It houses carvings from Oberammergau, earth from Jerusalem, and stone from Canterbury, and the wood for its crucifix was taken from a tree near Serenje in Zambia underneath which the heart of David Livingstone is buried.

Lake Fishermen

BRIAN MOSER

MOZAMBIQUE

Mozambique conjures a beautiful image of beautiful beaches, calm lagoons for sailing and paddling to tropical islands with diving, fishing, and dinners of prawns cooked in piri-piri (hot) sauce under waving palm trees. But Mozambique is only reopening to tourists slowly, and only through package tours. Casual visitors are not permitted.

The national political party, Frelimo cut off all tourism at independence in 1975, and made clear that in future it was not prepared to divert scarce resources to cater for casual tourists. Some tourist facilities have been rehabilitated in response to internal demand, and 1981 saw successful experimental package tours and safaris. The government is committed to increasing these tours, and is now contracting with foreign firms to rehabilitate hotels and promote tours.

South Africa has launched a major undeclared war against Mozambique. It arms, trains, and directs an anti-government force which makes travel dangerous in much of the centre of the country. The security situation varies considerably, but two of the country's main tourist attractions, the Gorongosa National Park and Santa Carolina Island, were inaccessible in mid-1985, and safaris had been suspended.

Package tours are sometimes advertised in newspapers, and more information may be available from the new state tourist company, Empresa Nacional de Turismo (CP614 Av 25 Setembro 1203, Maputo, telex: 6303 ENTUR), or the Star travel agency in Portugal. It is sometimes said, even by government officials, that individuals can apply to the government for visas; in fact, such applications are never even acknowledged. People living and working in Mozambique can sometimes obtain visas for relatives or friends, and embassies occasionally issue visitors visas, but individual tourism is officially not permitted.

The Land

The vast, low plateau, rising towards mountains in the west and north, accounts for nearly half the area of Mozambique. The coast, nearly 2,500 km long, is generally sandy, with long beaches often bordered by lagoons, coral reefs and strings of islands in the north, where the plateau narrows considerably. Mangrove and marsh vegetation is common in coastal areas, especially in the estuaries and delta of the Zambezi.

Behind the coastline, the plateau supports a landscape dominated by savannah – more or less dry and open woodlands with occasional tracts of short-grass steppe. The western and northern highlands are patched with

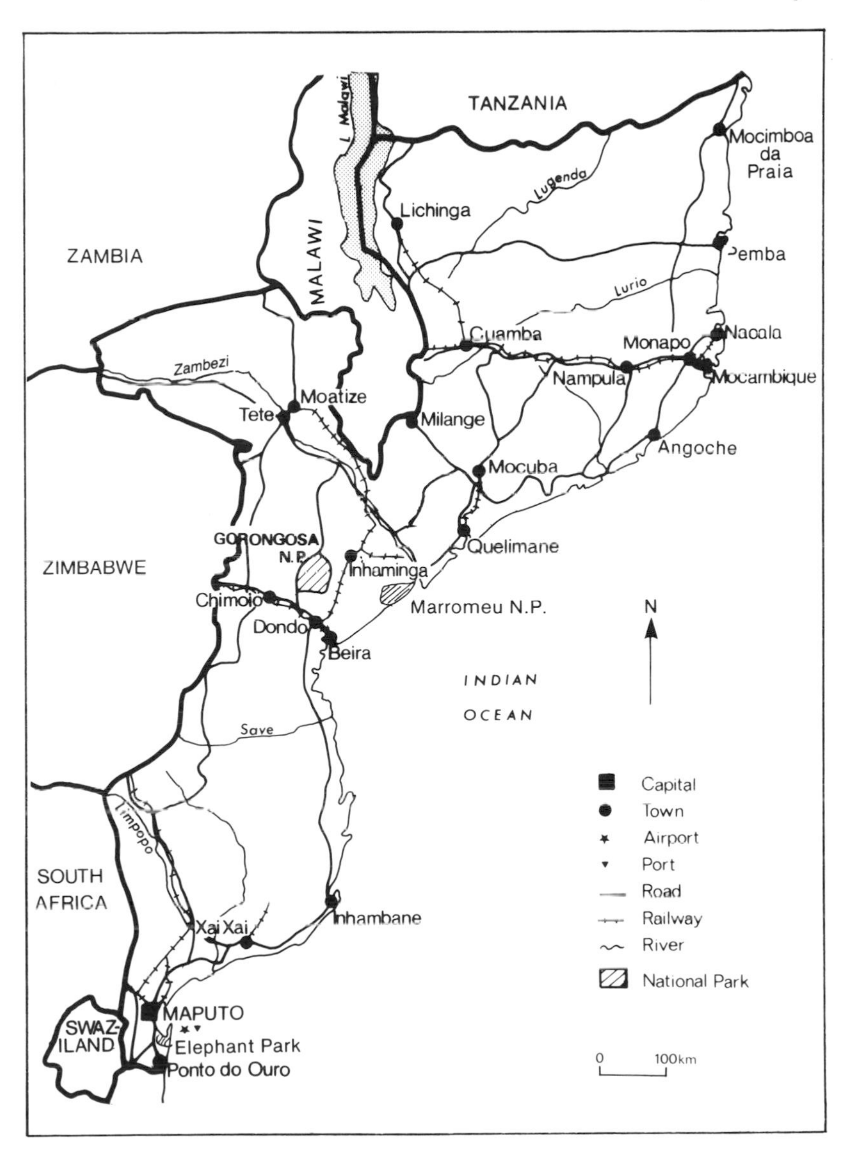

Area: 785,000 sq km
Population: 15.4 million (World Bank 1989)
Capital: Maputo

forest, sometimes of needle-leaf trees. The highest points are Monte Binga (2436 m) on the Zimbabwe border, Monte Namuli in the Zambezia province, Monte Gorongosa in Sofala province, and several massifs which are a continuation of the Malawi Shire Highlands into northern Mozambique.

The Zambezi is the largest and most important of the 25 main rivers which flow through Mozambique into the Indian Ocean. Rising in Eastern Angola, it traverses the country for over 800 km, 460 of which are navigable. In the colonial period it provided the Portuguese with access to the African interior. It also has the massive Cabora Bassa dam project sited on it. Other major rivers contributing to the development of the country through hydro-electric and irrigation schemes are the Save, the Incomati and the Rovuma, which forms the northern frontier with Tanzania.

The dramatic upheavals of the Mozambique revolution had added to an already complex population structure, with the flight of all but 20,000 whites, and the return of political refugees from Tanzania, Zambia and Malawi. Several hundred thousand migrant workers continue to live in South Africa, Zambia and Zimbabwe. The vast majority of Mozambique's population are black Africans from many different tribal groupings. The other main groups are *mesticos,* Pakistanis, Indian and other Asian people. The major concentrations of population are along the coast and in the fertile and relatively productive river valleys, notably in the Zambezia and Gaza provinces. Frelimo's development programme, including the reorganisation of agricultural production, gradual industrialisation, support for the development of the fishing industry and the massive drive for literacy, are bound to further affect the distribution of population. Vast tracts of country are still little used, and the average population density is 10.6 people per square kilometre.

The Makua-Lomwe, who belong to the Central Bantu, probably account for about 40% of the population. They are concentrated in the areas north of Zambezia, Gaza, Niassa and Cabo Delgado provinces. Other major tribal groupings, which conceal an enormous diversity of smaller groups, are distributed as follows: in the southern lowlands are the Thonga, who provide much of the labour for the South African mines; in the Inhambane coastal district are the Chopi and Tonga; in the middle of the country, and closely related to the people of eastern Zimbabwe, are the Shona; and in the far north (on both sides of the frontier with Tanzania) are the Makonde, who provided the backbone of Frelimo's army of liberation against the Portuguese.

Culture

At independence, a grossly inadequate education system was faced with 85-90% illiteracy. Since then, primary school enrolment has almost doubled, and Frelimo's aim is to increase the numbers who can read and write by 100,000 a year. Under the slogan, 'to produce is to learn', education is intended to break down the barriers between intellectual and manual work, and to integrate education with production and theory with practice. The tremendous enthusiasm for education is reflected in the schools which run morning and afternoon shifts, and in the evening are open for adults who work during the day.

Mozambique is in the process of transforming an elitist and racially segregated system of health services – one that left the newly-liberated country with a total of 40 doctors – to a system which will make the essentials of health care, prevention and education available to the whole population. The government is undertaking a mass inoculation programme, organising preventive health drives in the rural areas, and training 'barefoot doctors' from the villages, whose job it is to continue with health education projects and primary health care among their own people.

History

The ancient principalities in this part of Africa developed flourishing trading systems at least as far back as the 10th century AD. By that time, Arab and Indian traders were visiting Sofala to buy gold which was brought down to the coast by Africans from the Manica hills and the goldfields beyond Great Zimbabwe.

In 1498 the Portuguese explorer Vasco de Gama landed on the Mozambique coast while seeking a new route to India. He missed Sofala but found a black Muslim community of traders at Quelimane and Mozambique Island. Among the earliest colonisers in Africa, the Portuguese took over these and other ports during the next century, though their control never ran much beyond the coastal enclaves and the internal trade routes. They extracted wealth from the existing African trading communities, in the form of gold, ivory, and later, slaves. They gradually replaced the Arabs in the Indian Ocean trading system, sending commodities back to Portugal or to Goa in India, which became the administrative centre of their eastern empire.

In fact Portuguese colonialism was chronically over-extended. Metropolitan Portugal was weak in comparison with other European powers, and its capitalism slow to develop. Its 'civilising' mission was therefore often carried out by proxy: from the 17th century onwards, soldiers and traders set up private agricultural estates (*prazos*), which were effectively self-governing feudal fiefdoms with large private armies of slaves. They derived their income from the labours of the African peasantry, and were able to maintain this form of exploitation until the end of the 19th century.

These forms of colonialism were inadequate to a Portuguese economy increasingly threatened by the superior technology of its European competitors, and weakened by unequal treaties it had not the power to resist. In the 1920's, Salazar's fascist New State sought to solve these problems by avoiding them: the need for a massive restructuring of capital was averted by a combined policy of repressing the Portuguese working class, and propping up the metropolitan economy by a new integration with those of its colonies.

An attempt was made to seal the colonies off from non-Portuguese investment and to operate a protectionist policy to tie the colonies and their trade to Portugal.

The effect of this isolationist policy was to fossilise an already moribund economy. 40 years later, increasingly uncompetitive and unable to contain the wars of liberation in its African colonies, Portugal was forced to turn to its allies and competitors for help, and open up to foreign investment.

In Mozambique the economy came more and more under the domination of South Africa, which by the early 1970's accounted for about two-thirds of the country's foreign currency earnings. Thousands of Africans were contracted as cheap labour to the South African mines. In exchange the Portuguese government received gold, a vital source of foreign exchange, and its revenue from South African traffic through Mozambican ports.

Final recognition that the colonial wars could not be won was a vital factor in the overthrow of the Lisbon regime in April 1974. An attempt by the new Portuguese government to impose a neo-colonialist solution in Mozambique came to nothing in the face of a unified and popular liberation movement, Frelimo. Having grown in strength and experience since its foundation in the early sixties, Frelimo had suffered serious setbacks in 1968/9 with the assassination of its president, Eduardo Mondlane.

The southward advance was greatly accelerated by the collapse of the Lisbon regime and the demoralisation of the Portuguese army. An attempted coup by white settlers in the autumn of 1974 was quickly crushed, and Mozambique moved from transitional government in September 1974 to full independence on 25 June 1975. In February 1977 Mozambique was formally constituted as a Marxist republic under the leadership of Frelimo.

In the post-independence period, as one of the 'Front Line' states alongside Tanzania, Botswana, Zambia and Angola, Mozambique shouldered a heavy responsibility in supporting the war of liberation in neighbouring Zimbabwe. Substantial resources were required to support Zimbabwean refugees, to reconstruct towns and facilities destroyed by bombing, and to resettle Mozambicans displaced by the undeclared hostilities between their country and the Smith regime. This meant delays for vital development projects, and the after-effects of the war are still being felt.

In 1980 President Machel launched a major campaign against incompetence, corruption and inefficiency in the huge labyrinth of bureaucracy which was a legacy from colonial days. Some shops and businesses which had been taken over by the state were re-privatised.

In 1984/85 the government was plagued by serious drought and the growing strength of the opposition guerrilla movements, the National Resistance Movement (NRM), which made travelling in rural areas dangerous. President Machel was killed in a mysterious plane crash just over the South African border on 19 October 1986. President Joaquim Chissano assumed power and pursued the same policies.

CAMERAPIX

Maputo street market.

Economy

The newly independent state inherited an economic crisis of massive proportions: sabotage, flight of capital (especially small and medium owners), and withdrawal of technical and management expertise, with farms abandoned, cattle slaughtered or left to starve, machinery and equipment smashed or smuggled out of the country.

Sanctions against the Smith regime weighed heavily on the Mozambican economy, as did the cost of undeclared hostilities and the disruption of the western provinces. The termination of gold payments by South Africa in 1978 was a further blow. Disastrous flooding in the valleys of the Limpopo (1977) and Zambesi (1978) displaced more than a quarter of a million people in the provinces of Zambesia, Tete, Manica and Sofala. The results were a dramatic fall in production, serious food shortages in the towns and a slump in foreign currency earnings. Floods were followed by serious drought.

Agriculture was and is the basis of the Mozambican economy, accounting for an estimated 42% of GNP, 80% of the labour force and 80% of total export value. In the period before independence white settlers, less than 1% of the farming population, controlled half the cultivated land, including the most fertile areas.

The second major agricultural sector consisted of company plantations and estates, again European-controlled, and geared primarily to production for export. Cashew nuts, tea, sisal, and other crops including sesame seeds, sunflower seeds, and groundnuts, were exported to the US, UK, India and

Europe. Portuguese monopolies controlled the production of sugar, copra and cotton. All these commodities have continued in production since independence, but nearly all at substantially lower levels than in 1973/74.

Mozambique's mineral deposits were not fully explored or exploited in the colonial period and workings were confined to coal and certain rare minerals. However, recent mineral discoveries including coal, iron ore, bauxite, manganese, uranium, asbestos, diamonds and natural gas await exploitation. Another area of tremendous economic potential is hydroelectric power, including the Cabora Bassa dam, the largest hydroelectric project on the continent and one with important political implications since it is a major source of power for South Africa.

Industrial production has been mainly geared to the processing of primary export products, such as sisal and sugar, and the production of luxury goods for the settler population. In the period before independence there was a good deal of foreign investment in mining, and although export industries (including steel, fertilisers, chemicals and plastics) were set up under Rhodesian, South African, British and Italian ownership in addition to those owned by the Portuguese, these investments remained piecemeal, and the economy is still heavily dependent on South African industrial products.

In the economic as well as the political sphere, the transformation of social relations is seen to lie at the core of the reconstruction process. Thus in agriculture the emphasis on increased production has gone hand-in-hand with that on collective organisation. It has meant the development of three main sectors: the state farms (usually taking over old plantations), co-operatives, and communal villages (*aldeias communais*), the key element in the rural development programme, where families retain plots of their own but work is organised communally. More scope has been granted to the private sector in recent times in trade, agriculture and small industry, but the economy remains crippled by the civil war.

Wildlife

Mozambique has a rich and varied wildlife, which is protected in Reserves and National Parks, the most famous of which is the Gorongosa. Other areas with easy access to wildlife are Maputo province, Gaza, Inhambane and Sofala. Deep sea fishermen find fish such as marlin and swordfish, especially off the Bazaruto archipelago. Big-game hunting has been reintroduced in Mozambique, although it is strictly controlled with quotas of certain species only.

National Parks

The Gorongosa National Park is regarded as one of the finest game parks in southern Africa. The scenery varies from wide grassland to forest, savannah to marsh and river, all occupied by large herds of buffalo, lion, elephant, hippopotamus, kudu and many other species.

It is open except when rains make trails impassible (generally January through March). Booking is through Safrique (CP 216, Beira, tel 23686) who will meet visitors at Beira Airport and provide transport and guides. Visitors can also use their own cars, and the trails are well marked. Accommodation is found only at the main camp at Chitengo, where there are comfortable bungalows and a restaurant. There is an airstrip at Chitengo and air taxis can sometimes be hired in Beira. Gorongosa has been closed due to the security problems, but facilities at Chitengo are being rehabilitated to permit reopening as soon as possible.

Two other reserves are worth mentioning: the **Maputo Elephant Park,** which lies on the right bank of the Maputo River, south of Maputo; and the **Marromeu** at the mouth of the Zambesi River, which has great herds of buffalo.

Collecting mussels at low tide.

LARRY HERMAN

General Information

Government

The development of democratic and participatory processes is apparent in the new political structure: in December 1977, 27,000 new Deputies, of whom 13% were women and many were peasants and workers, were elected to a system of Popular Assemblies rising in pyramid form to a 210-member National Assembly. This consists of the Central Committee of Frelimo, the Executive Committee, ministers and vice-ministers, provincial governors, representatives of the armed forces, two representatives from each of the provinces and ten other citizens. Above this is a Council of Ministers presided over by the Head of State, President Joaquim Chissano, who is also Commander-in-Chief of the Mozambique People's Liberation Forces.

Languages

The official language is Portuguese, and the chief ethno-linguistic groupings are the Makua-Lomwe, among whom there are many tribal variations. There are still Asian minorities in Mozambique, and a Swahili-speaking people on the coast of Cabo Delgado and Mozambique districts.

Religion

Religious beliefs and practices are extremely diverse with strong animist traditions. Most rural people do not practice an organised religion, except in areas influenced by Catholic missions during colonial times. Two other rural exceptions are a strong Protestant influence in the Limpopo River Valley, and a strong Muslim influence in the northern coastal regions. Most religions can be found in urban areas, including evangelical and Hindu.

The Republic is a secular state in which there is absolute separation between the state and religious institutions. Chapter 33 of the Constitution guarantees individual freedoms, "including the freedom to practice or not to practice a religion".

How to Get There

By air: Regular flights to the international airport of Mavalane (8 km from Maputo centre) by the Mozambican airline LAM from all nearby capitals (Maseru, Manzini, Johannesburg, Lusaka, Harare, Blantyre, and Dar es Salaam) and several European cities (Lisbon, Paris, Sofia, Berlin). Swazi Airways, Lesotho Airways, South African Airways, Air Malawi, Interflug, TAP and UTA (from Paris). In addition Varig serves Luanda and Rio de Janeiro, Aeroflot serves Moscow, and Taag serves Luanda.

Some flights from Harare, Blantyre, and Dar es Salaam also land at Beira airport.

There is an airport tax on departure of 50 meticais. Taxis are rarely available at the airport and the visitor should arrange for someone to meet him if possible.

By sea: British, European, American, Japanese and South African cargo vessels call frequently at Maputo and Beira, but there are no regular passenger services.

By road: There are road links to all neighbouring countries except Tanzania, and a twice weekly bus service to Swaziland.

By rail: Daily passenger services run from Johannesburg to Maputo. At the Malawi frontier, trains from Nampula and Beira meet trains for Blantyre, but the connections are irregular and there is no accommodation at the border.

Entry Regulations

All foreign citizens must have a visa obtained in advance of their arrival. Usually these can be obtained for tourists only by friends or relatives already in Mozambique, or by tour agencies. For people travelling on business, the visa should be arranged by the company or ministry that takes responsibility for the visitor. Occasionally Mozambican embassies abroad issue visas. The visa application requires the names and nationalities of both parents, the names of relatives in Mozambique, and two photographs of the applicant.

Visitors should have valid international certificates of vaccination against yellow fever and cholera. It is advisable to be protected against typhoid and hepatitis, and to take malaria prophylaxis.

Customs Regulations

Entry into Mozambique of bank-notes and coins which are legal tender in foreign countries is permitted when carried by travellers in reasonable amounts for tourist expenses, provided it is in compliance with regulations in force in countries where such bank-notes and coins are legal tender.

Travellers when entering Mozambique are required to declare in writing on a proper form, in duplicate, the amounts of all currencies in their possession in banknotes, travellers' cheques and coins, specifying the respective monetary units. The declaration should be handed over at Exchange Counters found in the Customs Precincts at ports, airports and territorial boundaries. After being stamped at the Exchange Counters, the duplicate copy of the declaration will be returned to the traveller, in whose possession it must remain during his or her stay in Mozambique. It is very important that the declaration should be filled in with care and be as accurate as possible.

Travellers cannot take Mozambican coins or banknotes into or out of the country. The Bank of Mozambique only can change money, at border posts, the airports, the Hotel Polana in Maputo, two foreign currency shops in Maputo, the special foreign exchange bank on Rua Joaquim Lapa in Maputo, and the main banks in Beira and Nampula.

All travellers except those holding passports issued in Mozambique or those living in Mozambique under residential permits must change the equivalent of 1,000 meticais per person. On departure they can buy foreign currency equivalent to that originally changed less what they should have spent to maintain themselves during their stay.

Tobacco (up to 100 gm), personal clothing, sports and camping equipment, cameras, radios, typewriters etc. for personal use are exempt from duty. Visitors carrying any electrical goods, typewriters, cameras or tape-recorders are advised to register these articles at customs on arrival. To avoid paying duty the form registering the above should be presented at customs on departure.

Carved ivory, jewellery and precious stones, and sculptures in precious wood cannot be exported unless they have been purchased at official state-run shops and paid for in foreign currency. Receipts must be shown to customs officials on exit.

Climate

The interior is always cooler than the coast and the rainfall, too, is greater as the land rises. There are two seasons. From April to September the coast has a temperate climate, sunny and pleasantly warm (average 19°C in Maputo in June/July) and mainly dry. The best season for a visit is May and July.

The hot, wet season lasts from October to March. Most of the rain falls between January and March but it is extremely variable from one year to the next, averaging 750 mm in the south, more in the north and rising inland to even 1.7 m per year. Temperatures on the coast average 27°C-29°C, and humidity can be 80% when there is no wind from the sea. Inland the temperature averages about 21°C.

What to wear: In the hot season light, tropical clothing, preferably of pure cotton rather than synthetic materials because of the humidity, will suffice; but take some kind of wrap for the evening. A light raincoat will also be needed. In the cool season wear lightweight clothing and woollens, especially inland.

Health Precautions

Precautions should be taken against malaria. Bilharzia is endemic in rural areas and sleeping sickness is found in the rural north. The water supply in the major cities is good and there is no need to boil or filter tap water. Medical facilities in Mozambique, not least in the capital are extremely limited, due to the departure of most Portuguese medical personnel (this includes dentists). It is advisable to carry some drugs.

Banks and Currency

Banco de Mocambique is the central bank and has branches throughout the country. The other state bank is the Banco Popular de Desenvolvimento (People's Development Bank). One private bank remains: Banco Standard Totta de Mocambique. Foreign exchange is handled only at branches of Banco de Mocambique listed in Customs Regulations. It is impossible to change money except at border posts and in the three main cities.

Currency: Metical (plural meticais). There is a half metical (officially 50 centavos) which is usually called a quinhentao. 1000 meticais is often called a conto. Exchange rates p.10.

Business Hours

Offices: 0730-1200 and 1400-1700 Monday-Friday and 0730-1200 Saturday.

Banks: 0800-1115 Monday-Friday plus either Friday evening or Saturday morning for one hour. **Shops:** 1400-1830 Monday; 0830-1300 and 1500-1830 Tuesday-Saturday. Closed Sunday. Markets open longer hours.

Public Holidays

New Year's Day, 1 January
Heroes' Day, 3 February
Mozambican Women's Day, 7 April
Labour Day, 1 May
Independence and Foundation of Frelimo Day, 25 June
Victory Day, 7 September
Armed Forces Day, 25 September
Family Day, 25 December

Embassies in Maputo

Germany FR: CP 1595
Sweden: CP 338
UK: CP 55, tel: 26011
Other embassies in Maputo include those of Algeria, Belgium, Bulgaria, China PR, Cuba, Czechoslovakia, Denmark, Egypt, France, German DR, Guinea, Hungary, India, Italy, Lesotho, Malawi, Netherlands, Nigeria, Portugal, Rwanda, Somalia, Spain, Tanzania, USSR, USA, Yugoslavia and Zambia.

Transport

By air: LAM flights link seven of the provincial capitals: Maputo, Beira, Quelimane, Tete, Nampula, Lichinga, and Pemba. TTA operates small planes on scheduled flights which link these capitals to smaller cities, and also provides air taxi services. TTA flights can only be booked at the city or town of departure. TTA flights from Maputo serve the beach resorts of Inhaca, Inhambane, Vilanculos, and Santa Carolina.

By road: Tarred roads still do not link the entire country. There are two systems: Ressano Garcia (South Africa)-Maputo-Inhambane-Beira-Chimoio-Mutare (Zimbabwe)-Tete and Pemba-Nampula-

Nacala-Mocambique. The Chimoio-Tete and Beira-Inhambane roads are often closed, due to guerilla activity.

There are regular bus services covering most of the country. Carry food and water on long journeys. There are frequent controls on the roads to check passengers' papers, especially in the north and near the border with Zimbabwe. Bus travel is the cheapest form of transport in the country.

Car hire: Cars are sometimes available from the foreign exchange shop, the Loja Franca.

Taxis: Meters are fitted to taxis in Maputo but for a journey out of town, special arrangements must be made with the driver. It is necessary to telephone for a taxi, and they are often not available.

By rail: There is no rail connection between Maputo and Beira. Trains from Maputo go to the Limpopo Valley and South Africa. Trains from Beira go to Chimoio and Tete. Trains from Nampula go east to Nacala and west to Lichinga and the Malawi border. Three small lines, running from Quelimane, Xai Xai, and Inhambane carry passengers and still use wood-burning steam locomotives.

No food or water is sold on trains and, unusually for Africa, nothing is sold at stops; so carry provisions.

Accommodation and Food

Hotels of international standard are to be found in Maputo and Beira, and accommodation is adequate in smaller towns. There are camp-sites along the beaches and one rest camp with a restaurant in Gorongosa Game Park.

The cuisine is basically Portuguese, enriched by Far East recipes. Specialities the famous Delagoa Bay prawns which are grilled and served with piri-piri sauce. Many snack bars, coffee shops and sidewalk cafes can be found in various parts of Maputo and Beira. However, restaurants too are subject to frequent shortages and menus vary accordingly.

Dress is casual and tipping is neither expected nor refused.

Hotels

NAME	ADDRESS	TELEPHONE	TELEX
MAPUTO			
Cardoso	Avda. Patrice Lumumba, CP 35	741071	
Polana	Avda. Julius Nyerere, CP 1151	741001	
Tivoli	Avda. 25 de Setembro, CP 340	22005	
Turismo	Avda. 25 de Setembro, CP 1393	26153	

▶

[Hotels]

BEIRA

Don Carlos	CP 139	711158
Embaixador	CP 1249	23121
Mocambique	CP 1690	25011

Maputo

Maputo is an attractive city with wide tree-lined streets, pavement cafes and restaurants, and colourful Central Market. There are lovely areas for strolling in the steep zone by the sea, stretching from the Ponta Vermelha to the Polana Hotel. On the elegant outskirts of Somerschield there are huge houses surrounded by crowded, exotic gardens. The avenues are lined with jacaranda, acacias and mimosa and whole areas abandoned by the former wealthy occupants are now inhabited by residents of the shanty towns.

Worth a visit are the Museu da Moeda (money museum) on Oraca 25 de Junho downtown; the Museu Nacional Des Artes in Av Ho Chi Minh which houses good paintings and sculptures by Mozambique's best known artists; the Museu da Revolucao, recently opened in Av 24 Julho which shows the four stages of the history of the liberation struggle in Mozambique; the National History Museum in Av Patrice Lumumba, which has a natural history section and a collection of varied artwork from different parts of Mozambique.

There is an extensive bus service to all parts of the city but long waits between buses are to be expected.

Restaurants: The following is a selective review of restaurants in Maputo.

Costa do Sol, large restaurant at the end of Costa do Sol coast road, a car is necessary to get there.

Mini-Golf, quite expensive, near the beginning of the Costa do Sol road.

Matchedje, Av Mao Tse Tung, serves Mozambican dishes, including Matapa (sauce of ground peanuts and casava leaves) with rice or Wusa (stiff maize porridge). The Matchedje has now opened a second restaurant next door which specialises in prawns and shell fish.

'SELF', opposite the Tica Tica, self service cafeteria of the University of Eduardo Mondlane, very cheap, sometimes good food. you need to be connected to the University or come as a guest. A good meeting place, friendly atmosphere.

Polana Hotel Restaurant, old-fashioned dining room, good prawns, barbeque lunches, fairly expensive.

Grelha, Av Julius Nyerere, best steak in Sanzala, Av 25 Setembro near the Facim trade fair, is now one of the better and more expensive restaurants. The airport restaurant is open to the public and serves good pizza.

Taverna del Rei, Av Julius Nyerere,

fado-type Portuguese music.
El Greco, Av Julius Nyerere (with cocktail bar), good fish meals.
Piri-Piri, Corner of Av 24 Julho and Av Julius Nyerere, no atmosphere but serves prawns and beer.
Princesa, Av 24 Julho, old-type restaurant.
Zambi, the Baixa (downtown), fine setting on the sea-front, food served in the open air.
Vela Azul, off Praca 25 Junho, near the fort, in the style of a French transport cafe, excellent seafood and good steak. Advisable to go early as closes its doors at 2000 hrs.
The Cardoso Hotel, Av Patrice Lumumba, good restaurant more expensive than most, self-service luncheon on Sundays.
Ponto Final, Av Eduardo Mondlane (on the corner of the airport road), serves Chinese meals, friendly and efficient service.
Caxemira, Av Ho Chi Minh, inexpensive good East African curries.
Entertainments: There are a number of nightclubs or *boites* in Maputo where dress is casual and which offer a small dance combo plus singer and variety show. The style of music varies from typical Mozambican ballads to Western pop music. The most popular *boites* are, Sanzala and Zambi (both near the Facim fair ground), **Folkore** (beside the old bullfighting ring Av Guerra Popular),

View of Maputo.

MAGIC

Stacking rice in the Limpopo Valley.

Costa do Sol (Costa do Sol, Friday and Saturday only – very crowded).

Shopping and Markets: The Central Market (also called the Bazaar) set amid nineteenth century buildings, in Baixa, sells fresh produce, fish and meat as well as fine basketwork, wood carvings, masks, and inexpensive leather articles. The market is open every day except Sundays from 0700-2000. There is another market at Xipamine which is more interesting. It is an attractive open air market with fresh produce and basketwork which you can see being made on the spot.

Tourist Information: Empresa Nacional de Turismo, CP 614, Av 25 Setembro 1203, tel: 25011, telex: 6303 ENTUR. The only available map of Maputo is the one in the front of the telephone directory.

Beira

The modern port of Beira has good beaches and is the base for trips to the Gorongosa National Park. To the south, Nova Sofala has a beautiful beach surrounded by tropical scenery near the site of the famous Arab and Portuguese gold-trading town of Sofala, which has since been destroyed by the sea. Far inland are the interesting ruins of the Vila

de Manica area and of Sena.
Restaurants: There are several good restaurants serving seafood, piri-piri chicken and Portuguese dishes.

The Coast

Four resorts easily accessible from Maputo are specially recommended. **Ponta Malangane** and **Ponta do Ouro** lie at the southern-most end of Mozambique's coast and have beautiful, unspoiled beaches. Accommodation is in motel or bungalow units and there are lounges, bars, and restaurants. It is a two hour drive on a sand road, difficult in the rains. **Inhaca** is on an island just a 20 minute flight from Maputo. It has swimming and fishing in the bay, and walks through dunes and a nature reserve. Only a two hour drive north on a good paved road is **Bilene.** It's crystal clear lagoon is safe for swimming and dingy-sailing. These four have been given priority by the tourist authorities and have some of the best food in Mozambique, and must be booked in advance. Bilene is booked at Organizacoes Turisticas do Bilene (Av Karl Marx 174, tel 25173) and the other three at the Empresa Nacional de Turismo (Av 25 Setembro 1203, Maputo, tel: 25011, telex: 6303 ENTUR). The flight to Inhaca is booked at the TTA office at the airport.

Further north but still easily reached by paved road are **Xai-Xai** and **Chonguene,** which have pleasant beaches and reasonable hotels. There is a danger of sharks, however. Continuing north, **Zavora's** coral reef provides excellent skindiving, and there are rondavels and bungalows available for rent very cheaply. There is also a good camp-site. Water is available. The beach is 16 km along a sand road which is passable in an ordinary car.

Further north **Inhambane** is one of the pleasantest of Mozambican cities. It is reached by road on a branch off the main Beira road and there are several hotels and pensions in the town. The local beach resort is Tofo about 20 kms out of town which has a lovely unspoilt beach and good skindiving. **Vilanculos** is 20 kms on a good tar road off the main road to Beira. It is a quiet spot for swimming and fishing. There is a very good hotel with excellent food and well-appointed camp-site close to the beach.

The **Bazaruto Archipelago** of four islands is the country's most famous game-fishing area. There are large and plentiful marlin, barracuda, sailfish and swordfish. There is good accommodation and lovely coral on **Santa Carolina.** The island is being revived as a tourist centre. The north of the country has several good beaches. Just 5 km from the centre of **Pemba** is an idyllic cove with Mozambique's finest coral and one of its best beaches. Near Mozambique Island is a picture postcard beach on another cove, **Chocas.** Houses can be booked at the main office in Nampula of Organizacoes Chocas Mar (Av Eduardo Mondlane 37).

Mozambique Island

Mozambique was for many years the capital of the province, but was replaced in 1898 by Laurenco Marques, now Maputo, and has now lost importance to Nampula and the new port at Nacala. The coral island is joined by a 3.5 km long bridge to the mainland. The fortress of Sao Sebastiao was built in the sixteenth century. Most of the island's churches, mosques, residences and palaces date from the seventeenth and eighteenth centuries, when the town flourished on colonial trade. Many are now derelict and the visitor can wander in and out. But the government has given special priority to restoring the island to its former glory. Some buildings are now being rehabilitated, and tourist facilities have been improved. The one hotel, Pousada de Mocambique, has been rehabilitated and serves good food.

NAMIBIA

Area: 824,292 sq km
Population: 1.29 million (World Bank 1989)
Capital: Windhoek (Otjomuise)

Namibia is a vast, rugged country with clean air, baking hot by day in summer (and often in winter) and cool at night. Drought is endemic, but Namibia, often described in tourist literature as the land 'God made in anger', is more appropriately described as one of Africa's last and most bitterly contested colonies. The internationalisation of Namibia's struggle for independence dates back to the 1919 League of Nations mandate. For the last 30 years, the territory's international status has been disputed at the United Nations by South Africa which continues its illegal occupation with the aid of an army of more than 50,000 and a repressive state apparatus as ruthless as that in South Africa itself.

Negotiations by the five Western members of the UN Security Council led in 1978 to the UN plan for UN-supervised elections, but they were not held, instead South Africa held its own unilateral and limited elections at the end of 1978. South Africa hoped to consolidate the position of its internal settlement with the formation of a 'transitional government of national unity' in July 1985.

South Africa plans to continue to maintain its power in Namibia through its appointed Administrator-General, and the key areas of defence, law and order and foreign affairs remain directly under its control.

SWAPO, the Namibian liberation movement, has pledged itself to continue the armed struggle until genuine independence is achieved. This has led to an increasing militarisation of the country, and makes the north of the country in particular unsafe for the tourist to visit.

The Land and the People

Namibia stretches along 1,280 km of the most desolate and lonely coastline in the world. Along its whole length the vast shifting sand dunes of the Namib Desert spread inland for distances of 80 to 130 km. The country is bound to the north by Angola, with the Caprivi Strip in the east sharing a border with Zambia; to the east by Botswana; and to the south by South Africa. Inland, the escarpment of a north-south plateau, on average 1,000 to 1,700 m in altitude slopes away gradually to the east and north into the vast interior sand basin of the Kalahari. The coast is bisected by the closely situated towns of Walvis Bay, the country's major port, and Swakopmund, the major seaside and summer resort.

Inland, along the escarpment of the high central plateau, rainfall increases slightly. The plateau slopes down to the Kalahari Desert, on the Botswana border, and can generally support little more than yellow grass and 'bush' vegetation. The country's highest rainfall, about 600 mm, is in the swamplands of eastern Ovamboland and the Okavango, but this tails off to only about 150 mm in the south west near the Namib. Rainfall is unreliable, and droughts can last for as long as seven years.

In the far north-west, in the largely unmapped 66,000 sq km of the 2,500 m Kaokoveld Mountains live 10,000 pastoral Ovahimba, Ovajimba and Herero. To the east of the Kaokoveld lie the plains of Ovamboland. Its northern border with Angola is a military fence dividing the Ovambo on both sides of the frontier. The Ovambo comprise nearly 50% of the total population, with two closely-related languages, Ndonga and Kwanyama.

Further to the east, the Ovambo plains give way to swamps of the great Okavango, a river which carries more water than all the rivers of South Africa combined and yet does not flow into the sea. To the south of it live the 56,000 Kavango. The last part of Namibia's northern border, leading from the Okavango to the Zambezi, is also fenced in. It contains the strategically important Caprivi Strip, where South Africa maintains its northernmost air defence systems.

The second largest indigenous group are the 75,000 Damara, a negroid people who mostly speak the Nama language. Both they and the Nama themselves, a Khoisan people, live largely in the so-called 'Police Zone' (the white-inhabited area) where they have been allocated 'homelands'.

Perhaps the best-known of the black peoples are the Herero, who were decimated under German rule before World War One; they now number only 60,000. Their main reserve is in the Waterberg region south of Tsumeb, while Namibia's oldest people, the Bushmen, live in the Kalahari along the border with Botswana.

South of the capital, Windhoek, lies the Rehoboth Gebiet, home of the Rehobother (once known as the Basters, or 'Bastards'). They are an intensely religious and conservative mixed race who migrated from the Cape Colony in the 18th century.

Namibia's ruling whites number above 100,000. They are predominantly engaged in ranching, mining and commerce. Two-thirds are Afrikaans-speaking, a quarter German, and the rest English-speaking.

Culture

Colonisation, first by Germany and then South Africa, has done much to destroy many of rich and diverse cultural traditions of Namibian society. As African society was brought under the yoke of apartheid, with its repressive and racist ethic, so the free expression of the people has been undervalued and denied. However, Namibia still retains a strong cultural character of its own and the indeigenous peoples have preserved their distinctive identities.

One of the most colourful and moving festivals is the annual ceremony during August full moon, when the Herero gather to mourn their departed chiefs at Okahandja, about 70 km north of Windhoek.

Some of the finest Bushmen paintings are in the Brandberg – scene of the famous 'White Lady' – to the north of Windhoek and at Bushmen's Paradise, near Usakos on the road to Walvis Bay. The Bushmen, who still live in the Kalahari, were painting in the country until about 60 or 70 years ago.

The oral literary traditions, music and craft skills of the peasant societies only survive in the more remote rural areas while the culture of the blacks in the urban areas, where they have been made migrants in their own country by the needs of an apartheid economy, reflects the stultifying nature of the South African imposed system; only European forms of expression are accorded any value, although the 'black consciousness' movement has had an impact on urban youth.

The white German-speaking settlers maintain a close identity with German traditions, have their own newspapers and cultural events. Other white settler communities likewise pursue the traditions of their own societies. Their privileged position gives them the possibility to pursue the 'great outdoor life' of the colonisers of southern Africa and has not encouraged them to absorb anything of the culture of Africans, but rather plays a major role in keeping alive a distinct frontier spirit.

However, after nearly a century of colonialism, the culture of the masses is slowly being regenerated through their resistance to the occupying South African regime. In recent years, it is finding new expression in the songs and dances, poetry and art that has grown out of the liberation movement. For the visitors, at present however, it is difficult to have access to either past or present African culture. The museums have concentrated on the artifacts of the colonisers, and the rigorously segregated nature of the ruban areas does not permit any degree of entry into the black communities. In addition, the war situation particularly in the north of the country, makes travel through the rural peasant communities impossible.

Religion, and in particular Christianity, play an important role in the lives of all the communities, and the Church takes an active part in political events.

History

Namibia has been inhabited since pre-historic times by Khoisan-speaking San (Bushmen) and Nama in the southern plateau, joined in the distant past by the Damara of the central plateau. In the 16th and 17th centuries Bantu-speaking Herero migrated into north-western and central Namibia, while in the far north the Ovanbo settled in dense clusters on the inland flood plain along the Okavango valley. Society in much of Namibia was nomadic, stateless and organised into patriarchal clans, based on hunting and gathering (the Kalahari sandveld), sheep and goats (the south) and cattle (the central plateau). In the far north, where cultivation as well as stock-raising was possible, strong monarchies formed.

The immigration across the Orange River of the Orlams, pushed out of the Cape Colony by encroaching Boertrekkers, militarised the whole region and caused overcrowding in the south. Between 1830 and the early 1860s a conquest state under Jonkar Afrikaner dominated much of Namibia from Windhoek south before collapsing in on itself.

The first recorded encounter between Europeans and the inhabitants of Namibia took place near Walvis Bay in 1670. Although there were occasional expeditions into Namibia over the next two centuries, it was not until the second half of the 19th century that white traders and missionaries began to arrive in any numbers. The 1870s and 80s saw a growing colonial influence, first by the Cape Government and then by the Germans, who were quick to exploit divide and rule tactics in their interference in local politics.

By 1890 Namibia's present international boundaries had been agreed amongst the imperialists. The Herero attempted to preserve their autonomy by defensive diplomacy, the Nama by sporadic guerrilla warfare, the Ovambo by armed neutrality and skilfully playing off German aspirations against Portuguese. In 1904 the Herero rose in rebellion but were brutally crushed, and after a year of open genocide, nearly wiped out. The Nama resistance was not finally defeated until 1909. Some 60% of the black population in the 'Police Zone' perished in the holocaust. The Ovambo avoided conquest until the First World War brought a crushing defeat by Portuguese forces in 1915 and an unprovoked South African military campaign in 1917.

The war brought Namibia a new colonial master. A South African military force compelled a German surrender in 1915, and the Treaty of Versailles confirmed the South African occupation under a C-class mandate of the League of Nations. For the next four decades, it was the tribal leaders of the Police Zone who kept up a sustained passive resistance campaign to the new colonisers. From the middle 1950s two new social forces emerged. The one was formed by the uniting of a small group of students and intellectuals with white-collar workers and urban youth to become the South West African National Union (SWANU) in 1969. The second, expressing the growing militancy of the contract workers emerged as the Ovamboland People's Congress, later Organisation (OPO), with the primary objective of ending the contract labour system. In 1960, recognising that the ending of the contract system meant the overthrow of colonialism itself, the OPO reconstituted itself into a national liberation movement, the South West Africa People's Organisation (SWAPO).

At first, SWAPO waited on decisive action by the United Nations, who had assumed the League of Nations Mandate over Namibia when the League was formally dissolved in 1946. Proceedings against South Africa at the International Court of Justice (ICJ), begun in 1960, finally produced a non-judgement in 1966. In the same year the UN General Assembly terminated South Africa's mandate over the territory. Henceforth, the South African occupation was illegal, and in 1967 the UN established the Council for Namibia to administer the territory. On the day of the 1966 ICJ verdict, SWAPO declared 'We have no alternative but to rise to arms and bring about our own liberation'. From then on, the liberation struggle was fought by SWAPO on three fronts: international lobbying, guerrilla war, and a mass mobilisation campaign inside the country.

In 1969, the UN Security Council endorsed the General Assembly's termination of South Africa's mandate, and set October 1969 as the deadline for South Africa's withdrawal. South Africa's response was to implement the Odendaal Plan, which reduced Namibia to the status of a fifth province of South Africa, and transformed the 'reserves' into 'homelands'. In 1971, the year in which the ICJ finally upheld UN sovereignty on Namibia, as mass upsurge of popular resistance erupted throughout the country, culminating in a nationwide strike, involving over 20,000 contract workers.

Although the strike achieved little more than token reforms, which were quickly followed by an ever greater degree of repression, it helped to give momentum to the political struggle. The churches, always a powerful body in Namibia, took an increasingly active part in the struggle of the people against colonialism.

The 1973 Bantustan elections in Ovamboland saw over 97% of the electorate support SWAPO's call for a boycott. This was despite the systematic political repression and state of emergency declared in Ovamboland. South Africa now embarked on a unilateral exercise in self-determination in Namibia in an attempt to head off increasing international pressure. A constitutional conference was convened in the old Turnhalle drill hall in Windhoek in 1975. The conference was composed of 11 ethnic delegations, in the main selected from South African appointed tribal administrations of the reserves and Bantustans. The Turnhalle finally came up with a constitution in March 1977 and set December 1978 as the date for 'independence'. Continuing debates and resolutions at the UN however made it quite clear that the Turnhalle internal solution was not a package the West could hope to sell internationally. With vast economic interests at stake, the five Western members of the Security Council in 1977 set up the 'contact group', which for the next 18 months assumed the role of mediator between South Africa and SWAPO. SWAPO had in 1973 been recognised by the UN General Assembly as the 'sole authentic representative of the Namibian people' and accorded full observer status at the General Assembly.

The 'proposal for a settlement' of the contact group, accepted by both SWAPO and the South African Government, was endorsed in the UN Security Council in July 1978. The Commissioner for Namibia, Martii Ahtisaari, was appointed UN Special Representative in Namibia, and a plan for UN supervised elections was drawn up. But South Africa objected to key aspects of the proposed implementation of the plan and decided to proceed with its own unilateral elections in December 1978. The Turnhalle, which had been dissolved, was immediatley reconstituted as the Democratic Turnhalle Alliance (DTA).

The DTA won 41 out of the 50 seats in the Constituent Assembly, but this result remains unrecognised by the international community. Negotiations on the settlement plan were resumed in mid-1979, and focussed on the idea of a demilitarized zone 100 kms wide along the Angola-Namibia and Zambia-Namibia borders, to be patrolled by a UN peace-keeping force. SWAPO forces would disarm under UN supervision before being allowed into Namibia to participate in UN-supervised elections. South Africa continued to raise difficulties about the plan and no agreement was concluded, despite a series of peace talks from 1981-83.

Inside Namibia, the transfer of responsibilities to the new Council of Ministers continued, with the establishment of a separate central budget and civil service, while a SWA Territorial Force was constituted out of South African units serving in Namibia. But in January 1983 Dirk Mudge, the Chairman of the Council of Ministers, resigned and Willie van Niekerk was established as Administrator-General. Louis Pienaar took the office on July 1 1985. A "transitional government of national unity" was installed on July 17 1985.

Meanwhile the level of fighting along the border significantly escalated from 1979, with large-scale South African attacks on SWAPO bases in Angola and Zambia, and draconian security restrictions throughout northern and central Namibia.

After a series of meetings at the end of 1988 South Africa finally agreed to the independence for Namibia. It agreed to implement United Nations proposals under UN resolution 435. The country came under joint UN/SA administration while the first democratic elections were organised for November 1989. After this a constitution is to be drawn up followed by independence.

Economy

South Africa's primary objectives in Namibia have been two-fold: to appropriate the main natural resources for commercial exploitation (which they continue to do despite a UN decree prohibiting it without permission from the UN Council for Namibia); and secondly, to guarantee the employer a long-term supply of cheap labour. The conditions under which the vast majority of Namibia's black workers are forced to live, and the restrictions that bind them to their employers have often been described as akin to slavery. Up to two-thirds of the labour force are migrants, permitted to remain in the country's white industrial and farming areas only so long as they are required by the apartheid economy. The vast majority of Namibians, whether directly caught up in the contract labour system or not, live in conditions of extreme poverty – in a country which possesses some of the richest and most abundant natural resources in Africa.

Namibia's commercial economy has been built almost entirely on the export of raw materials and animal products. The mining industry is almost completely owned by foreign corporations, mainly South African, British and American. Gem diamonds, base metals (copper, lead, zinc and cadmium) and uranium are the main minerals exported. Production at Rossing, the world's largest uranium mine, began in 1976; output peaked at 4,800 tonnes in 1980. It was valued at R413m in 1982.

The fishing industry, based on the nine modern factories at Walvis Bay which process pilchards and anchovy, has been ruined by overfishing by South African companies. Settler agriculture consists almost entirely of ranching-cattle on the central plateau, and karakul sheep in the arid south. Commercial cereal production is minimal, and the peasant areas have been so underdeveloped that they have had to become importers of maize flour.

The impact of this massive foreign orientation on the economic structure and on income distribution is extreme. Manufacturing industry is almost non-existent; and finance, commerce and services are overwhelmingly geared to the needs of the corporations and white colonists.

In 1977 South Africa annexed Walvis Bay to the Cape Province, a unilateral move contested by SWAPO and the international community, depriving Namibia of direct control over the port.

Wildlife

Proclaimed game reserves account for roughly one-seventh of the total land surface, and with the closed diamond mining areas along the coast, game is effectively protected in about one-fifth of the country. With these vast open spaces Namibia has some of the last great migratory herds remaining in Africa. The animals most commonly seen are kudu, springbok, warthog, zebra, gemsbok, impala, hartebeeste, wildebeeste, eland as well as lion, leopard, giraffe and elephant.

National Parks

There are now ten national parks under the Department of Tourism and Nature Conservation. The two best known game reserves however, are the Etosha Pan Game Reserve and the Kalahari Gemsbok Park. The latter is actually part of South Africa and lies between the tip of the North-Western Cape, the border of Namibia, and Botswana. However, a good direct route leads directly from the Park to Keetmanshoop and Windhoek in Namibia.

Etosha Pan Game Reserve, some 400 km north of Windhoek by tarred road, is one of the finest game parks in Africa. The Pan itself is flat and devoid of vegetation, but the surrounding grasslands and bush support vast quantities of animal and bird life. Vast herds of buck or wildebeest can frequently be seen. It is wild, hot and very dusty, but there are well-equipped rest camps with comfortable rondavel type accommodation and excellent camping facilities. The Reserve is open from mid-March until approximately the end of October.

The Kalahari Gemsbok National Park must be entered from South Africa and is open throughout the year. The park on the south-east corner of the Kalahari desert consists of typical desert terrain – dry riverbeds and dunes scattered with shrubs, thorn-trees and tsamma melons. Temperatures vary enormously especially in winter when the days are warm, but the nights bitterly cold. In summer it is uncomfortably hot. Gemsbok, springbok, kudu, and wildebeest traverse the desert and enormous communal nests of the weaver birds are of particular interest.

General Information

Government

In 1989 the country came under joint United Nations/South African administration while preparations were made for the first democratic elections scheduled for November 1989. After that a constitution had to be agreed, followed by independence.

Languages

English, German and Afrikaans are the official languages, the latter being the most widely used. Within certain 'homelands', the local language has been given official status. The languages spoken by the black population fall into two groups – the Khoisan and the Western Bantu. Both divide further into two sub-groups, speakers of the former being the San and the Nama/Damara, and of the latter, the Herero and Ovambo/Kavango. There are also small groups of Tswana and Lozi speakers.

Religion

Although animist traditions survive amongst the northern peasantry, the people are strongly Christianised. Nearly 80% belong to recognised churches, with well over 50% belonging to the two ex-mission Lutheran churches.

How to Get There

By air: Three South African Airways flights between Johannesburg and Frankfurt (twice), and Johannesburg and Zurich (once) pass through Windhoek each week. Lufthansa also operates a direct link between Frankfurt and Windhoek. SAA's internal service connects Windhoek with Cape Town and Johannesburg. Namib Air also flies internally and to South Africa.

By road: From the south, through Uppington in South Africa to Karasburg, there is a tarred road. From the east, there is an untarred road from Botswana to Gobabis. The road from Luanda in Angola through Namibia to South Africa is now completely tarred, but it is advisable to check if the road is open to tourists in northern Namibia through Ovamboland, as this area has been under a state of emergency.

By rail: The only cross-border line from South Africa runs up central Namibia through Windhoek to terminate at Tsumeb and Grootfontein, with branches to Walvis Bay and Luderitz and eastwards to Gobabis. Passenger trains run each way twice a week and there are daily goods/passenger services. Rail travel however, is neither quick nor particularly comfortable.

Entry and Customs Regulations

South African regulations apply. See under South Africa: General Information in this guide.

Climate

The cold Benguela current keeps the coast of the Namib Desert cool, damp and rainless, with the shoreline fogbound for much of the year. Inland, the rainfall, all of which falls during the summer months (October to April) as thundery showers, increases from south to north. Daytime temperatures in the summer are high, sometimes exceeding 40°C. The high altitude keeps the summer nights cool, and the winters are cold (15°C maximum in central parts).

What to wear: Cool summer clothes are needed most of the year, with warm woollens for the winter nights.

Health Precautions

Malaria prophylactics are recommended if planning to visit a game park. Visitors are recommended not to swim in inland rivers and dams as they contain bilharzia. Those going on long safaris or hikes should beware of snakes and scorpions and are advised to carry an anti-bite serum.

Banks and Currency

Namibia is fully integrated into the Rand monetary system, and most of the principal South African banks operate branches in the main towns.
Currency: South African Rand, divided into 100 cents.
Exchange rates p.10.

Business Hours and Public Holidays

See under South Africa in this guide.

Embassies

There are no embassies in Namibia.

Transport

By air: Because of the vast distances, flying is the quickest, and often the most economical, way to get around. Namibair has daily scheduled flights within the country between Windhoek, Walvis Bay, Swakopmund, Tsumeb, Keetmanshoop, Grootfontein, Luderitz and Alexander Bay.
By road: Heavy investment by South Africa in strategic roads to back up its war effort has given the country a nationwide network of all-weather roads, many of them tarred.
By rail: There are branches off the main central line to Walvis Bay and Luderitz, and eastwards to Gobabis.

Accommodation and Food

Most towns have modest hotels, while Windhoek and Swakopmund have several of a more luxurious nature. Many of the cafes and restaurants reflect the German influence on Namibia. The last few years have seen some relaxation in the apartheid legislation, allowing blacks into some, though by no means all, hotels and restaurants.

Windhoek

Founded in 1890 by a German officer, Windhoek is situated in the Khomas-Hochland Mountains at the centre of the country. Like all southern African cities, Windhoek is actually two cities: the modern shopping and business centre with its spacious white suburbs, and the

Hotels

NAME	ADDRESS	TELEPHONE	TELEX
WINDHOEK			
Continental	Kaiser St	2681	
Kalahari Sands	Kaiser St	–	
Thuringerhof	Kaiser St	6031	▶

[Hotels]

SWAKOPMUND		
Panorama	PO Box 630	336
Strand	Strand St	2605
WALVIS BAY		
Flamingo	7th St	3011
Mermaid	6th St	2541 ■

adjacent black township of Katutura, with its oppressive hostel compound and small match-box houses. The white part of the city has fashionable shops, hotels, German cafes and restaurants, cinemas, a theatre and museum. The Alte Feste (Old Fort), which houses the Cultural History Museum, the three German castles at Klein Windhoek, and the Tintenpalast are all reminders of the German occupation of Namibia.

Swakopmund

The Germany legacy can best be seen at Swakopmund. The attractive seaside resort on the edge of the Namib Desert used to be the German administrative capital during the hot summer months. The architecture is still predominantly German colonial, with fine examples in the Lutheran church and government buildings. The black township is made up of the usual matchbox houses, and is constantly encroached upon by the sands of the Namib.

Walvis Bay

Annexed by the British in 1878, Walvis Bay is still claimed by South Africa to be part of the Republic – a situation hotly contested by SWAPO. It is Namibia's only deep-water port, and is currently a major military base for South Africa. Apart from the nearby lagoon which has a large population of flamingoes, Walvis Bay is an ugly town permeated by the smell of fish.

The North

Okahandja, 72km north of Windhoek, is the spot where the Herero gather every August to mourn their departed chiefs. The town has a picturesque mission house and church and a private zoo. Near Karibib, 114 km west on the Swakopmund road, is the vast extinct volcano of Erongo, whose surroundings are particularly rich in Bushmen paintings. The famous Bushman painting 'White Lady of the Brandberg' is, however, much less accessible, lying about 210 km north west of Karibib on a rough dirt road. In this area, too, are Bushman rock engravings at Twyfelfontein; the Burnt Mountain, completely bare of plantlife and composed of rainbow-coloured lava rocks and the Petrified Forest, 45 km from Welwitschia on the road to Torra Bay. Further east, near Kalkfeld, are the footprints of a dinosaur. North west of Usakos, rising out of the Namib, is the 2,000 m Spitzkoppe, the country's 'Matterhorn', where there are well known rock paintings and good mountaineering.

The South

South of Windhoek the main road passes

through Rehoboth to Mariental. Nearby is the Hardap Dam Park, and to the west, 72 km from Maltahohe in the Namib, is the remarkable and immaculately preserved Schloss Duwisibery, a German-built castle. Also in the west is the Nauklauft Mountain Zebra Park. Between Mariental and Keetmanshoop is Mukatos – 'The Finger of God' – a spectacular 30 m weathered stone tower near Asab. Further south is Brukkaros, a 1,500 m high extinct volcano.

At Keetmanshoop, the centre of the country's major karakul farming area, there are hotels, shops and an airport. The Kokerboom Forest is nearby.

The main places of interest towards the South African border are the hot springs at Ai-Ais and the dramtic Fish River Canyon, which some claim is an even finer sight than the American Grand Canyon. In the midst of a desolate mountain landscape the earth suddenly falls away dizzyingly to the sandy river bed winding 600 m below, over a distance of 110 km. Approach the Canyon with care – it is difficult to see the lip until you are within only a few metres of it. It can be visited at any time of the year, but walking tours of the Canyon only take place in winter because of the danger of summer flooding. Visitors to the Canyon can stay at Keetmanshoop; there are also camping facilities at Ai-Ais. A permit to visit the springs there must be obtained from the Magistrate at Karasburg.

Part of the area surrounding the Canyon has been declared a national park – the home of leopard, zebra, kudu, ostrich and several species of antelope.

Windhoek

CAMERA PRESS

RWANDA

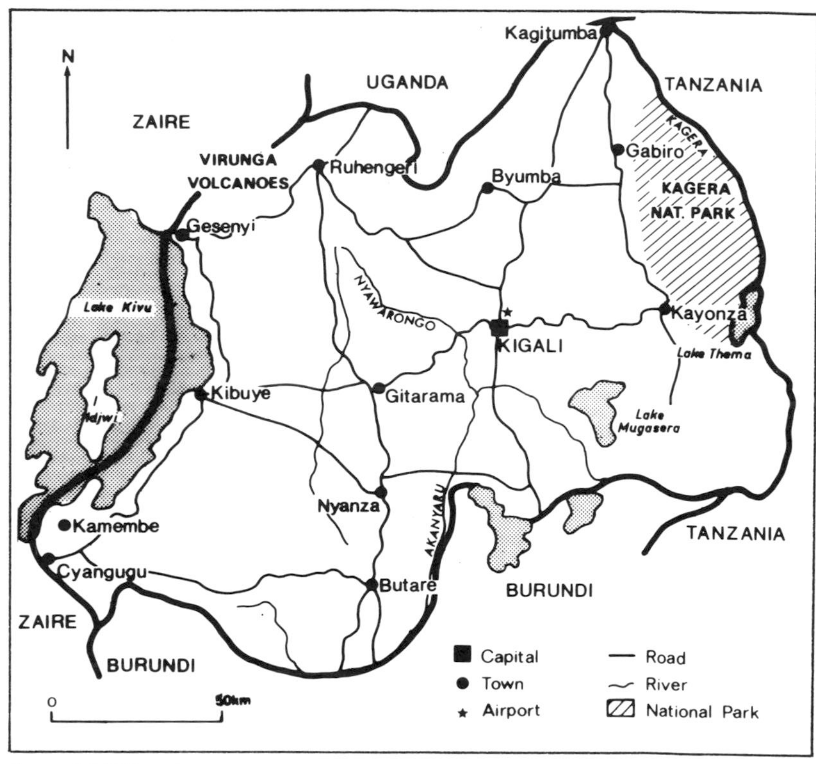

Area: 26,338 sq km
Population: 6.88 million (1989 World Bank)
Capital: Kigali

To the traveller undaunted by Rwanda's physical isolation, the country offers rich dramatic scenery and a sense of peace. In the midst of seemingly endless hills and mountains cultivation is unusually intense with subsistence farmers using every available square metre of land whether valley or hilltop.

Land of a Thousand Hills

Rwanda lies in the dramatic, remote centre of Africa, split by the Rift Valley. Lake Kivu, one of the chain of lakes running from Lake Tanganyika to

Ethiopia, forms the western border with Zaire. Steep, forest-clad slopes rise above it to the Nile-Zaire watershed; great peaks of up to 3,000 m run through the country from north to south.

From the great Nile-Zaire divide the land falls eastwards in distinctive hills, separated by rivers, lakes and swamps. The landscape of eucalyptus trees, banana groves and fields alternating with luxuriant pasture shows that although Rwanda is financially poor it is still a wealthy country in terms of sustenance. The traditional way of life continues to be based on agriculture and cattle.

The Rwandese, densely settled in scattered homesteads in the fertile areas, do not form villages. Each family is surrounded by its own fields. Every hill was a traditional unit where pasture rights were controlled by local Tutsi, once the ruling caste, but now forming only 9% of the population. Many fled as refugees in the uprising of the Hutu peasant majority in 1959 and in subsequent disturbances, but the country has succeeded in establishing a degree of ethnic tolerance in the last decade. Tutsi still herd their cattle and live freely in the towns.

Culture

Music and dance play important roles in traditional cultural life. The Rwanda National Ballet is famous for its traditional dancing and singing and displays can be seen either at national ceremonies or, perhaps more satisfatorily, on request in the villages. Stringed instruments, xylophones and drums are made by the musicians themselves.

The pygmy Twa are the traditional potters. Their work is simple and fine, and uses no artificial colours or mechanical devices. Rwanda's basketwork is the most beautiful of the inherited crafts. There are official museums and shops at Butare, Nyundo and Nyabisindu (Nyanza), where prices are fixed and quality excellent.

History

The pygmy Twa people were probably the first inhabitants of Rwanda, living as hunters and gatherers. They still survive in very small groups but have been completely outnumbered by the growth of the agricultural Bantu Hutu population whose ancestors arrived around 1000 AD, and the Hamite Tutsi, who arrived as cattle-rearing overlords from the 15th century onwards during the great migrations of central and eastern Africa.

The history of the old Kingdom of Rwanda can be traced back through the oral traditions to about 1386, but it did not expand to its present size until the conquests of the ruthless, absolute monarch Mwami Rwabugiri (1860-1895) who centralised his kingdom under non-hereditary Tutsi bureaucrats appointed by him. The Rwandan Mwami's authority was far greater than that of his counterpart in Burundi; he was an absolute ruler in every sense.

The Tutsi of Rwanda developed a system of feudal overlordship unsurpassed outside Ethiopia. The master-client relationship between Tutsi and Hutu was perfected in economic, political, ceremonial and religious forms. The Tutsi maintained that they came from another world, did not consume the same 'profane food' as the Hutu and emphasised the concepts of power and authority constantly in their culture. Tutsi chiefs enforced their will through their superior wealth in cattle, and in exchange for Hutu pasture rights and the use of some cattle, they controlled the allocation of land and exacted rental in the form of forced Hutu labour.

Swamps, mountains and their fearsome reputation kept the Rwandese isolated from the Zanzibari slave and ivory trade of the 19th century. It was not until the late 1890's that German explorers from the east coast entered and annexed the country. Both the Germans (1890-1916) and then the Belgians who took over in 1916 under a League of Nations Mandate and administered the territory or Ruanda-Urundi together with the Belgian Congo, accorded authority and power to the Tutsi, while none of the 'benefits' of colonialism accrued to the Hutu peasantry, whose conditions of existence deteriorated. Hutu feelings of resentment multiplied, until in 1957, they called for an end to the Tutsi monopoly and urged radical reforms in the administration of the colony. In July 1959, a widespread Hutu uprising involving massive bloodshed was provoked when a ruthless Tutsi clan seized power on the death of Mwami Matari III. The new Mwami, Kigeri V, fled the country.

The Belgian colonial government belatedly introduced political concessions, and in September 1961, parliamentary elections brought the Hutu majority party to power, with Gregoire Kayibanda as the first President of Rwanda. Under his leadership, Rwanda became independent in July 1962 and separated itself from the still Tutsi-dominated Burundi.

Kayibanda ruled cautiously with some degree of political stability until the early 1970's when there was a resurgence of anti-Tutsi feeling echoing the tension in neighbouring Burundi, where Tutsi rulers still clung to power. Disturbances in various parts of the country prompted the head of the army, General Habyarimana, to oust Kayibanda in a coup d'etat in July 1973. The general has since retained power, and there is presently a fairly calm atmosphere in the country. In 1978, the military announced measures to return the country to 'constitutional government' with presidential and legislative elections. General Habyarimana was the only presidential candidate and his political party the MRND, the only party. In December 1983 he was re-elected President. Tensions between the church and state led to the resignation, from the central committee, of Archbishop Vincent Nsengiyumva in December 1985. Leaders of religious sects, imprisoned for inciting rebellion against the government in October 1986, were granted presidential pardon in July 1987 to commemorate the 25th independence anniversary.

Economy

Although Rwanda has no towns or cities (apart from the small capital Kigali) it has the highest population density in Africa. About 90% of the population live on small family farms scattered over every hillside which is intensively cultivated.

87% of Rwanda's cultivated land is under subsistence food crops – but farms are decreasing in size annually owing to overpopulation and ecological damage to farmland. Fuel shortages have developed as woodlands have been destroyed and there are still too many cattle to allow for more productive use of the arable land.

Most families subsistence farm and some cash crops such as tea and pyrethrum are grown – but the latter are not economically very significant. Coffee is grown in some areas and the boom in coffee prices in recent years has marginally boosted the generally low average income. Some mining is carried on, largely by primitive methods; the chief minerals produced are tin and tungsten.

National Park

Kagera: The north east of Rwanda is covered by 2,500 sq km of savannah and hilly plains beside the great Kagera River and is devoted to game preservation – mostly lion, zebra, antelope, hippo, the biggest species of buffalo in Africa, as well as impala, tapir, warthog, waterbuck, eland, leopard, crocodile, monkeys and a fascinating varied waterbird population of crested crane, heron, fish eagle and cormorant.

One passes through plains and marshy valleys to reach the series of lakes along the river by a 150 km track. For some days or even weeks (especially in December, March and April) the route may be impassable because of rains.

The visitor arrives at the entrance to the park at Gabiro by air or road and buys a permit at the office of the Conservateur there, picking up a Rwandan guide. No accommodation facilities exist within the park but there is a guest house on the edge of the reserve – Gabiro Hotel, Byumba. Accommodation should be booked in advance.

The Virunga Volcanoes: Between Ruhengeri and Gisenyi lies a range of volcanoes that is of special interest to both geologists and photographers. The Zaire border runs along the peaks of the mountains on the other side of which stretches the great Virunga National Park of Zaire. Fair roads lead from Gisenyi into the beautiful mountains of the Zaire-Uganda frontier.

Of the volcanoes, Karisimbi (4,507 m) is the most imposing. Mahabura (4,127 m) above Ruhengeri is the main haunt of gorillas. The still active Nyiragongo in Zaire (3,470 m) is the most commonly climbed from Gisenyi.

The visitor can take special air trips from Gisenyi to view the craters. No real climbing is involved and assisted by Rwandan guides the expedition takes two or three days. Rest huts are provided.

General Information

Government

Presidential, single party government under Maj. Gen. Juvenal Habyarimana and the Mouvement Révolutionnaire National pour le Développement (MRND).

Languages

Kinyarwanda and French are the official languages. Swahili is used for trade and commerce.

Religion

Traditional (50%), the remainder predominantly Roman Catholic.

How to Get There

By air: There are flights by Sabena, Air France or Air Zaire to the international airport of Kanombe, 12 km from Kigali. There are also flights from Bujumbura (Burundi). Taxis from the airport are few. The Rwanda Travel Service runs a bus from the airport to the main hotels.
By road: There are main roads from Burundi, Uganda, Tanzania and Zaire.

Entry Regulations

Visitors to Rwanda must have a valid passport and visa. Visas of up to three months' duration are obtainable from Rwandan embassies abroad. They should be applied for at least six weeks in advance. A visa may be obtained at Kigali airport on arrival for those countries where there is no Rwandan representative, or can be applied for directly from Ministère de l'Intérieur, Service de l'Immigration, BP 63, Kigali, Rwanda.

Visitors must possess a valid international certificate of vaccination against yellow fever. Inoculation against cholera is also advisable.

Customs Regulations

Customs formalities are not strict for short-stay visitors. Usual amounts of tobacco and spirits can be taken in duty-free. Personal effects are not subject to duty.

Climate

Close to the equator but very high, Rwanda has a delightful, equable and healthy climate. The average temperature is 23°C over most of the country but in the mountains it can fall to 15°C. There are two rainy seasons: mid-January to mid-May and mid-October to mid-December when rainfall is generally heavy, especially on mountain slopes.

Health Precautions

Malaria prophylactics should be taken, although at Lake Kivu itself there are no mosquitoes and allegedly no bilharzia. Tap water should not be drunk.

Banks and Currency

Banque Commerciale du Rwanda, BP 354, Kigali, Bd de la Revolution, tel: 5591, telex: 505 (Branches in Cyangugu and Gisenyi)
Banque de Kigali, 63 Avenue du Commerce, BP 175, Kigali, tel: 6391, telex: 514 (Branches in Kigali and Ruhengeri)
Central Bank: Banque Nationale du Rwanda, BP 531, Kigali, tel: 4282, telex: 508
Currency: Rwanda Franc
Exchange rates, p.10.

Business Hours

Banks: Monday-Friday 0830-1200 for cash transactions; 1400-1500 for other business.

Government offices and commerce: Monday-Friday 0800-1200 and 1400-1700.
Shops: Dawn to dusk.
Post offices and Airline offices in Kigali: Monday-Friday 0800-1200 and 1400-1700; Saturday 0800-1200.

Public Holidays

New Year's Day, 1 January
Holy Thursday, 12 April 1990
Good Friday, 13 April 1990
Easter Monday, 16 April 1990
Labour Day, 1 May
Whit Monday, 4 June 1990
National Holiday, 1 July
Assumption, 15 August
Government Holiday, 26 October
All Saints' Day, 1 November
Justice's Holiday, 24 November
Christmas Day, 25 December

Embassies in Kigali

Belgium: BP 81, Kigali
Burundi: BP 714, Kigali
China: BP 1345, Kigali
France: BP 53, Kigali
Germany FR: BP 355, Kigali, tel: 5222
Switzerland: BP 597, Kigali
Uganda: BP 656, Kigali
US: BP 28, Kigali
USSR: BP 40, Kigali
Zaire: BP 169, Kigali

Transport

By air: Internal services are operated by Air Rwanda, BP 177, Kigali, between Kigali, Kamembe and Butare. There are non-commercial airports at Ruhengeri, Nemba, Gisenyi and Gabiro which can be reached by chartered two-engine planes for up to seven passengers, but the cost is high.

By road: Roads are very poor and the terrain difficult; these should be attempted only by adventurous and experienced drivers. The main north-south is being tarred.

Bus services are being introduced slowly by **Autobus,** BP 619, Kigali, tel: 5404-5411. Hitchhiking is more reliable but one is usually expected to pay some sort of fare.

Car hire: Rwanda Links, BP 573; Agence Solliard, BP 335, tel: 5660; and Rwanda Motor, BP 448, tel: 5924.

Accommodation and Food

Hotels in Kigali tend to be expensive. More reasonably priced are those at Butare, Gisenyi and Ruhengeri (the Muhabura). Camping is now forbidden.

Hotels

NAME	ADDRESS	TELEPHONE	TELEX
KIGALI			
Hotel des Diplomates	BP 269	5579	
Hotel Kiyovu	BP 1331	5106	
Hotel des Mille Collines	BP 1322	6530	
Meridien Hotel	BP 874	2176	
Motel	BP 276	5673	

►

[Hotels]

GISENYI		
Hotel Edelweiss	BP 82, Ave du Progrès	7082
Hotel Palm Beach	BP 142	–
Hotel Regina	BP 63	7063
BYUMBA		
Gabiro Hotel*	–	–
BUTARE		
Hotel Faucon	–	–
Hotel Ibis	–	–

* Guest house on the edge of the Kagera National Park. No accommodation facilities exist within the Park itself.

Kigali

An administrative and commercial centre, the tiny capital has little to offer in the way of tourist attractions.

Restaurants: There are restaurants at the main hotels. Others in town include Chez John, La Sierra, Le Picket. There are many small bars such as Aux Delices, Café de Kigali, La Bonne Source, Lumiere, Terminus, Panorama, Come Back, Venus.

Tourist Information: Office Rwandais du Tourisme et des Parcs Nationaux, BP 905, Kigali, tel: 6512.

Travel Agencies: AMI (tours), BP 262, tel: 5395; RTS (Rwanda Travel Service, public transport), BP 140, tel: 6512; Sabena, BP 96, tel: 5294; Agence Solliard (tours and car hire), BP 335, tel: 5660; Star (air taxis), BP 177, tel: 5238; Transintra-Transafricair, BP 383, tel: 5287; Taxis Aeriens de Bry (air taxis), BP 352, tel: 5318.

Butare

Butare, on the main north-south road, is the university town and centre of scientific research. There is an interesting craft museum and shop. The forest of Nyungwe lies between Butare and Cyangugu on a very rough road, which passes through the forest of exotic trees and shrubs. Troops of monkeys can be seen from the road, and a small elephant herd inhabits the forest.

Gisenyi

Gisenyi, the attractive town on Lake Kivu, has an avenue of flowering trees and a sandy beach on one of the most beautiful lakes of Africa. Swimming is safe (no crocodiles or hippos) and one may water-ski. The lake itself is lined with banana plantations rising steeply to high hills, making access difficult. The road from Kigali is high and winding but in fair condition. The road down the lake to Cyangugu gives beautiful views of the lake but is very rough. This is the centre, too, for expeditions to the national park of the Virunga Volcanoes (see above).

SOUTH AFRICA

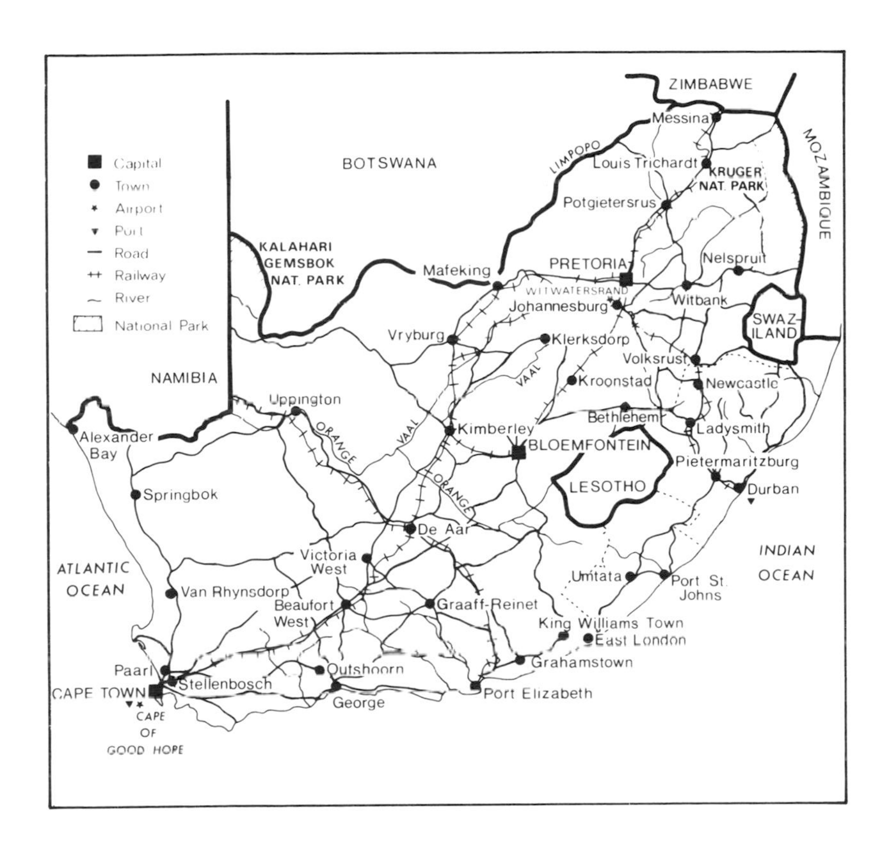

Area: 1,221,037 sq km
Population: 34.0 million (1989 World Bank)
Africans 24.5 million; Whites 5.2 million;
Coloureds 3.2 million; Asians 1.1 million
Capitals: Pretoria (administrative), Cape Town (legislative), Bloemfontein (judicial)

South Africa is a land of great and often stunning contrasts; of fertile green valleys and harsh near-desert conditions; of rugged mountains and endless silver beaches along two oceans; of hot summers and cold winter conditions; of bustling 20th century cities and settlements of hovels; of great wealth and bitter poverty; of dynamic growth and artificial restrictions to growth; of freedom for some and denial of basic human rights for the majority.

It is a country of surging confidence and of deep fears – a land in which millions of people are being forcibly uprooted to create a more rigidly, racially divided society in pursuit of the country's official policy of apartheid. This quite simply means separation: physically separating whites, blacks, Coloureds (people of mixed race) and Asians. Both socially and politically it is a unique country.

The sharp contrasts will affect visitors differently – a black traveller, if he could secure a visa, would find himself seriously restricted in his freedom of movement; the white traveller, by contrast, will find an open welcome from a hospitable country: neither will find it easy to see what lies behind the economic dynamism of the society, or beyond the unsurpassed physical splendour. The travel posters are misleading only in what they don't tell.

The Land and The People

South Africa has three major natural regions; the plateau, the mountains and the coastal belt. The high plateau has sharp escarpments which rise above the flat plains, or *veld*, broken up only by the characteristic flat-topped hills. These are some of the oldest hills on earth, flattened by constant weathering. Occasional outcrops of granite are sometimes associated with immensely rich mineral deposits, particularly gold, of which the most famous is the ridge rising gently from the plateau known as the Witwatersrand (the Ridge of the White Waters). The vegetation is open grassland, changing to bush in the northern Transvaal and to thornveld in the arid south west.

Despite two main rivers systems, the Limpopo and the Orange, most of the plateau lacks surface water. On the eastern rim of the plateau soar the Drakensberg range (the Dragon Mountains) whose highest peak, the Mont-aux-Sources, rises to 3,482 m. Rainfall is abundant in these mountains.

The coast is lined with fine sandy beaches and rocky coves. The Mediterranean climate gives Cape Town and the south western Cape Province dry summers (October to March) and wet winters with shrub-type vegetation such as the pink protea – the national wild plant. The Cape Range, which includes the famous landmark of Table Mountain, runs along the sea.

Inland is the arid Karoo which rises to the high plateau. Further north, the dramatic Wild Coast of the Eastern Province, the Ciskei and Transkei softens into lusher sub-tropical forests.

South Africa is the most highly urbanised and industrialised country in the continent, a development it owes mainly to its rich mineral resources, its pool of cheap black labour and its extensive network of communications and power. The major conurbation is the string of towns along the golden Reef, or Rand, which centres on Johannesburg. The Reef forms one side of the Vaal Triangle, the industrial-mining 'Ruhr' of South Africa. The administrative capital, Pretoria, is by contrast quiet and spacious.

The country's other major industrial centres are in and around its ports – Cape Town, Port Elizabeth, East London and Durban.

Of the 26 million people in South Africa some 4 million are officially classified as 'whites', of whom one third are English-speaking and nearly two thirds are Afrikaans-speaking. The Afrikaners (or Boers, meaning farmers), are a mixture of Dutch, French Huguenots, Germans and English.

The bulk of the population is officially classified 'non-white' – comprising Africans, Coloured and Asians. The 2.8 million Coloureds evolved in the early colonial society of the Cape Province from the Dutch settlers, the brown-skinned San (Bushmen) and Khoikhoi (Hottentots), who were the original inhabitants of that area, and from the Malay slaves of Indonesia. Most of the Coloureds live in the Western Cape. Predominantly Afrikaans-speaking, their culture is largely European.

The Asian community of almost a million consists mainly of Indians, found mostly in Natal where they were brought to work on the sugar plantations in the 1870's. Many subsequently turned to trade, market-gardening and to skilled and semi-skilled labour. The majority are Hindu.

Two out of every three South Africans are black (about 21 million). Officially designated as Bantu (which simply means 'the people') the blacks themselves prefer the term 'Africans' or 'blacks'; they regard 'natives' as a term of opprobrium and 'Bantu' as meaningless and politically offensive.

Under the policy of apartheid – known as 'Separate Development' – the entire country has been divided into racially exclusive areas to keep the people socially apart. Over 87% of the land is designated for white occupation – and is known as the 'white area'; the other c. 13% is for black occupation: these are the reserves which have been divided into 10 'Bantu Homelands' or 'Bantustans' which, in the ripeness of time, are supposed to achieve their separate independence. There is no land exclusively reserved for Coloureds or Asians. However, every village, town and city is sub-divided into separate areas reserved exclusively for one of the four racial groups. It is a crime for a member of one group to live in a different racial area.

Africans are deemed to be citizens of their own Homeland and have no rights in the 'white areas' where they are officially treated as temporary sojourners under the Government policy of making all black workers into migrants – moving between the work-starved Homelands and the worker-starved 'white areas'. The black workers may stay there only as long as they are 'deemed' to be of useful service to the whites. If they are no longer of use they are declared 'surplus labour appendages' (an official designation) and are 'endorsed out', that is, forcibly repatriated to the

Homelands where they must go through the process of finding new employment. Only a privileged minority of black urban dwellers are partially exempt from this migratory system.

Since the adoption of apartheid as a policy in 1948, over two million blacks, Coloureds and Asians have been uprooted from their former homes to achieve racially exclusive neighbourhoods. Official policy is to allow only African males to come and work for contract periods in the towns leaving their families behind; or, in the case of women, they may not be accompanied by their children. This policy makes migrants of the black workers and furthers the breakdown of African family life. Special privileges are, however, issued to wives to visit their husbands in the 'white areas' for a strictly limited period of 72 hours for the purpose of conception – a phenomenon possibly unique in history.

The Homelands are scattered around the periphery of the 'white areas'. With the partial exception of the Transkei all the others are made up of fragmented areas of land – sometimes, as in the case of the Zulus, over 80 in number; or, as in the case of the Tswana, three areas separated from each other by up to 300 miles. Attempts to reduce this degree of fragmentation have not, so far, proved successful except in minor areas. Half the Africans live in 'white areas' and others commute daily from the Homelands to work in the white 'border industries'.

The Homelands stretch along the east coast and the northern borders with Botswana, Zimbabwe and Mozambique, where the African population is densest. Travelling up the east coast from Grahamstown, one finds the Xhosa people in the Ciskei and Transkei; the Zulu in Kwazulu (in Natal); and the Swazi on the borders of Swaziland. All these speak closely related Nguni languages, some of which have 'click' sounds absorbed from their Khoikhoi and San neighbours long ago. Most of the other black groups in South Africa are related to the Sotho, the Tswana along the Botswana border (in Boputhatswana), the Northern Sotho of Lebowa in the Transvaal, and the Southern Sotho of Basothoqwaqwa in the Orange Free State near Lesotho. Other groups in the Transvaal are the Venda and, near the Zimbabwe border, the Tsonga who are joined with the Shangaan in the Gazankulu Homeland. The Ndebele are joined to Lebowa.

Culture

South Africa is as diverse culturally as it is racially. Its cultural history can be traced on the African side to the San (Bushmen), and on the European side to the early Dutch settlers. Bushman art – mainly realistic portrayals of animals and people painted in reddish, yellow and black tints on cave walls – was prolific. In contrast to the hunters the pastoral Africans traditionally made polychrome pottery, blankets of sheep's wool, elaborate ornaments out of tiny, coloured beads whose patterns had distinct meanings, as well as weapons and tools. Their art still survives.

On the European cultural side, the principal, and perhaps the most original, flowerings of culture were the simple, but elegant, 18th and 19th century Cape silver of immigrant German and English smiths, whose work can be seen in collections of Cape Town's Cultural History Museum and Johannesburg's Africana Museum, and in the superb Cape Dutch architectural style and furniture.

Afrikaans literature has been created in under a century. It is vigorous, experimental and richly redolent of the local atmosphere, owing very little to its Dutch origins, and has been a crucial element in the nurturing of Afrikaner nationalism.

The South African English writers have produced a number of outstanding poets, novelists and playwrights, from Olive Schreiner, whose *Story of an African Farm* is a minor classic, to Nadine Gordimer, Dan Jacobson, Alan Paton (author of *Cry, the Beloved Country*) and Atholl Fugard.

Oral literary traditions among the different ethnic black groups, continue in the rural areas of the country, while black South African writers have used literature and poetry as a strong form of protest against the Apartheid system. Among the best known black writers and poets are Alex La Guma, Es'kia Mphahlele, Dennis Brutus, Nonnie Jabavu, Bessie Head, Peter Abraham, Oswald Mtshali and Fatima Dike. Several avant-garde literary magazines publish prose, poetry, drama and graphics from an increasingly articulate group of local black and white writers and artists.

All the major cities have flourishing theatres, which produce mostly imported plays performed by white actors for white audiences. However, the African Music and Theatre Trust has been largely responsible for enabling the country's black talent to break out of the limits imposed by the rigid system of segregation. There are also independent alternative theatres which have sprung up during the past few years in Johannesburg and Cape Town with racially mixed groups of actors promoting local plays with a strong political bias.

History

South Africa has produced the most complete series of Stone Age remains in Africa, dating from a pre-Acheulian culture of about 1.8 million years ago. At that time an ape-man of the Australopithecine type – lightly built and about four feet tall – lived in the Transvaal, where bones and fossils have been found, notably in the Sterkfontein and Makapan caves. From these tool-users evolved Stone Age men who made their own tools of stone, wood and bone (from about 40,000 BC). Their sites have been found in the far south as well as in the Transvaal. The late Stone Age culture shows some affinities with that of the Khoisan peoples, who were later driven out or absorbed by Bantu-speaking iron-miners in the north or Europeans in the south.

The Khoisan were a brown-skinned people speaking a variety of 'click' languages. The name is an amalgam of Khoikhoi ('Hottentot') and San (the Khoikhoi name for Bushman). The main distinction between the two was that Khoikhoi were herders of sheep and cattle whereas the San were hunters.

San sometimes attached themselves as servants of Khoikhoi, scouting and hunting for them; sometimes they raided and stole from them. The Khoikhoi had sheep, but cattle were probably introduced from Bantu-speakers in about the 15th century. They used the cattle for riding as well as for dairy products.

From early times mining and barter added to the subsistence economy of the Transvaal but the metals mined were copper and iron rather than the gold for which the area has since become famous. Copper may have been mined at Phalaborwa (near the Kruger National Park) as early as the 8th century, and certainly from the 11th to the 14th centuries Mapungubwe (on the Limpopo above Beit Bridge) became an important centre where archaeologists have found copper and gold ornaments. Copper mining continued in the area (especially at Messina) under Venda chiefs who came perhaps in the 17th century from Rhodesia, so that the Limpopo came to be known to the Portuguese as the Copper River.

Much further inland in the Transvaal the Sotho also mined copper and iron and sold it to the Tswana in the west and, through Tsonga middlemen, to the Portuguese in the east. The Sotho and Venda have left many small stone ruins, huts as well as enclosure walls. They and the related Tswana lived under powerful chiefs in large villages.

The foothills of the Drakensberg were inhabited by cattle-keeping Nguni peoples certainly by the 16th century and probably by the 14th. These people also grew millet, made their huts of reeds and their sandals and shields of skin. Cattle were of vital significance for their religious ceremonies as well as their economy. Originally living in scattered groups they were united in the 19th century into the great Zulu nation by Shaka.

The Dutch at the Cape (1652-1795): In 1652 Jan van Riebeck arrived at the Cape of Good Hope to set up a revictualling station for Dutch ships on their way to the East. He built a fort around which soldiers and servants of the Dutch East India Company, for which he acted, began to grow vegetables and fruit. This they sold to some 33 Dutch ships a year passing through. Later settlers were producing enough wheat for the whole Dutch Eastern empire and owned large cattle ranches.

As the Dutch spread, the Khoikhoi lost their grazing lands and many became servants of the whites, learned Dutch and eventually produced a Eurafrican (Coloured) population. The San, less amenable to the new order, were exterminated or fled to the desert.

More settlers were not encouraged at this time as the hinterland was poor agriculturally and transport was difficult, but some Huguenot refugees from France settled in 1688. During the 18th century a number of slaves were imported from West Africa and Malaysia. The isolated white community became closely united, all speaking the new language, Afrikaans, and all members of the Calvinist Dutch Reformed Church.

In about 1770 began the long series of Xhosa Wars ('Kaffir Wars') when the Europeans and Xhosa, both expanding and in search of land, met and fought on the Great Fish River.

The Cape was a bone of contention in the Napoleonic Wars and in 1806 it finally became British so that the period of Dutch rule ended and British settlers and governors began to arrive.

The 19th century was a time of violent expansion by Xhosa, Zulu, Afrikaner and British to produce the triangular struggle between 'Boer, Briton and Bantu'. The Africans were defeated by superior fire-power and the Afrikaners were eventually subdued by the British in the Anglo-Boer War (1899-1902), a war so bitter that the victors lost public support and soon afterwards made concessions.

Among the Northern Nguni in Natal, three great leaders had arisen one after the other – Dingiswayo, Shaka and Dingaan – to conquer a large kingdom and unite it to form the Zulu nation. With tough discipline, new tactics and weapons (like the short stabbing *assegai* instead of a throwing spear), they annihilated all opposition. The repercussions of Shaka's wars in Natal (the *Mfecane* wars) were felt right across the Highveld where refugees like the Ndebele conquered new kingdoms and much land was abandoned as people fled Shaka's armies – indeed some fled as far as Tanzania, Malawi, Zambia and Mozambique. Nearer home the Sotho and later the Swazi united in mountain strongholds and successfully defended their independence against Zulu and Afrikaner, with the aid later on of British protection. They now form the independent countries of Swaziland and Lesotho.

Both Ndebele and Zulu were in their turn defeated (1837-1840) by the Afrikaner (Boer) *Voortrekkers*. The historic Great Trek in 1836 of many Afrikaners away from the Cape was caused by the introduction of British rule and also by the British law of 1834 ordering the emancipation of 40,000 slaves in the colony. They set out in wagons to find new land where they could be independent, speak their own language and live according to their own customs. They sought farm land with access to the sea at either Lourenco Marques or the as yet unclaimed Natal coast. Malaria, tsetse fly and the Tsonga, however, barred their way to the first port and in the 1850's English settlers and their Indian labourers occupied Natal. The Boers succeeded, however, in seizing large tracts of land and established the two independent Republics of the Orange Free State and the Transvaal.

Until 1870 South Africa had been a purely agricultural country, but during the last part of the century the economy was revolutionised by the discovery first of diamonds, then of gold. The wars of conquest, which were waged against the indigenous people from the 1860's to the end of the century helped to bring a labour force into existence to serve these industries. As a result of these wars the various African communities came to be restricted to small areas of land, the 'Reserves', where they were subjected to crippling taxes and thus forced to seek wage labour on the mines.

In Hopetown someone picked up a diamond by chance in 1867 and adventurers rushed in the Kimberley area to exploit the biggest concentration of diamonds in the world. Gradually Cecil Rhodes's company, De Beers, bought out smaller miners and the Cape Colony quickly annexed Kimberley before the Afrikaners could claim it. In 1886 the Witwatersrand gold deposits were discovered. This resource was indisputably in the Transvaal but large numbers of foreigners (*uitlanders*), many of them British, flooded in to seek their fortunes. Their complaints against the Afrikaner government and the ambition of Cecil Rhodes, then Prime Minister of the Cape Colony, led to the disastrous Jameson Raid of 1896 in which Jameson tried unsuccessfully to stir up *uitlander* rebellion in the Transvaal to give the Cape an excuse to annex it.

The final military conflict between Britain on one side and the two Boer Republics on the other came in the terrible South African War of 1899 to 1902 (known in Britain as the Boer War). The Afrikaners had no outside help and were subdued only with concentration camps and the burning of their farms. The War Museum at Bloemfontein vividly recalls the period. This struggle brought out a fierce Afrikaner national consciousness.

After the peace, Britain quickly made concessions and by 1910 has given self-government to the resulting Union of all the provinces. This created the conditions for the strict control over black labour which has characterised South Africa ever since. Especially important in this regard were the 1913 Land Act which legalised enforced restriction of Africans to the 'Reserve' areas; the Pass Laws and Masters and Servants Laws which penalised desertion and which rigidly controlled the movements of Africans; and the extension of labour recruitment drives beyond the borders of South Africa. The Afrikaners had their final revenge when in 1948 they won the general elections which ensured their political supremacy and enabled them to embark on their policy of Apartheid.

The main architect of Apartheid (in theory the separate but equal development of each of the four main racial communities – white, black, coloured and Asian – but in practice ensuring the preservation of white, particularly Afrikaner, supremacy over two-thirds of the country) was Dr Hendrik Verwoerd, Prime Minister of the ruling Nationalist Party from 1958 to 1966, when he was assassinated. His successor, B.J. Vorster, continued Verwoerd's basic policies.

In 1961 South Africa's racial policies were so far out of step with the multi-racial Commonwealth of Nations, that it was forced to withdraw to avoid being voted out. It became a Republic on 31 May 1961.

In keeping with the 'Homeland' policy, the Transkei 'Homeland' (under the leadership of Chief Kaiser Matanzima) was granted its so-called independence in October 1976, Bophuthatswana (under Chief Mangope) in December 1977, and Venda in the latter half of 1979. The Ciskei followed in 1981 and Kwandebele in 1986.

The mass of discriminatory laws which regulate the lives of the Republic's African, Coloured and Asian populations have led to the detention without trial of many of the Government's opponents, the banning of Africa political organisations outside the 'Homelands', and the forced removal of thousands of Africans under the Group Areas Act and the 'Homelands' policy.

By the late 1960's, a coherent movement based on the ideology of Black Consciousness had begun to develop. After the Natal strike in 1973, and the violence of black workers on the mines in 1974, African discontent finally boiled over in the Soweto riots of June 1976, when black residents in the urban township of Soweto outside Johannesburg rose in revolt against Apartheid. The revolt quickly spread across the country. Vorster used the virtually limitless powers conferred by the Internal Security Act to crush the riots and several hundred people died in confrontations with the police. Political unrest and African protest continued through 1977 – exacerbated by the economic recession and the rising cost of living. In an attempt to destroy the opposition movement, the State intensified its repression. On 17 September 1977 Steve Biko, a black community leader, became the 45th person known to have died while in detention under the security laws in South Africa.

In September 1978 Vorster resigned as Prime Minister and was succeeded by Pieter Botha, his Minister of Defence, who had argued in favour of South Africa's disastrous intervention in Angola in 1975. The South African Government, however, suffered a severe blow to its image of a patriotic and united Afrikanerdom when the 'Muldergate scandal' broke in 1978.

The findings of a commission investigating the affair led to the resignation of Dr Vorster from the Presidency and helped provoke a split in the ranks of Afrikaner nationalism.

This widened considerably with the adoption of an increasingly reformist stance within the ruling Nationalist Party by Prime Minister Botha. However, Botha's promised changes do little more than refine the cruder manifestations of apartheid, and have yet to be put into effect. The most dramatic changes planned by the government involved a relaxation of the restrictions on the movement of black workers. The changes are clearly designed to produce a more mobile black workforce to accelerate economic expansion, as well as to create a stable black urban middle class who would serve as a buffer to the demands of black workers.

The government abolished the all-white Senate in June 1980 and replaced it by a President's Council on which Whites, Indians and Coloureds sit. Blacks are to have their own council which can make recommendations to, but will not have representation on, the main body. This futile constitutional change has had a negative reaction from the Indian and Coloured population.

From 1980, political unrest in the black, Coloured and Indian communities throughout the country escalated. Black and coloured schools in Cape Town and the Eastern Cape were boycotted to draw attention to the disparity

This was the background to the much increased social unrest starting in September 1984, leading to the declaration of a state of emergency in July 1985, followed by the arrest of more than a thousand political opponents and escalating violence in the black townships of the major cities.

During 1988 hundreds of detainees who had been arrested under the state of emergency in July 1985 were released. President P. W. Botha suffered a stroke in February 1989 and stood down from the leadership of the party. His successor F. W. De Klerk promised a fresh approach to South Africa's problems.

Economy

Mining originally formed the basis of the modern South African economy. The country has large reserves of chromium ore, platinum, vanadium, manganese ore, fluorspar, and 50% of the world's gold reserves. Gold is the major mineral export and although there has been a gradual decline in gold output since 1970 rising gold prices have increased the value of sales.

The establishment of the South African Iron and Steel Industrial Corporation (ISCOR) and the South African Coal, Oil and Gas Corporation (SASOL) laid the foundations of the heavy engineering, chemical and petroleum industries. The textile and food processing industries are also growing. During 1978, unrest in Iran, from which South Africa had been importing 90% of its petroleum, led to a search for alternative fuel sources. South Africa is already successfully extracting oil and gas products from coal. Following Iran's decision in 1979 to stop petroleum supplies, the search for indigenous sources has been intensified – but no petroleum has yet been found in commercial quantities.

Much livestock is reared in South Africa and there are significant fruit, wine and fishing industries, as well as major exports of wool, maize, sugar and karakul pelts.

Industrial development has been dependent on the white population for management, administrative and higher technical skills. Statutory job reservation has ensured that certain jobs may be held only by Europeans, while the unskilled labour force is made up of Africans, Coloureds and Asians. Certain categories of reserved jobs were removed in 1977 owing to the decline in white emigration to South Africa. But average European real earnings are still five times greater than African earnings, and black unemployment is rising.

A special feature of the South African economy is its vast permanent migrant labour population. The countries around South Africa, as well as the 'Bantustans', have functioned as labour reserves for the past century. It is this, vast supply of constant cheap labour that has supported the growth of the economy. The reserves are overstocked and overpopulated and the traditional economy no longer operates, forcing thousands of people to move to the urban areas in search of employment.

South Africa has made moves to establish and confirm its economic power over neighbouring states by promoting the concept of a 'Constellation' of states from South Africa to Zaire. The constellation would guarantee South Africa supplies of vital raw materials and formalise her use of black labour, while the Pretoria government would offer financial aid and joint agricultural and commercial ventures. However, this plan is being strongly resisted by the frontline states who are attempting to reduce economic dependence on South Africa.

The political troubles of 1984/85 and the refusal of foreign banks to reschedule national debts led to a collapse in the value of the South African rand. This led to inflation, massive disinvestment, a drain on reserves and balance of payments problems, but the economy began to improve by 1989 as the trade balance moved into surplus.

Wildlife

Most wild animals of any size have long since been hunted out, except in the national parks. The Kruger National Park, which can be explored from rest camps at all times of the year, has most of the larger species including lion, leopard, elephant and giraffe. The Kwazulu game reserves are noted for different kinds of white and black rhino and in St Lucia and Umfolozi one can go on Wilderness Trails by boat and on foot. On nearby ranches Zululand Safaris organise hunting safaris as well as the more usual photographic expeditions.

The Gemsbok Kalahari National Park provides more adventurous holidays, giving a real insight into the wild, lonely desert, inhabited only by gemsbok, springbok, lion and ostrich. By contrast, the Drakensberg reserves (Giant's Castle and the Royal Natal National Park) are set in magnificent mountain scenery where one can ride or walk amid fascinating wild flowers, birds and baboons.

The best season for flowers is the southern spring (September and October) when the Cape blossoms with arum lilies, red aloes, wild geranium, Namaqualand daisies and the pink protea bushes. Altogether 16,000 species of plant are found in South Africa. The Kirstenbosch National Botanic Gardens in Cape Town are well worth visiting at any time of the year.

National Parks

Kruger National Park is the largest and most popular game reserve in South Africa. The best time for visiting is from June to the end of September when the dryness drives the animals to waterholes where they can easily be seen.

The park contains a remarkable collection of animals with buffalo, elephant and lion predominating. There are plenty of giraffe, ostriches, crocodiles, all kinds of buck and a profusion of bird life including the

grotesque hornbill, the eagle, the vulture and red-eyed oxpecker.
Accommodation: There are 11 rest camps. The largest ones have well-appointed restaurants and shops. Bookings should be made in advance through the National Parks Board of Trustees, Sanlam Bldgs, Andries and Pretorius Sts, Box 787, tel: 44-1194, cable NATPARK, Pretoria.

The Lion Inn complex is under construction and will provide a hotel-motel and caravan park at the gate to the park, 3½ km from Phalaborwa. At Phalaborwa: Impala Inn, Box 139, 49 rooms.

Kalahari Gemsbok National Park: This northern Cape park has abundant game and is the home of vast herds of springbok, eland and red hartebeest. It is also the only place where the gemsbok, with its sword-like horns, is to be found in profusion. There are three rest camps and a small store selling some tinned food; anything else needed should be brought.

Other South African game parks include the **Addo Elephant Park,** about 72 km north of Port Elizabeth on the Garden Route, while there are five game reserves in KwaZulu (northern Natal): **Hluhluwe, Umfolozi, St Lucia, Mkuzi** and **Ndumu.** They fall under the control of The Natal Parks, Game and Fish Preservation Board, with a central reservations office in Pietermaritzburg: PO Box 662, Pietermaritzburg 3200, tel: 51514, telex: 6-43481 SA. Petrol and oil may be bought in the reserves but there are no restaurants or stores and visitors must take their own provisions.

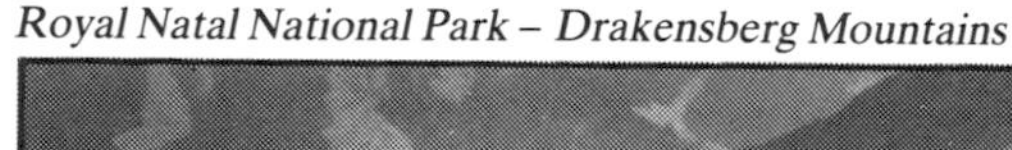

Royal Natal National Park – Drakensberg Mountains

General Information

Government

The President and the House of Assembly are elected by whites, and only whites may stand for election. The all-white Senate has been replaced by a President's Council which includes White, Asian and Coloured representatives. There is a Coloured People's Representative Council and a South Africa Indian Council respectively, with very limited legislative and administrative powers. Blacks are supposedly represented by their 'Homelands'.

Languages

English and Afrikaans. African languages include Zulu, Xhosa, Sotho, Tswana, Shangaan, Ndebele, Swazi and Venda.

Religion

Christianity, in various denominations, with Muslim, Jewish and Hindu minorities. Also traditional religions.

How to Get There

By air: South African Airways and 16 other international airlines operate frequent services to and from Europe, North and South America and Australia. Flights direct to South Africa from other countries within Africa are at present available only from Zimbabwe, Malawi, Kenya, Lesotho, Botswana, Swaziland, Mozambique, Mauritius and Zambia.

The main airport for Pretoria and Johannesburg is Jan Smuts Airport about 15 miles from Johannesburg. Services go to Cape Town, Durban, Port Elizabeth, East London, Kimberley and Bloemfontein.

By sea: There are regular services to most overseas countries and also connections between the ports of South Africa. Many shipping companies reduce their fares from February to July.

By rail: There is transport from Mozambique, Botswana, Zimbabwe and Namibia.

By road: There is a twice weekly coach service from Salisbury to Johannesburg. If one is travelling by car, a triptyque (or carnet), South African third party insurance (available at border posts) and a valid driver's licence incorporating a photograph are required. Opening hours of border posts vary but all posts are open at least from 0800 to 1600. For further information contact The Automobile Association of South Africa, AA House, 42 de Villiers St, Johannesburg.

Entry Regulations

Most visitors to South Africa require visas in addition to valid passports, except holders of passports from UK, Ireland, Switzerland, West Germany and Lichtenstein. These are obtainable at the local office of the South African diplomatic representative. In countries having no representative, apply to the nearest South African representative or direct to the Director General: Home Affairs, Private Bag X114, Pretoria Telex 321353 SA/321358 SA 0001 (Teleg: INTERIOR PRETORIA). Apply well in advance, on the correct form, sending your passport. Non-white tourists are advised to make careful enquiries before embarking. Some visas are valid for one entry only; if so, a re-entry visa must be obtained if the visitor wants to make a trip to an adjacent country such as Swaziland and then to return.

Those visitors intending to visit the Transkei require a valid passport and a visa. Visitors are furthermore requested to enter the Transkei at specified border posts, viz Great Kei Bridge, Umzimkulu Bridge and on the Lesotho border at Qacha's Nek, Ramatsilitoses Gate and Telle Bridge. Applications for visas may be made direct to the Secretary, Department of the Interior, Private Bag X 5006, Umtata 5100, at least four weeks in advance. There are no entry formalities between South Africa and Bophuthatswana and Venda.

All visitors to South Africa must satisfy the officials on arrival that they have sufficient means to maintain themselves for the period of their visit and either a return ticket or funds to obtain one.

Everyone should carry a valid International Certificate showing vaccination against yellow fever.

Customs Regulations

Travellers may import personal effects, used cameras, radios, firearms, camping equipment etc, 1 litre of spirits, 2 litres of wine, 50 ml of perfume, 250 ml toilet water, 400 cigarettes or 250 grammes of tobacco, but all other articles are dutiable. For a firearm a permit is necessary, issued by customs officials at the point of entry. The firearm must have a number stamped in the metal.

There is no limit to the amount of foreign exchange a visitor may take into South Africa.

On arrival visitors must complete special customs forms listing all their holdings of currency, and a stamped copy is retained by them. On departure from the country visitors are allowed to take out as much foreign exchange as is shown on the customs form.

Up to R200 per person may be taken into or out of the country in bank notes.

Climate

South Africa has a sunny, pleasant climate. The Western Cape has a Mediterranean climate with dry summers (October to March) when the temperature averages around 20°C. Most of the rain falls in winter. The rest of the country lies in the temperate zone. Along the coast of Natal, February may be extremely humid with temperatures over 38°C, but elsewhere it is seldom too hot. On the plateau in summer a little rain may fall in an afternoon shower and in winter the nights are cold and crisp. Snow falls in the Drakensberg. In Johannesburg in June the temperature averages 15.5°C. The best time to visit is between September and May.

What to wear: In summer (October to March) lightweight clothes are essential, with a light sweater sometimes for evenings. Take a raincoat and umbrella for the short sharp showers. In resorts, casual clothes are normal but in cities in the more exclusive hotels – and often in those that are not – ties and jackets are worn. From April to September cool clothes are also needed but it is advisable to take warmer ones for the Cape or the mountains.

Health Precautions

Water is drinkable throughout South Africa but many rivers and lakes are not suitable for bathing as they may be contaminated with bilharzia. When swimming in the sea, great care should be taken to read notices on safety and one should always swim within the shark nets. Precautions against malaria are necessary in the Kruger National Park and St Lucia Game Reserve. Keep your eyes open for snakes and scorpions.

Banks and Currency

Barclays National Bank Ltd, 84 Market Street, PO Box 1153, Johannesburg 2000
Nedbank Ltd, 81 Main Street, PO Box 1144, Johannesburg 2000
Standard Bank of South Africa Ltd, 78 Fox Street, PO Box 7725, Johannesburg 2000

Volkskas Ltd, PO Box 578, 229 Van Der Walt Street, Pretoria 0001
Trust Bank of Africa Ltd, Trust Bank Centre, Heerengracht, PO Box 2116, Cape Town.
Currency: Rand divided into 100 cents (see currency table, page 10.)

Business Hours

Banks: Monday, Tuesday, Thursday and Friday 0900-1530; Wednesday 0900-1300; Saturday 0830-1100
Government Offices: Monday-Friday 0800-1630
Offices: Monday-Friday 0800-1630
Post Offices: Monday-Friday 0830-1700; Saturday 0830-1200
Shops: Monday-Friday 0830-1700; Saturday 0830-1230

Public Holidays

New Year's Day, 1 January
Founders Day, 6 April
Good Friday, 13 April 1990
Easter Monday, 16 April 1990
Ascension Day, 24 May 1990
Workers Day, 1 May
Republic Day, 31 May
Settlers' Day, 7 September
Kruger Day, 10 October
Day of the Covenant, 16 December
Public Holiday, 17 December
Christmas Day, 25 December
Boxing Day, 26 December

Embassies

Australia: 4th Floor Mutual and Federal Centre, 220 Vermeulen Street, Pretoria PBX150
Austria: 10th Floor, Apollo Centre, 405 Church Street, PO Box 851, Pretoria
Belgium: 275 Pomona Street, Muckleneuk, 0001 Pretoria
Canada: PO Box 26006, Arcadia, Pretoria 0007
Finland: 171 Esselen Street, Sunnyside, PO Box 443, Pretoria 0001
France: 807 George Avenue, Arcadia, Pretoria
Germany FR: 180 Blackwood Street, Arcadia, PO Box 2023, Pretoria
Greece: 995 Pretorius Street, Pretoria
Israel: Apollo Centre, 405 Church Street, Pretoria
Netherlands: 1st Floor, Netherlands Bank Building, Church Street, PO Box 117, Pretoria 0001
Portugal: 261 Devenish Street, Muckleneuk
Spain: 240 Vermeulen Street, PO Box 1633, Pretoria
Sweden: PO Box 1664, Pretoria
Switzerland: 818 George Avenue, Arcadia, Pretoria
UK: Greystoke, 6 Hill Street, Pretoria, tel: 433121
USA: 7th Floor, Thibault House, 225 Pretorius Street, Pretoria.

Transport

By air: South African Airways fly several flights a day linking Cape Town, Johannesburg, Durban, Port Elizabeth, East London, Kimberley and Bloemfontein. The SAA internal services are supplemented by scheduled flights offered by private companies.
By rail: Except for express trains, most others are slow. The Blue Train is a luxury express running from Johannesburg/Pretoria to Cape Town, offering air-conditioned comfort, excellent cuisine and shower baths. Reservations should be made well in advance.
By road: Modern freeway systems take the traveller out of the major cities, and 61,000 km of tarred roads lead to almost all places of tourist interest. A wide variety of coach tours is available. The major operators are South African Railways, Atlas Tours, Grosvenor Tours and Springbok Safaris. Bookings can be made through travel agents outside the country, as well as on arrival.

Visitors who decide to drive themselves are advised to take extra care –

South Africa has among the highest road accident rates in the world. They should watch their speed, particularly on the many rural dirt roads, and on fast tarmac roads with soft gravel edges. Maximum speed limits of 60 kph in urban areas and 90 kph elsewhere are in force. Fines for breaking the speak limits are very heavy and all limits are enforced by provincial traffic police who have the power to make spot fines. Visitors hiring cars should not under-estimate fuel costs and distance charges – fuel prices have risen very steeply, especially since Iran stopped supplying petroleum to South Africa. Filling stations are open from 0700-1800 Monday to Friday, and on Saturdays from 0700-1200. On Sundays they are closed owing to fuel restrictions. Bona fide visitors to the country can get a weekend petrol purchase permit from the Airport Police Station, Jan Smuts Airport, Johannesburg. Petrol may not be carried other than in the tank of the vehicle.

As elsewhere, hitch-hiking is the cheapest way of travelling – but women should beware of hiking on their own.

Car hire: South African Airways arranges car hire to connect with flights. There is also a large number of care hire firms operating from all cities.

Accommodation

There is a large number of hotels for whites in South Africa graded by the Hotel Board on an exacting one- to five-star formula. They range from the modern international hotels in the large cities, through medium-sized, and price, tourist hotels to unpretentious but comfortable hotels in country towns. The visitor should refer to the annual *Where to stay – National Accommodation Guide* available from South African tourist offices in most western countries or at SATOUR PBX164, 0001, Pretoria, tel: (012) 47-1131, telex: 3-20457 SA, for a full list of hotels and restaurants throughout South Africa.

There are restaurants to suit all palates and pockets in all the major cities. These cater for white visitors only as restaurant facilities are strictly segregated except in international hotels.

Black travellers must make special arrangements for accommodation if they are not staying in international hotels.

There are many first-class motels along main highways, on the outskirts of the Kruger National Park and along the Garden Route. The game and nature reserves are well provided with rest camps of rondavels (round huts). South Africa is also well organised for the caravan and camping holidaymaker. Complete lists of camp-sites may be obtained from the South African Touring Corporation. For the young, there are also some youth hostels. Full information on the facilities available can be obtained from the South African Youth Hostels Association.

Tipping: It is customary to give a ten per cent tip to porters, taxi drivers, waiters and petrol pump attendants. Some hotels and restaurants add a service charge to the bill. In these establishments extra tipping is optional.

Rules to remember

While whites love talking politics, they frequently equate the midlest dissenting or 'liberal' view with communism, so it's as well to be careful what you say, and to whom you say it. Visitors should avoid taking political books, magazines or leaflets into the country with them. They should also leave behind any form of erotica or pornography. There's a long list of banned books and publications.

Under the numerous residential and 'influx control' laws it can be an offence to stay overnight in another race's 'group area'. Although some petty Apartheid legislation has been abolished, mainly in the Cape, it is an offence to use public amenities reserved for a different colour.

Other offences include the carrying of liquor in unwrapped containers, and the buying and selling of liquor on Sundays. Under the Sunday Observance Laws, hotel visitors can generally drink only when they buy a meal as well; cinemas, theatres and nightclubs are closed, and all organised sports are forbidden on Sundays. Most bars are reserved for white men only. 'Pot', known locally as 'dagga', is in plentiful supply, but the use of this drug carries penalties of up to 25 years' imprisonment.

Anyone may travel freely along the through roads and the tourist routes of the Homelands, but if visitors wish to digress they must obtain permits three months in advance from the Secretary for Bantu Administration and Development, Bantu Affairs Building, cnr Paul Kruger and Jacob Mare Street, Pretoria.

Organised bus tours are run around Soweto (South Western Townshops) by Johannesburg's Non-European Affairs Department at 81 Albert Street. To enter other black locations (townships), applications must be made to the local magistrate who may in turn refer the visitor back to Pretoria. For reasons of political sensitivity, permits are increasingly difficult to obtain.

For the black tourist visas are needed. There are African hotels in some towns and some for Coloureds, and all international class hotels now have permission to take black tourists.

Some beaches are still strictly segregated.

Cape Town

Founded in 1652, Cape Town is the country's oldest white settlement. A port with a sheltered bay, beaches, fishing grounds, old trees and beautiful gardens, it nestles below the craggy Table Mountain and Lion's Head. As the seat of South Africa's Legislature, it is home for Members of Parliament from November/December to June/July.

Hotels

Only four or five star hotels listed, for others see *Where to Stay – National accommodation guide*, available from South African tourist offices in most Western countries or at Head office, SATOUR, Menlyn Drive, PB X164,0001 Pretoria, S. Africa, Tel (012) 47 1131/348 9521, Telex 32-0457 SA.

NAME	ADDRESS	TELEPHONE	TELEX
CAPE (WESTERN & SOUTHERN)			
CAPE TOWN			
Cape Sun	Strand St, Box 4532	021 23884	522453
Mount Nelson	Orange St, Box 2608	021 231000	527804
Capetonian	Pier place	021 21150	520000
De Waal	Mill St, Box 2793	021 451311	520653
NEWLANDS			
Newlands	Main Rd	021 611105	520686
SEA POINT			
President	Beach Rd, Box 62	021 441121	526620

[Hotels]

NORTHERN CAPE, WESTERN TRANSVAAL

KIMBERLEY

Kimberley Sun	120 Dutoitspan Rd	0531 31751	58689
EASTERN CAPE			
PORT ELIZABETH			
Elizabeth Sun	Laroche Drive, Box 13100	041 523720	243498
ORANGE FREE STATE			
BLOEMFONTEIN			
Bloemfontein Sun	East Burger St, Box 2212	051 301911	267039
Holiday Inn	1 Union Avenue, Box 1851	051 301111	267645
NATAL, DURBAN			
Royal	267 Smith St	031 3040331	622454
Maharani	Marine parade, Box 10592	031 327361	622485
Edward	Durban beachfront, Box 105	031 373681	622318
Elangeni Hotel	63 Snell parade	031 371321	620133
Beverley Hills	Umhlanga rocks Box 71	031 561221	622073
Tropicana	Marine Parade Box 1035	031 376261	622381
TRANSVAAL			
TZANEEN			
Coach house	Box 544, Agatha	01523 22326	
JOHANNESBURG			
Carlton/Carlton Court	Box 7709, Main St	011 3318911	486130
Protea	120 De Korte St Braamfontein	011 4035740	430620

[Hotels]

Devonshire	Box 31197, Jorissen St, Braamfontein	011 3995611	422052
Gold Reef City	Gold Reef City	011 4944200	486749
Down Town Holiday Inn	Box 11026	011 281770	484092
Rosebank	Tyrwhitt Av, Rosebank	011 7881820	422268
Sun and Towers	84 Smal Street, Box 535	011 297011	482327
SANDTON			
Sandton Sun	5th Street, Sandhurst Box 784902	011 7838071	430338
VEREENIGING			
Riviera International	Vereeniging Box 64	016 222861	427427
PRETORIA			
Burgerspark	Minaar St, Box 2301	012 3227500	322525

Although there is still plenty to remind the traveller of the city's Dutch period, much of its most attractive architecture has been demolished to make way for high-rise buildings serving the needs of modern business and trade.

On fine days Robben Island is clearly visible from Cape Town. It has had an interesting history, but today it is once again a prison island where many of the Republic's non-white political prisoners serving life or long-term sentences are confined. They include prominent black nationalists.

The Cape Town Castle dates back to 1666, and its State Rooms house period furniture and paintings. There are many fine examples of Cape Dutch architecture, notably the Koopmans-De Wet Museum and the Old Town House, built in 1755. The Malay Quarter is still the home of descendants of Malay slaves, although coloured inhabitants have been forcibly evicted from much of the area commonly known as District Six, and it has been flattened by the authorities and proclaimed as a 'white' area which is to be redeveloped. On New Year's Day the Coloured population parade with both traditional and modern singing and dancing in the 'Coon Carnival'.

In Newlands, on the slopes of Table Mountain, are the world-famous Kirstenbosch National Botanic Gardens, open daily from sunrise to sunset. Table Mountain itself may be ascended by cable car from the station off Kloof Nek. It affords superb views of Table Bay and the country around.

Further examples of fine architecture are Groot Constantia, an old Cape farmhouse, and, further inland, Paarl, a typical Western Province town set in orchards and vineyards with a backdrop of the Hottentots Holland Mountains.

All round the Cape Peninsula coast are beaches, fishing villages and popular resorts like Muizenberg, St. James, Kalk Bay and Simonstown on the warm Indian Ocean side, or Clifton and Llandudno on the cold Atlantic coast, where one can swim, surf, sunbathe, or enjoy excellent fishing.

Tourist Information: National Tourist Bureau, 3rd Flood, Broadway Centre, Heerengracht, PO Box 6187, tel: 47-1646.

Outside Cape Town

Two beautiful towns within easy reach of Cape Town are **Paarl** and **Stellenbosch,** seat of the foremost Afrikaans university, Lanzerac, in Stellenbosch, is an hotel converted from a Cape Dutch winery which offers first class accommodation and food. Reasonably priced wine and cheese lunches are available on weekdays. Both Paarl and Stellenbosch are on the South African Wine Route.

Further away from Cape Town lie three picturesque mission stations. **Genadendal** (near Caledon), **Elim** (near Bredasdorp) and **Wuppertal** (near Clanwilliam). **Hermanus** is a famous seaside resort, and **Caledon** is the main centre for the Cape's spectacular wild flowers.

The Eastern Cape Province still retains something of its early 19th century flavour. **Grahamstown,** a cathedral town, is also the seat of Rhodes University. Nearby is **Alice,** a wooded area below the Hogsback. Here, too, is the oldest African university in the country, Fort Hare.

The Garden Route

One of the world's last havens of unspoilt natural wilderness, the Garden Route extends from Mossel Bay to the spectacular Tsitsikama National Park at Storms River Mouth – a distance of about 200 kms. It also runs inland to the little Karoo, including both Graaf-Reinet and Oudtshoorn. The trip offers the lovely Tsitsikama and Outeniqua mountain ranges, unspoilt beaches that extend for miles, enormous forests of yellowwoods and stinkwoods which harbour the last of a herd of wild elephants, and a chain of lakes and lagoons unsurpassed along South Africa's coastline. In order to preserve this area there have been suggestions – so far unheeded by the State – to turn the entire area into one vast nature reserve.

The Transkei

Although the Transkei is impoverished and suffers from bad soil erosion due to overgrazing, it is also very beautiful. One drives through attractive undulating downland and although some of the Xhosa people keep their elaborate traditional costumes and ornaments, the Tourist Corporation lays on highly artificial dances for visitors. The rocky seashore here is called the Wild Coast and is intersected by broad, unbridged rivers. Angling in the rivers and sea is particularly good.

Natal Coast

The Natal Coast is the most popular holiday area among white South Africans. It offers a wide choice of resorts with warm all-year-round swimming and surfing.

The coast south of Durban is the more developed, especially the Hibiscus Coast around Margate. Sugar fields, which in places run almost into the sea, give the coast an incredible lushness when the cane is growing. Most beaches are reasonably well protected from sharks, and it is wise to avoid any which are not.

Durban

As the centre of the Natal coast and the country's major port. Durban is a vast sub-tropical resort: very humid in summer and warm in winter. It is the main town of the only predominantly English-speaking province of the Republic.

The Eastern influence on Durban is everywhere – Hindu temples and mosques, the Indian market full of Oriental curios, tropical fruit and spices. The fantastic dress and ornaments of the *rickshaw* pullers brighten the streets. The city dwelling Zulu perform Ngoma Dances most weekends in the African recreation grounds off Somtscu Road.

Two interesting rural festivals occur nearby: the Festival of First Fruits at the March new moon in Mafunza, near Elandskop, 40 km from Pietermaritzburg, and the Shembe Festival, a mixture of traditional and Christian ideas, in the week before full moon at the end of July at East Kupakumein, near Inanda, 32 km from Durban. The Durban Visitors' Bureau arranges tours to the latter, but a permit is needed if you wish to use private transport because it lies in the restricted area of a Homeland.

Entertainments: Safe bathing and excellent surfing: all kinds of sport, theatres, cinemas, amusement parks, nightclubs. It is an important horseracing centre – the country's classic horse race, the July Handicap, is run there on the first Saturay of July.

Tourist Information: National Tourist Bureau, 3rd Floor, 320 West Street, PO Box 2516, Durban, tel: 304-7144, telex: 621205 SA.

Kwazulu

The Zulu Homeland, unlike the Transkei, is scattered all over Natal, interspersed by large 'white' areas. Like the Transkei, however, it is generally dry, eroded, and overpopulated. The most solid concentration of land is in northern Natal, with the administrative centre at Nongoma, but even here are 'white spots' like the developing port of Richard's Bay – a point of conflict between the Homeland and the Government since it would provide the only natural seaport for the Zulus if ever they became independent.

The Drakensberg

The 'Dragon Mountain', snow-covered in winter, spreads from Lesotho (where it is known as the Malutis) along the border of the Orange Free State and Natal, to the Lebombo range which, in places, divides the Transvaal from Mozambique. The mountains provide walks, riding, climbing, fishing, flowers and some game as well as superb scenery. The hotels also have swimming, tennis and bowling facilities.

Mont-aux-Sources, at 3,482 m, is the highest peak in the Republic. It is the source of the Orange, Caledon and Tugela rivers – hence its name. There are countless streams and waterfalls, wild flowers, small buck and baboons. The Giant's Castle reserve organises riding tours in the surrounding mountains where a variety of mountain flowers and some game, notably the rare Cape eland, can be seen. There are fine Bushman paintings in the caves.

Johannesburg

The country's wealth is based mainly on the golden Reef which forms the Witwatersrand (Ridge of White Waters) of which Johannesburg (pop. 1,446,000) is the centre.

The Witwatersrand, known mostly as the Rand, has two radials – the East Rand with the mining and industrial towns of Germiston, Boksburg, Benoni, Brakpan, Springs and Nigel; and the West Rand with Florida, Roodeport, Krugersdorp and Randfontein. It has extended with the discovery of newer goldfields to the Far West Rand town of Klerksdorp – where the gold reef submerges to appear again in the Free State goldfields. To the south of Johannesburg are the coalfields and industries of Vereeniging and the steel and oil processing complex of Sasolburg. Nearby is the huge steel complex of Iscor (the Iron and Steel Corporation). Together this area forms the Vaal Triangle, the South African Ruhr.

The Rand is traversed by enormous mine dumps, the man-made range of hills dug up from some of the deepest mines in the world. Lying at 2,000 m above sea-level Johannesburg has an invigorating climate – hot in the summer, cold when the sun goes down in the early dusk of winter. It is a city of extremes – of political reaction and of progressive ideas; of a vibrant culture and of brash philistinism; of white affluence and of black poverty; of violence and lawlessness which take their toll indiscriminately among whites and blacks.

The city is strictly segregated. The western, eastern and southern suburbs are mostly occupied by white artisans or middle-classes; the northern suburbs have among the finest and richest homes and gardens in the world. The million or so Africans are mostly concentrated in the great black city of Soweto on the southern periophery, or in the vast complex of bachelor compounds in Alexandra township – the home of many of the migrant workers, which has no parallel in the world. The Asians have been uprooted from their old homes and resettled in the segregated town of Lenasia on the southern outskirts.

Conducted tours of the gold mines take place three times a week, and the strenuous tour gives a fascinating insight into the surface and underground workings. Protective clothing is provided. It is necessary to book such a trip three months in advance, either direct through the Public Relations Department, Chamber of Mines, 5 Holland St, PO Box 809, Johannesburg, or through the Tourist Bureau.

Tourist Information: National Tourist Bureaux, Suite 4611, Carlton Centre, PO Box 1094, tel: 331-5241.

Pretoria

The administrative capital of South Africa is only 48 km from Johannesburg, but still retains its old-world atmosphere. The Union Buildings dominate the city, which is also the seat of the Transvaal Provincial Council and of one of the Afrikaner universities.

Pretoria holds many reminders of both Afrikaner and English history. The Boer military victories are commemorated in the massive Voortrekker Monument, 40 m high and visible for miles around, and a national shrine for Afrikaners. President Paul Kruger's house in Church Street is now a museum. The Transvaal Museum has a notable collection of geological, archaeological and natural history specimens from the Stone Age period and earlier. The Old Museum, next to the zoo, contains a rare exhibition of San (Bushman) art.

Umtata in the Transkei

SWAZILAND

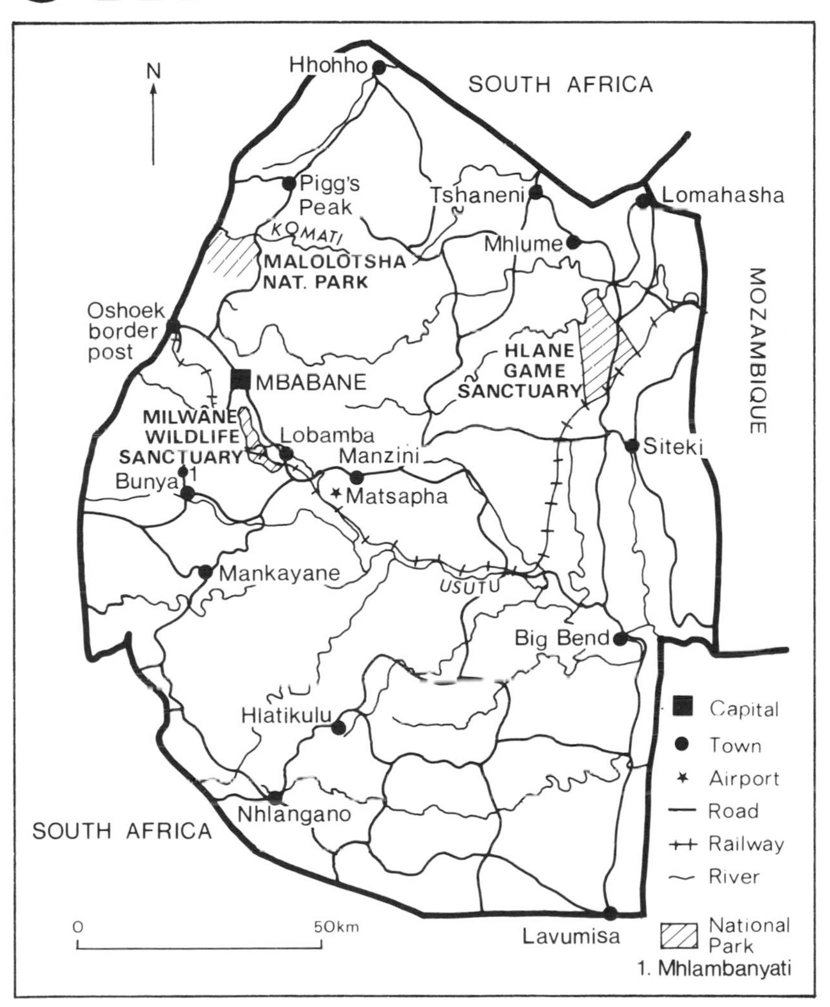

Area: 17,364 sq km
Population: 762,000 (1989 World Bank)
Capital: Mbabane

Swaziland contains within its small area nearly every example of African landscape, with the exception of desert. In a 160 km drive the road may pass through sugar cane plantation, rugged often mist-shrouded mountains, savannah and thornbush country, citrus orchards and pineapple groves.

Before its independence in September 1968, Swaziland formed part of the British High Commission Territories with Basutoland (now Lesotho) and Bechuanaland (now Botswana). Unlike most African States it emerged into independence under the firm guidance of its King, Sobhuza II, who began his rule in 1922 and died on 21 August 1982.

Known as the 'Switzerland of Africa', Swaziland, small as it is, is very beautiful. It has a thriving tourist industry, with 90% of its visitors coming from South Africa. They are drawn to Swaziland's casinos and its easier social and political climate.

Hills and Plateaux

Despite its smallness Swaziland has a rich variety of soils and vegetation and is one of the best-watered areas in southern Africa. Four major rivers – the Komati, Usutu, Mbuluzi and Ngwavuma – flow from west to east to the Indian Ocean. There are four well-defined topographical regions, extending longitudinally north and south in roughly parallel belts.

The Highveld (locally called *Inkangala*) is a wide ribbon of rugged country in which lie Swaziland's ore deposits. There are asbestos and iron ore mines in this area. Until the early 1970's, mining was Swaziland's leading export earner, but the mines are now being worked out. Although at one time the Highveld may have been wooded, deforestation and overgrazing have caused complete denudation in some places. However, this has been counteracted in other parts by successful re-afforestation schemes, as with the 40,000 hectares of Usutu pine in the Usutu forests, one of the largest man-made forests in the world.

The Middleveld rolling down from the Highveld through hilly country with well-watered valleys, supports mixed farming, the main crops being rice and sub-tropical fruits (citrus and bananas) grown under irrigation, and maize, cotton, beans, tobacco and pineapples cultivated on drylands. The rivers afford extensive irrigation schemes.

The Lowveld (known as *Liblanze*) is characterised by 'bush' vegetation, and has hills rising from 170 to 350 m. As well as cattle ranching, it now has large irrigation schemes and is an area of intensive sugar-cane, rice and citrus fruit cultivation. The sugar and citrus industries are centred at Big Bend and Mhlume where there are three large sugar mills. The sugar industry has rapidly become the country's leading export earner.

The Lubombo plateau is an escarpment along the eastern fringe of the Lowveld. It is mainly cattle country and good mixed farming land. The Lubombo has one town, Siteki. From the top of the escarpment at about 600 m, you can look across deep valleys to coastal flats on the Indian Ocean.

Nine-tenths of the Swazi people still live in the rural areas of Swaziland. The settlement pattern is one of scattered homesteads rather than the village settlements predominant in Lesotho and Botswana. Families often work in communal fields and the headman (*umnumzana*) of each homestead has authority over his dependents. tribal territory is divided into a number of districts, at the head of each of which is a chief (*sikhulu*). Aided by his mother, he centralises law, economics and ritual in his area. Local headmen constitute the council (*Libandla*) of each chief. The chief of each area is the responsible authority for the Ngwenyama. Apart from land under European concession, all land in Swaziland is owned by the Swazi nation and held in trust by the King.

Traditionally, the Swazi were peasants who cultivated crops, kept cattle, hunted, and gathered fruits and vegetables. The agricultural system of about 70% of the population is still centred around cattle rearing and the growing of maize and millet. The principal form of agricultural life, however, remains the pastoral rearing of cattle, and much of Swazi culture and tradition revolves around this. Cattle serve as potent symbols in a wide range of situations, both economic and ritual, in addition to their direct value as a source of food and clothing. Similar to other pastoral economies in different parts of Africa, soil erosion is severe, especially in the Highveld and southern Middleveld where overstocking and overgrazing is prevalent. Until fairly recently approximately 75% of Swazi land was devoted to grazing and only 10% to cultivation.

With the increasing emphasis on commercial farming and rural development schemes, more Swazi farmers are becoming involved in cash crop production of tobacco, cotton, citrus and sugar-cane. But, cashcropping still plays a very minor part in Swaziland's economy in comparison with the revenue from the plantations sugar and ore exports. One of the reasons for its slow expansion is that economic emphasis is directed instead towards the commercial production by large foreign corporations of raw materials for export. This policy is fostered by the government, as foreign investors, lured by a competitive tax structure, need cheap labour rather than middle-class consumers. The Swazi monarchy depends largely on peasant support and has not encouraged the growth of a rural trading class.

Traditions are Retained

Swaziland is a constitutional monarchy. The Swazi royal family goes back to the 'Nkosi Dlamini' who lived in the 15th century. Since the death of King Sobhuza Queen Regents have ruled while a minor Prince Makhosetive is being trained to become king.

The two major cultural and ritual events in the Swazi year are the Incwala ceremony (December-January) and the Reed Dance (July-August), both of which are held at the Lobamba Royal Kraal.

The Incwala ceremony is the most important and sacred of Swazi ceremonies and is spread over a period of about three weeks culminating in the six days of the Big Incwala. The ceremony is the sacrament of the first fruits, sanctifying the kingship which binds the nation together, and renewing strength and unity for the coming year. The monarchy represents a source of fertility for the nation. King Sobhuza had hundreds of children by dozens of different wives. The Incwala ritual includes every member of Swazi society. On the final day of the Big Incwala, objects representing the past year are burnt in a ritual fire in the Royal Cattle Byre at Lobamba. Rain is expected to fall and quench the flames (it has done so with remarkable consistency!) The Incwala ends with feasting and dancing and on the people's return home, new crops may be safely eaten. Visitors may attend the Incwala on certain days, but photographs may only be taken with permission from the Government. Requests should be made to the Swaziland Information Services in Mbabane.

The Umhlanga or Reed Dance lasts a week and is not a sacred ceremony like the Incwala. Its object is to encourage young Swazi girls of the same age-group to work in harmony, to preserve their chastity, and to show their respect in a practical way for the Queen Mother by collecting reeds to repair the windbreaks around her residence. Visitors are welcome to watch the Reed Dance itself which takes place at Lobamba in the National Stadium on the sixth and seventh days after the girls have returned from their reed collecting.

Traditional life is still strong in rural Swaziland. Singing and dancing are a part of everyday life and Sibhaca dancing remains popular throughout the country. There is an annual Sibhaca competition performed for the King, and visitors should have no difficulty in seeing a dance if they wish. The tourist office in Mbabane will provide the necessary information.

Unlike many other African peoples, musical instruments play a very small role in Swazi culture except for the individual use of flutes and musical bows. Among the latter, there are two belonging expressly to the Swazis – the *ligubu* and the *makhweyane*, strung bows with inverted calabashes as resonators. However, apart from these, Swazi music is almost exclusively vocal. Communal dancing is an important feature of Swazi social and religious life and Swazi dancers sing their own dance music for both traditional and secular dances. No drums or other instruments are used for accompaniment.

There is a rich tradition of oral lore in the forms of praise poetry, folktales and historical narrative.

History

Swazi history goes back to the end of the 16th century when Ngwane II (the first King commemorated in modern ritual) crossed the Lubombo mountains from the east coast of southern Africa and settled in south-eastern Swaziland. His grandson Sobhuza I established himself at the foot of the Mdzimba mountains which is the area to this day in which most of the royal villages are found. Sobhuza I demanded allegiance from the Nguni and Sotho people who already occupied the area, and he left his successor a strong kingdom, respected and feared by neighbouring tribes, with a centralised political system controlling several thousands of people.

In the 18th and 19th centuries tribal conflict and conflict between Africans and whites became inevitable owing to economic pressure on land. Sobhuza's heir, Mswati (1840-1868) was the greatest of Swazi fighting kings. Influenced by the Zulu, he reorganised his army into centralised age regiments and he welded the Swazi nation together, extending his dominions to three times the size of modern Swaziland. Mswati was the last truly independent ruler of Swaziland for the next hundred years.

The initial relationship between the Swazi and the whites was friendly and co-operative; the Swazi were prepared to treat both Boer and British as allies. The two white groups, however, expressed different interests in Swaziland. The Boers were searching for good arable land and also for a route to the east coast to establish their own port in order to escape contact with the hated British in the Cape. Britain, on the other hand, although not wanting to expand her colony any further, was reluctant to allow the Boers to gain control of a country of unknown potential and divert trade from her own ports.

Gold was discovered in 1882 in the north-west and hundreds of European fortune hunters descended on Swaziland. The sovereignty of the Swazi was frequently asserted but Mswati's successor, Mbandzeni, had no constitutional control over the whites and he was coerced into granting land concessions for grazing land and prospecting rights that clashed with the rights or customary land usage. Although accused later of granting concessions indiscriminately, Mbandzeni is remembered by his own people as a king of peace duped by unscrupulous Europeans.

In 1894, without consulting the Swazi, the two white powers, Boer and British, concluded a convention granting the South African Boer Republic of the Transvaal control over Swaziland. Swaziland was no longer recognised as an independent state and the original European conquest by concession was now backed by military force. After the Anglo-Boer War (1899-1902), Britain reluctantly made Swaziland a protectorate, and the Transvaal became part of the Union of South Africa.

Swaziland became an economic and political backwater. The Partitions Proclamation of 1907 confirmed Mbandzeni's land concessions of the 1880's, and the concessionaires who were often absentee landlords, remained in control of two-thirds of the land, a third being set aside for Swazi occupation. The British made no attempt to identify the traditional Swazi administration with the central administration, and government was by dual control rather than indirect rule. In 1922 King Sobhuza II took over office from his grandmother Gwamile, who had acted as Queen Regent, and at the age of 21 was installed as Paramount chief of Swaziland and King of the Swazi nation.

His first task was to contest the concessions originally granted to foreigners by Mbandzeni. After an initial protest failed the nation sent him to appeal to the Privy Council in London in 1922. The Swazi nation lost the appeal on a technicality. Finally, in 1941, a further petition resulted in the purchase by Britain of a number of freeholds which, together with Crown land, were handed over to the Swazi. Today, about 57% of Swaziland is owned by the nation, but the Swaziland government continues to press its case for the return of other land sold to Europeans to finance the British administration.

With the onset of decolonisation in the early 1960's, the Swazi monarchy with its political institutions of chiefs and headmen appointed by the King and organised into district councils (*tinkundla*) under the Swazi National Council, was still largely intact. King Sobhuza II and the Swazi National Council had strong support from the Swazi rural electorate, while the newly formed factional parties of the educational elite and black traders turned for support to the growing working class. The NNLC led by Dr. Ambrose Zwane had some popular support from both these groups until 1973. The King, who had previously entirely opposed the idea of political parties per se, was convinced by the 1963 strikes and pressure from both the British administration and from white settlers who promised support, that he should form his own political party, the *Imbokodvo* (grindstone) National Movement, for the 1964 elections. In 1966, however, the British recognised Sobhuza's authority as King of Swaziland, and placed responsibility for Swazi communal land and mineral rights in his personal trust, rather than vesting these powers in the State. Swaziland, which was the last directly administered British colony in Africa, finally became independent in September 1968.

Predictably, the King's Imbokodvo party had an overwhelming majority of votes in the national legislative elections of 1964, 1967 and 1972. However, in 1973, King Sobhuza repealed the constitution and dissolved all political parties. The monarchy promised a new constitution more suited to traditional Swazi values, but it has yet to be finalised. King Sobhuza continued to pursue his 'traditional' solution to Swaziland's political problems by abolishing the parliamentary system entirely in March 1977 and replacing it with the tribal institutions of the *tinkundla*. The new tribal 'parliament' (*libandla*) made up both of members elected by the *tinkundla* and appointed by the King, was opened in January 1979. The King was able to veto any parliamentary resolution and appoint and dismiss ministers at will.

After the King's 'coup' in 1973, there were intermittent outbursts of protest from the growing Swazi proletariat and the professional and white collar employees of the government who became increasingly powerless as policy decisions shifted to the monarchy. The Swazi military and paramilitary security forces have increased in numbers and exercise wide-ranging powers, including detention without trial. A large number of political detainees were released in late 1979, however, after the replacement of Maj.-Gen. Maphevu Dlamini, the hard-line Prime Minister, by a more liberal successor.

King Sobhuza died on 21 August 1982 after 60 years on the throne. This caused a struggle for succession and for political power. The heir apparent, Prince Makhosetive was still a schoolboy at Sherborne public school so the King's senior wife Queen Dzeliwe was appointed to rule as regent through the Supreme Council of State. However in order to end the power struggle between the various factions around the throne King Mswati III, though only 18 years old, was brought back from school and crowned king on 25 April 1986. He soon became politically involved and showed that he had a mind of his own.

In its external policies, Swaziland has taken a cautious line, with strong economic links and political co-operation with South Africa on the one hand, and trade agreements with the new Mozambique government on the other. South African political refugees and liberation movements are barely tolerated.

Wildlife

Once Swaziland was rich in wildlife but years of unchecked hunting ravaged the game population and many of the larger antelopes were in danger of becoming extinct. Animals still to be seen are zebra, hippo, kudu, water buck, impala, duiker and wildebeest. The establishment of extensive forestry has led to a return of some of the smaller antelope to the sanctuary of the trees. Crocodiles inhabit the lower reaches of the main rivers.

Birdlife is prolific and you will see the European stork, sacred ibis, blue crane, wattled crane and crested crane (the mating dance of cranes is a fantastic sight), hornbill, hammerhead, the lilac-breasted roller, bee-eaters, hoopoes and kingfishers. Several species of waterfowl including the spur-wing geese, congregate on the rivers and the Sand River Dam.

National Parks

Mlilwane Wildlife Sanctuary: A small game sanctuary in the Ezulwini Valley, Mlilwane was started by a keen conservationist to protect and foster the country's wildlife and flora. Earth roads, along which visitors can travel in their own cars, cross the reserve. There is a wide variety of wildlife to be seen but no elephant or carnivores.

Also in the Mlilwane Game Sanctuary is the Gilbert Reynolds Memorial Garden, containing a number of rare cycads and 230 aloe species collected throughout Africa and Madagascar. The gardens are particularly colourful in winter (mid-year). Accommodation consists of chalets and camping.

Hlane Game Sanctuary: This is located off the Manzini/Mpaka/Lomahasha main road about 70 kms from Manzini, and comprises 35,000 ha of unspoilt bushveld in the Lowveld. White rhino, wildebeest, zebra, impala, kudu, waterbuck, steenbok, grey duiker and giraffe can be seen as well as predators such as the spotted hyena and the black-backed jackal. Conservationists have been concerned with recent clearing of natural bushland on two sides of the reserve to make way for the new sugar mill project. No accommodation is yet available at Hlane, although there are plans to build a small motel/rest camp in the near future. Camping grounds are provided.

Malolotsha National Park: This new national park which has always been a popular hiking and picnicking spot in the Malolotsha Valley, lies north of Forbes Reef and borders the Komati River and Transvaal boundary. It has the attraction of the Malolotsha Falls which, at over 50 m are the highest in the country. Sections of the Park have been designated wilderness areas to be explored only on foot or horseback. Records show that in the past a great abundance of animals frequented the area, even elephant, and it is planned to reintroduce species such as rhino, kudu, zebra, waterbuck, impala and wildebeest. The only known colony of rare Bald Ibis nests in the Park. The Park is situated on the main Mbabane-Piggs Peak road.

Ndzindza National Park: This 12,000 acre property in the Lowveld bordering Mozambique was recently donated to the Swaziland Trust Commission. The reserve embraces the Imbuluzi Gorge between the Lubombo mountains and has an interesting variety of birdlife. It is planned to keep Ndzindza a wilderness area and although it will soon be open to visitors, at present access is only possible in four-wheel-drive vehicles.

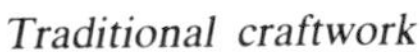

Traditional craftwork

DANIDA

General Information

Government

Monarchy. Rule is by King Mswati III crowned king on 25 April 1986.

Languages

Official languages – SiSwati and English.

Religion

Christian and traditional beliefs, with the majority of people being Christian (Roman Catholic, African Baptist and Protestant).

How to Get There

By air: Matsapha Airport near Manzini is the main air entry point. Royal Swazi Air flights connect daily with Jan Smuts (Johannesburg) and Durban airport. There are also schedule services to and from Dar-es-Salaam, Harare, Lusaka, Nairobi, Maseru and Maputo. Charter planes are available and details can be obtained from Tibiyo Travel Agency, Swazi Plaza, Mbabane, or directly from Matsapha airport.

By road: Numerous tourist buses visit Swaziland from Natal and Transvaal in South Africa. Information is available from the Swaziland Tourist Office in Mbabane. The quickest road route to Swaziland from Johannesburg is via Bronkhorstpruit, Witbank, Carolina (Oshoek Border post) Mbabane – some 340 km of tarred roads. From Durban there is a tarred road via Ladysmith, Volkrust, Ermelo, Oshoek or a shorter but rougher route, much of it on dirt roads, through northern Zululand and Lavumisa (border post). From Maputo, motorists' entry point is Namaacha/Lomahasha (border post) 130 km away including some 65 km of dirt road or via the Mhlumeni/Goba (border post) to Manzini, which includes 38 km of dirt road.

Border Posts and operating hours
Bulembu (Josefdal) 0800-1600
Gege (Bothashoop) 0800-1600
Lavumisa (Golela) 0700-2200
Lomahasha (Namaacha) 0830-1200 and 1300-2000
Lundzi (Waverley) 0800-1600
Mahamba 0700-2200
Mananga 0800-1800
Matsamo (Jeppe's Reef) 0800-1600
Mhlumeni (Goba) 0700-1200 and 1300-2000
Ngwenya (Oshock) 0700-2200
Salitje (Onverwacht) 0800-1600
Sandlane (Nerston) 0800-1600
Sicunusa (Houdkop) 0800-1800

Entry Regulations

All visitors to Swaziland require valid passports. There are immigration posts at Matsapha airport, Lomahasha, Goba on the Mozambique border, and the recently established immigration post at Oshoek. Visitors entering from South Africa at any other point must register with the Immigration Office in Mbabane or at any other police station within forty-eight hours of arrival. Visitors staying more than 60 days require a temporary visitors permit.

Citizens of Britain, or Commonwealth countries do not require visas for Swaziland, nor do the nationals of the following countries: Belgium, Denmark, Finland, France, Greece, Iceland, Italy, Israel, Portugal, Liechtenstein, Luxembourg, Netherlands, Norway and its Colonies, San Marino, South Africa, Sweden, Switzerland, Uruguay and the

United States.

Visitors must have sufficient resources to cover their stay and have a return ticket or the means to buy one.

Visitors who come from an endemic yellow fever area require a valid yellow fever inoculation certificate.

All travellers visiting the Kingdom from any part of the world should be in possession of a valid cholera vaccination certificate.

Customs Regulations

With South Africa, Lesotho and Botswana, Swaziland is part of the southern African common customs area, and visitors from South Africa are not subject to customs formalities. Those arriving from Mozambique have to comply with certain regulations. Vehicles registered in Mozambique may enter for up to six months without payment of duty. Those from other countries (excluding South Africa, Lesotho or Botswana) may also remain for up to 12 months without payment of duty if a deposit is paid to cover the duty, by using carnets de passage or triptyques from recognised international motoring organisations, or through temporary customs importation permits.

Tourists from outside the common customs area may bring in goods to the value of E50.00, and tobacco and wines subject to the usual limitations. Arms and ammunition may not be brought in without advance permission from Police Headquarters, P.O. Box 49, Mbabane.

Climate

Because of variations in altitude the weather is extremely changeable. Except in the Lowveld, it is seldom uncomfortably hot and no part of Swaziland is ever very cold although frosts occasionally occur in the Highveld.

The Highveld is near temperate but humid: temperatures can be as high as 32°C from October to February, with mid-year winter temperatures dropping to zero. Average rainfall varies between 1,000 and 2,000 mm. The Middleveld and the Lubombo are sub-tropical and drier, with annual rainfall of 750-1,150 mm. Most of the rain falls between October and March, but long periods of continuous rain are uncommon. In the Lowveld the terrain drops from 350 m-170 m above sea level and the mean annual rainfall is 660 mm, although in a drought year it can fall well below this. The Lowveld climate is particularly pleasant during the winter months (mid-year).

What to wear: Light, casual clothing is the norm, but the evenings can be cool, even in summer, and it is advisable to have something warmer. A light raincoat is necessary during the summer months (October-March).

More formal wear is customary at the casino and sophisticated hotels.

Health Precautions

If you intend spending any time in the Swaziland Lowveld during the wet months (September-March) you should take malaria prophylactics before, during and after your stay. Bilharzia is a hazard in most rivers and dams.

Banks and Currency

Mbabane

Barclays Bank, PO Box 667, tel: 42696, telex: 2096

Standard Bank, PO Box 68, tel: 43351, telex: 2041

Bank of Credit and Commerce International, PO Box 1337, tel: 43659

Swaziland Development and Savings Bank, PO Box 336, tel: 42555, telex: 2055

Manzini

Barclays Bank, PO Box 1, tel: 52411

Standard Bank, PO Box 11.

Bank of Credit and Commerce International, PO Box 645, tel: 53181

Swaziland Development and Savings Bank, PO Box 199, tel: 52431

Currency: Lilangeni (plural Emalangeni); 1 Lilangeni = 1 Rand (SA); Both are legal tender in the Kingdom.
(See currency table, page 10).

Business Hours

Banks: Monday-Friday 0830-1300; Saturday 0830-1100
Government offices: Monday-Friday 0800-1300 and 1400-1700
Immigration Office closes daily at 1500
Shops: Generally follow Government office hours but cafes and restaurants in Mbabane and Manzini stay open until 2230 or 2400.

Public Holidays

New Year's Day, 1 January
Good Friday, 13 April 1990
Easter Monday, 16 April 1990
National Flag Day, 25 April
Ascension Day, 24 May 1990
Commonwealth Day, 11 June
Umhlanga (Reed Dance) Day, July or August
Somhloto (Independence) Day, 6 September
United Nations Day, 24 October
Christmas Day, 25 December
Boxing Day, 26 December
Incwala (First Fruits) Day, December or January

Embassies in Swaziland

Israel: PO Box 146, Mbabane, tel: 42626
UK: British High Commission, Allister Miller Street, Private Bag, Mbabane, tel: 42581.
USA: Central Bank Building, Mbabane, tel: 22281
Republic of China, Box 56, Mbabane. Tel: 42379.

Transport

By road: Public transport is still in its formative stage. While there is a fair, if erratic, bus service between Mbabane and Manzini, the visitor would be well advised to hire a car, or arrange for transport through an hotel. But services meet scheduled air flights.
Car hire: There are three Hertz rental stations in Swaziland. Cars can be pre-booked at any Hertz office worldwide or on arrival in the country. Postal address: Hertz United, PO Box 360, Manzini, tel: 2404. Also at Matsapha Airport, tel: 52509 and Mbabane, tel: 42561.

All cars drive on the left and an upper speed limit of 80 kms per hour applies throughout the country. Most main roads in Swaziland have gravel surfaces of a good standard, while others are being upgraded prior to tarring.
A note to motorists: exercise extreme caution at narrow bridges on many of the country roads as approaches may be steep and warning signs are frequently absent. A blind rise is often followed by a deep descent. Herds of cattle using the road can also be extremely hazardous.

Petrol is available: Monday-Friday from 0600-1800 hours, on Saturday from 0600-1400 hours, and on Sunday from 1400-1800 hours. These are subject to alteration.

Useful Phrases

	SiSwati
Hello, good day	*Sawubona*
Yes	*Yebo*
No	*Cha!*
How are you?	*Unjani?*
I am well	*Ngikhona*
Thank you	*Ngiyabonga*
Goodbye (Stay well)	*Sala Kahle*
Go well	*Hamba Kahle*
I am hungry	*Ngilambile*
I am thirsty	*Ngomile*
How much?	*Malini?*

Accommodation and Food

Hotels offer a fairly wide range of accommodation, ranging from sophisticated international hotels to comfortable country inns. As Swaziland is very popular with tourists, existing hotels are hard put to meet the growing demand, so accommodation bookings should be made well in advance – and confirmed. Peak holiday periods are week-ends, South African public holidays and school holidays (Easter, June, September and December-January). The Royal Swazi Hotel with its casino, and the Ezulwini and Lugogo Holiday Inns, all in the Ezulwini valley, attract the most custom. However, the smaller country hotels are much more reflective of the country and offer a more personal service. All hotels are open to non-residents and some of the more expensive hotels aspire to having a high standard of cuisine. To be sure of a table in most Swaziland restaurants it is advisable to book in advance.

Camping sites exist in Mbabane and at Matsapha, and there are motels and caravan parks in the Ezulwini Valley. The Timbali Caravan Park in Ezulwini offers good facilities for campers, as does Milwane Game Park which also has comfortable, if simple, accommodation, in traditional Swazi beehive huts in the restcamp.

Meals at the majority of hotels and restaurants are mostly European, although good Greek, Hungarian and Indian food is available. Tipping should be ten per cent of the bill. The local market women run food stalls at the main market places in Mbabane and Manzini where they sell plates of traditional Swazi meat stew and maize meal or stamped mealies, and roasted corn on the cob (in season). Traditional Swazi beer brewed by market women is also on sale at the market. Water is safe to drink and alcoholic beverages are freely available.

Hotels and Rest Camps

NAME	ADDRESS	TELEPHONE	TELEX
MBABANE			
Jabula Inn	PO Box 15, Mbabane	42406	
Mountain Inn	PO Box 223, Mbabane	42461/2	
Swazi Inn	PO Box 121, Mbabane	42235	2135
Tavern Hotel	PO Box 25, Mbabane	42361	
Highland View Caravan Park	PO Box A231 Swazi Plaza, Mbabane	22989	
EZULWINI VALLEY			
Diamond Valley Motel	PO Box 247, Mbabane	61041/2 Lobamba 61146	
Ezulwini Holiday Inn	PO Box 123, Mbabane	61201 Lobamba	2147
Happy Valley Motel	PO Box 943, Mbabane	61061 Lobamba	

[Hotels]			
Lugogo Holiday Inn	PO Box 123, Mbabane	61101 Lobamba	2058
Mantenga Falls Hotel	PO Box 15, Ezulwini	61049 Lobamba	
Royal Swazi Hotel and Spa	PO Box 412, Mbabane	61001 Lobamba	2014
Smoky Mountain Village	PO Box 21, Ezulwini	61291 Lobamba	
Timbali Caravan Park	PO Box 1, Ezulwini	61156	
Yen Saan Hotel	PO Box 771, Mbabane	61051 Lobamba	
MANZINI			
George Hotel	PO Box 51, Manzini	52061	
Highway Motel	PO Box 546, Manzini	506140	
Uncle Charlie Hotel	PO Box 48, Manzini	52297	
Paradise Caravan Park	PO Box 614, Manzini	53057	
MHLAMBANYATI			
Foresters' Arms	PO Box 14, Mhlambanyati	74177/74377	
Meikle's Mount	PO Box 13, Mhlambanyati	74110	
MANKAYANE			
Inyatsi Inn	PO Box 21, Mankayane	12	
NHLANGANO			
Nhlangano Casino Hotel	Private Bag, Nhlangano	78211	2089
Robin Inn	PO Box 360, Nhlangano	78488	
HLATIKULU			
Assegai Inn	PO Box 30, Hlatikulu	16	
LAVUMISA			
Lavumisa Hotel	PO Box 9, Lavumisa	7	▶

[Hotels]		
BIG BEND		
Bend Inn	PO Box 37, Big Bend	36111
SITEKI		
Bamboo Inn	PO Box 84, Siteki	34118
Stegi Hotel	PO Box 33, Siteki	34126
[Hotels]		
TSHANENI		
Impala Arms Hotel	PO Box 34, Tshaneni	31244/5
PIGG'S PEAK		
Highlands Inn	PO Box 12, Pigg's Peak	12
REST CAMP		
EZULWINI VALLEY		
Mlilwane Wildlife Sanctuary	PO Box 33, Mbabane	61037/8
Rest camp planned at Hlane Game Sanctuary		■

Mbabane

A mixture of old and modern buildings, Mbabane (the largest town in Swziland) is the administrative capital and an expanding commercial centre. Attractively situated among the Dlangeni Hills, it overlooks the beautiful Ezulwini Valley.

Restaurants: Worth mentioning and worth a visit are:

The Mediterranean Restaurant, Allister Miller Street, tel: 43212. Indian and vegetarian dishes.

Lourenco Marques Restaurant, Top of Allister Miller Street, tel: 43097. Specialises in Portuguese food.

Plaza Restaurant, Swazi Plaza, tel: 22841. Serves good European food; especially recommended for lunchtime eating.

Jubilee Room, Tavern Hotel. French and Mauritian cuisine, tel: 42361.

"Red Feather" restaurant, Malegwane Hill, Swazi Inn Hotel, tel: Mbabane 42235/6. European food, à la carte menu.

Entertainments: There are three night clubs in Mbabane: D'Discotheque, Highland View Hotel, tel: 42461. Opens 2000 every night.

Nite Club 701, Johnstone Street – except Mondays, opens 2000 every night. Live music.

Studio 21 Discotheque, Allister Miller Street, (adjacent to the Jabula Inn). Live music tel: 42406.

Shopping and Markets: Below Allister Miller Street, just south of the town, is the **Swazi Plaza,** a large and attractive shopping complex providing virtually every type of shopping and ancillary service facility. Opposite the Swazi Plaza at the bottom of Allister Miller Street, is the **Mbabane market** selling both local produce and Swazi craft – well worth a visit.

For those interested in good quality craft, the government-sponsored Small Enterprises Development Co. (SEDCO) has opened an estate on the Mbabane-Manzini Road where you can watch Swazi craftsmen at work and buy their products. Items available include a wide variety of beadwork and basketwork, grass and sisal mats, copperware, leatherwork, wooden bowls, local gemstone jewellery, wooden and soapstone carvings, calabashes, knobkerries, battleaxes, walking sticks, drums, karosses (animal skin mats), python skins, hand-woven fabrics, clothing using characteristic Swazi techniques, from batik to tie-and-dye.

Tourist Information: Swaziland Tourist Office, PO Box 451, Mbabane, tel: Mbabane 42531, telex: 2232.

King Sobhuza II

Ezulwini Valley

After leaving Mbabane and winding down the Malagwane Hill, one reaches the Ezulwini Valley 20 km away. Situated in the valley is the Royal Swazi Hotel (Swazi Spa) and Casino, one of Swaziland's main tourist attractions. This luxurious complex belonging to the Holiday Inns group has included many facilities and entertainments which visiting South African tourists particularly enjoy; there is a casino, a cinema showing films unlikely to be seen in South Africa, a discotheque and nightclub often with international stars or cabaret, and an 18 hole golf course. Young Swazi women are frequently lured by the superficial glamour and sophistication of 'The Valley', and prostitution is unfortunately a thriving profession owing to the racial and sexual taboos of white South Africans.

Restaurants: There is a varied selection of restaurants and bars serving à la carte and buffet meals in all 3 Holiday Inn Hotels in the valley.

The Calabash Restaurant, alongside The Timbali Caravan Park, tel: 61187. Good Austrian food – must book.

The First Horse, alongside the Yen Saan Hotel. Good continental cuisine, tel: 61137.

The Yen Saan Chinese Restaurant, Yen Saan Hotel, tel: Mbabane 61051, excellent Chinese food.

Diamond Valley Steakhouse, Diamond Valley Motel, tel: Mbabane 61041/61146, convenient medium priced steakhouse.

Paulino's at Smokey Mountain Village,

tel: 61291. Good Italian food

Entertainments: The main attraction for South African tourists is the Casino at the Royal Swazi Hotel. The casino opens at 2000 hrs from Monday to Friday, at 1400 on Saturdays, Sundays and public holidays. It closes when the last player leaves.

There is a popular nightclub in The Royal Swazi Hotel – 'Gigi's' – with resident band and dancing every night. They also stage regular cabarets.

Why Not Discotheque, Happy Valley Motel, tel: Lobamba 61061, well frequented discotheque both by local Swazis and expatriates. Open every night. Good music.

Sports: The Royal Swazi Hotel boasts a Health Studio built alongside the nearby hot mineral springs where saunas and massage are available. However, less developed and still in their natural setting are the hot springs at Siphofaneni (70 km away on the main Manzini – Big Bend road) a saline chloride spring with a high concentration of solids. There is a very attractive 18 hole golf course with lovely views of the Ezulwini Valley attached to the Royal Swazi Hotel, and there are facilities for tennis, squash, horseriding and swimming at all three Holiday Inn Hotels. For children, a novel adventure playground, designed by a young Swede, is open alongside the Lugogo Holiday Inn on the main Mbabane – Manzini road. There is walking and hiking country in the Ezulwini Valley – a popular hike is up 'Sheba's Breasts', a fairly strenuous climb but which offers superb views of the valley.

Markets: Situated at Mantenga Falls adjacent to the Mantenga Falls Hotel, is **Mantenga Craft,** a unique handcraft complex set up by Pan African Handcrafts, part of a private development corporation which operates all over Africa. The centre produces pottery, woodcarving, hand-forged silver, silk screen and block-printed cloth, and handweaving in wool and local cotton. The staff of the centre attempt to produce and promote Swazi craft of high quality as well as introduce new skills. This is one of the few labour intensive development projects in Swaziland.

Lobamba

This is the traditional home and spiritual capital of the Swazi nation. It is also the legislative capital and the parliamentary buildings are situated here. The Queen Mother's village is at Lobamba which was the traditional headquarters of the King. Before his death he had a new official residence built at vast expense at Lozitq, near the University of Swaziland and the Botswana (U.B.S.) campus at Kwaluseni; his successor could choose a new headquarters. The Somhlolo National Stadium, built in 1968 for the Independence celebrations is also to be found at Lobamba. The annual Reed dance is performed here.

Parliament: The House of Parliament may be visited.

Museum: Situated near the House of Parliament is well worth a visit and would be of interest to anyone interested in Swazi culture and traditions. There is a section on the geology and archaeology of Swaziland and a collection of traditional dress, implements and weapons. There are also examples of traditional Swazi handcraft in wood, grass and clay. The museum also supports contemporary culture in Swaziland and presently has modern sculptures by young Swazi artists on display.

The State Palace: King Sobhuza did not live in the palace but used it to receive important dignitaries. Turn left off the main road to the House of Parliament and continue along a tarred road for about 14 km. No one other than authorised visitors may approach or photograph the Palace.

University of Swaziland and Botswana – Kwaluseni Campus: The university campus is found about 2 km off the main

Mbabane-Manzini road. From Mbabane, turn off left at Matsapha. The campus is attractively set into the surrounding hills and open to visitors.

Restaurants: Los Cabanas Restaurant (near Matsapha Industrial site and opposite the turn off to Kwaluseni campus), tel: Manzini 52884. One of the few gourmet restaurants in Swaziland. Run by a highly individual Hungarian. Should book for the evening.

Markets: Mahlanya market is a large country market selling mainly local food produce on the main road shortly after Lobamba royal village. There is a bus station at the market place and buses can be caught to both Mbabane and Manzini.

Tsheshwe Craft is a small and highly innovative privately run craft centre in the Malkerns valley. Handmade clothing in local African cotton prints, batik, patchwork, basketry, unusual clay beadwork and leatherwork all produced by local craftsmen. Tsheshwe is found on the Malkerns road. Take a right turn at Mahlanya Market travelling on the main road Mbabane to Manzini. Thatcher's Silverware, near the First House restaurant and Yen Saan Hotel, specialises in individually hand-crafted work in silver.

Manzini

Situated 40 kms south of Mbabane, Manzini is the industrial hub of Swaziland and an agricultural centre. The town itself offers comfortable hotels, well-stocked shops and a Swazi market where traditional handcrafts can be bought at modest prices.

Restaurants: George Hotel, tel: Manzini 52061. Has two restaurants – one of which opens attractively onto the hotel garden. Continental cuisine

Mozambique Restaurant, tel: Manzini 52489. Specialises in Portuguese food.

Siteki

The only town on the Lubombo escarpment, Siteki is a convenient stopping place to or from Mozambique; the Mhlumeni border post is 28 km away. The old-fashioned but comfortable Bamboo Inn is one of the oldest in the country.

Big Bend

In the sugar growing area of the southern Lowveld, Big Bend is situated on a bend of the Great Usutu River. Besides the sugar estates which cover vast tracts, the surrounding countryside is very attractive, particularly in winter when the aloes are in bloom.

Places of Interest

Mbabane, Ezulwini, Manzini area

Pine Valley: This is on the Luve road from Mbabane; there is a series of waterfalls on the Black Mbuluzi river to the left. On the right is the bald rock, Sibebe.

Dlangeni Hills: Take the turning to Fonteyn on the Pine Valley road and drive up to the radio mast. There is a wonderful view of Mbabane.

Tea Road: This is signed off on the east side of the main highway at Ezulwini about 10 kms from Mbabane. This road to the tea growing areas gives marvellous views of the Mdzimba mountains.

Mantenga Falls: These are spectacular; ask for the directions at the Mantenga Falls Hotel 18 kms south of Mbabane.

Ngwenya and Pigg's Peak area

Lion Cavern: This 10 m cavern and other ancient excavations cut into the cliff-face of Ngwenga mountain near Kadake, date back to BC 43,000. It is probably the oldest mine in the world. Permission to explore the workings may be obtained on application to the Swaziland Iron Ore Development Company Limited, PO Box 444, Mbabane (43311).

Malolotsha Falls: This is the highest waterfall in Swaziland. Take the Motshane/Pigg's Peak road and follow a

track to the left about 15 kms (there are two sharp bends in the road and the track is just beyond the second bend). When you come to a rocky hill (about 2 kms from the road) park and walk northward for about 4 kms. Hard going and difficult to find but well worthwhile.
Sotho Ruins: These are near the Barytes Mine just beyond Kadake Station.
Rock Paintings: There are over 20 examples of rock paintings in Swaziland, all but one of which are attributed to Bushmen. The most famous painting is at the Nsangwini Shelter near Pigg's Peak; ask the District Office at Pigg's Peak for a guide. Visitors interested in seeing other rock paintings should ask the Swaziland Archaeological Society for advice.
Magonigoni Falls: Take the Balegane road from Pigg's Peak and turn left towards Matsamo after 37 km. After a further 20 km turn right opposite a signpost to Jacks on the left, and drive down to the falls, on the Mpofu river.
Phophonyane Falls: These are found about 18 km from Pigg's Peak on the Matsamo road.

Forbes Reef 'Ghost Town': About 10 km along the Motshane/Pigg's Peak road on the left are the remains of an early gold-mining centre, with cemetery, hotel and old workings.
Emlembe: This is the highest point in Swaziland (1862 m). To climb Emlembe, take the steep road to the left by the gate of the Havelock Golf Course, follow a path which peters out and then go straight up the face of the mountain. No mountaineering skill is needed.
Nginamodvolo Falls: These are on an impressive gorge on the Komati river. Ask the District Office, Pigg's Peak for a guide.

Hlatikulu and Hhlangano area
Khubutha Shelters: These are clusters of small caves 2½ kms to the west of Khubutha, once thought to be ancient mine workings, but now considered to have been shelters or strong-points used during Zulu raids, and possibly tombs. Many artefacts are found here.
Ndlozane Gorge: Turn right to Mashobeni on the road from Nhlangano to Gege and walk down to the very impressive gorge on the Ndlozane river.
Mahamba Gorge: This is a short walk behind the Mission station at Mahamba; ask for directions at the Mission.
Tshedi: A few kilometres to the south of Mbulungwane are three enormous vertical boulders to the east of the road. Tshedi means 'High Boulders'. They are called 'The Three Sisters' – said to be the 'Three Silent Ones' of H. Rider Haggard's 'King Solomon's Mines'.
Bulunga Poort: This is a splendid waterfall on the Great Usutu river. In Manzini take the Sidvokodvo road to Hlatikulu and turn left after 15 kms. Park your car after 14 kms. The local Swazis will willingly guide you to the falls which are a short walk from the road.

ZAIRE

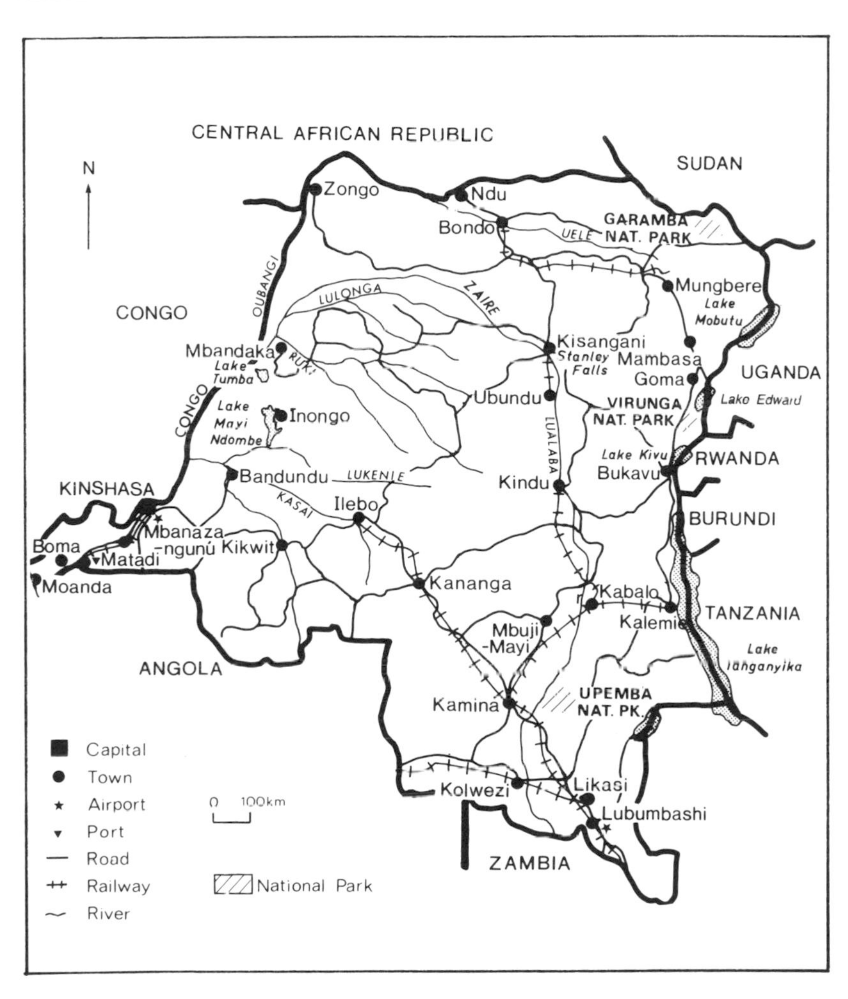

Area: 2,345,000 sq km
Population: 34.71 million (1989 World Bank)
Capital: Kinshasa

Zaire is not the easiest country in Africa for conventional tourism, but the rural areas are well worth a visit for those who have a spirit of adventure and are looking for out-of-the-way, unspoiled places. The Kivu, on Zaire's eastern border, with its lakes, mountain ranges and game parks, offers a variety of safari circuits for tourists. In the government capital Kinshasa and the copper capital of Lubumbashi, visitors are exposed to the international lifestyle of the black and white elite as well as to the impoverished Zairean masses in their daily struggle for survival.

The Land and The People

Zaire is the third largest country in Africa, about eighty times the size of its former colonial power, Belgium. The country's size has endowed it with a tremendous variety of assets including vast mineral resources, almost unlimited agricultural potential and abundant wildlife. There are mountain ranges, equatorial forests, vast plains, highland plateaux and many picturesque lakes, rivers and valleys. However, because of its size, Zaire is also crippled by transport problems, and tribal and ethnic differences.

The tremendous Zaire river dominates the country and has played a vital role in human settlement and economic development. This river has the second largest volume of water of any river in the world, being fed alternately by rains in the northern and southern hemispheres.

There are between 200 and 250 tribes in Zaire, yet despite differences, there exists a certain unity which distinguishes the peoples of Zaire from peoples of other African cultures. Most of the inhabitants of the rural areas of Zaire gain a precarious living from agriculture. The collapse of Zaire's infrastructure in recent years has made it almost impossible to market agricultural produce, and there has been a widespread return to subsistence farming. Crops produced include cassava, corn, bananas, groundnuts, papayas, sugar cane, coffee, tea and palm oil. Generally the men clear the land, and then the women plant and cultivate the crops. Fishing is also important for those people who live along Zaire's numerous rivers and lakes.

Special mention should be made of the pygmies, a peaceable nomadic forest-dwelling people, easily identifiable by their unique physical features. Despite attempts by the Belgian government before independence and the Zairean government after, to integrate the pygmies of the forests into modern life, many have managed to maintain their hunting and gathering existence.

Culture

Zaire has a strong artistic tradition and the National Museum is making a determined effort to conserve this cultural heritage. During the past few years, thousands of valuable objects have been collected, identified and classified at the National Museum headquarters at Mont Ngaliema in

Kinshasa. The museum also has an impressive collection of traditional music recordings and photos taken on numerous trips into remote areas of the country. Though the museum's storerooms are not open to the general public (special permission can sometimes be obtained), a small but impressive exhibition of traditional Zairean art has been established temporarily at the Beaux Arts Academy, until sufficient funds are available for a full-scale museum.

Though traditional Zairean music is basically vocal, a large assortment of musical instruments exists, the most important of which is the drum – the source of rhythm. The museum in Kinshasa has a vast assortment of drums, one of the most interesting of which is the type used for relaying messages, the 'telephone drum'. Other traditional instruments include the harp, zither, lute, horn, flute, whistle and xylophone. Modern Zairean music is the most popular in Africa. The songs have an urgent rhythm but a curiously sad and lilting melody. The instruments used are straightforward and familiar, drums and guitars, but more and more traditional instruments are being rediscovered.

Traditional dance is sometimes very complex. The most famous is probably the ballet 'bobongo' of the Konda tribe, but there are many others, including the Intore dancers of Kivu and the dances of the Bapende and of the Lunda.

In addition to the museum of traditional art, the Beaux Arts Academy of Kinshasa holds an art exhibition every Sunday morning from 1000 am to 1200 noon. Visitors can admire and purchase, at reasonable prices, modern art ranging from wood sculpture to paintings, and ceramics to beaten copper plaques. Various banks, embassies, hotels and commercial centres often organize exhibitions as well. Though the sale of genuine traditional art is rare, fairly good copies of traditional masks and carvings can be found or ordered at the art market in Kinshasa, near the railway station on the main boulevard.

History

The tropical forest which covers the whole central area of Zaire presented a formidable barrier to pre-Iron Age peoples who were unable to cut paths through it. Even now most habitation is confined to the river banks and the main mode of transport is the canoe. Along these rivers grew up small-scale kingdoms such as that of the Kuba people near Ilebo on the tributaries of the Kasai. In the far interior in the Ituri forests near the Uganda border the pygmies still live by hunting and gathering the fruits of the forest.

The Kongo kingdom became powerful in the 14th century before the arrival of the Portuguese in 1482. It was highly centralised under an autocratic king who controlled the currency of the country which was a particular kind of shell – the *nzimbu* – found only on Luanda Island and collected only by his officials.

The great expansion of East African trade in the mid-19th century had a major influence on most of eastern Zaire, and this is why Swahili is widely understood there. Traders seeking slaves, ivory and Katangan copper normally stayed many years in the interior raiding and trading, some even establishing their own kingdoms.

In the 1870s Livingstone reached Nyangwe; Cameron crossed the continent from Bagamoyo, through Nyangwe and Katanga to Benguela; and Stanley finally travelled right down the Congo from Nyangwe (1874-77). He was so impressed with the economic potential of the country that he urged European countries to take over the area. King Leopold of Belgium was the only ruler interested at the time, so from 1879 to 1885 Stanley made treaties with various peoples to establish a Belgian sphere of influence.

The country's present boundaries were established following the Berlin Conference of 1884-5 which brought together representatives of the European powers. The 'Congo Free State', as it was then known, was personally ruled until 1908 by King Leopold of Belgium (who never visited the territory); it then became a full colony of Belgium.

The establishment of plantations and the discovery of great mineral wealth led to large-scale recruitment of labour, in its scale and nature not far removed from the horrors of the slave trade that King Leopold claimed to have eliminated. In some districts there was a serious depletion of the population.

From the 1930s onwards the urban centres grew rapidly. Congolese town-dwellers were divorced from their traditional ways of life which found no substitute in the cities. It was the emergent class of European-educated urban Congolese, or *évolués* that led the nationalist movement. The Belgian failure to recognise their aspirations until too late was responsible for much that followed.

The Congo became independent in June 1960. Within a week of independence a mutiny occurred within the *Force Publique* (the combined army and gendarmerie) which still did not have a single Congolese officer. Subsequent events led to the temporary flight of most European residents, the collapse of the administration and the new Government's appeal for United Nations' intervention. The Province of Katanga, under Moise Tshombe (backed by Belgian financial interests and European mercenaries) seceded.

Crisis followed crisis for the next six years. The first Prime Minister, Patrice Lumumba, was early removed from office and then murdered. His supporters set up a rival government in Stanleyville (now Kisangani). The secession of Katanga was finally ended by UN military action at the beginning of 1963.

When the UN forces left in 1964 a nation-wide rebellion challenged the Government. Tshombe, switching roles, became the Prime Minister of the central government – but he did not last long. A military coup brought young General Mobutu to power in November 1965. Thereafter law and order was gradually restored, the foreign mercenaries were expelled, a new constitution set up, and President Mobutu began to consolidate his power through his single party *Mouvement Populaire de la Révolution (MPR).*

General Mobutu's search for new national objectives was responsible for the renaming of the country in 1971, followed by changes in the names of many regions, towns and institutions and even of Zairean citizens.

In 1973 a policy of Zaireanisation led to the take-over of 1,500 foreign-owned enterprises which were given to Zaireans chosen by the State. This measure proved a fiasco; many of the new Zairean owners merely emptied the bank accounts of their newly acquired enterprises. In an effort to patch up the damage and punish the greedy and corrupt political elite, in 1974 President Mobutu declared 'radicalisation'. This measure returned to the State most business which had been Zaireanised. They were in turn given to other Zaireans. At the same time Zaireans were forbidden to maintain foreign bank accounts or own property abroad and their children were forbidden to attend foreign schools. Religious-run schools within the country were closed. These measures, accompanied by falling copper prices, the closing of the Benguela Railway (vital for the efficient export of Zaire's minerals), galloping inflation and increased oil prices, produced such disastrous consequences for Zaire, that in 1976 the State asked the former expatriate owners to return. The response, however, was less than enthusiastic.

During the Angolan Civil War, Zaire supported Holden Roberto and the CIA-backed FLNA. This effort proved costly and unsuccessful. In 1977 and 1978 Zaire got a dose of its own medicine when FLNC (Front National pour la Libération du Congo) rebels invaded Zaire's mineral-rich Shaba province from their bases in Angola. In the first invasion the rebels were dispersed by a joint Moroccan/Zairean military effort. However, during the second invasion of May 1978 the rebels took the key mining town of Kolwezi and were only repulsed when the Zairean army retook Kolwezi airport and French Foreign legionaires were parachuted into the town. Before peace was restored about a thousand people were killed. The expatriates were evacuated from the town and a 2,500 man Inter-African peace-keeping force was brought in to maintain security. The mining industry suffered setbacks due to the disruption and the loss of expatriate technicians.

Following the second Shaba invasion, President Mobutu took steps to improve relations with Angola. In an effort towards national reconciliation, he declared a general amnesty for all Zaireans living outside the country as refugees. This amnesty offer was remarkably successful as an estimated 150,000 refugees, most from Angola, decided to return to Zaire. However, hopes among Western supporters of the regime that some liberalisation might follow proved completely unfounded. Mobutu declared that there would not be another political party in Zaire as long as he lived.

No end was in sight in the country's political and economic problems. Some ministers and heads of State enterprises, accused of fraud and corruption, was relieved of their posts, but no real cleansing was possible as the President himself was known to be deeply implicated in illegal exports and other lucrative operations. The Zairean people continue to suffer the effects of falling production and high inflation; IMF-controlled measures to restore Zaire's finances were not designed to relieve the sufferings of the people. Malnutrition is rife, especially in the towns as successive devaluations of the currency have reduced the already low purchasing power of the inhabitants. Still, there is no sign of an end to Western financial and military support for Mobutu, without which he could not remain in power.

Economy

While Zaire has tremendous natural resources, development has been hindered by the country's size, insufficient human and institutional resources, and an inadequate transport infrastructure. Economic investment has been generally concentrated on large, capital-intensive projects, particularly mining. Governmental corruption is endemic and has had a disastrous effect on development.

Since independence, agriculture has been seriously neglected and the Zaireanisation measures taken in 1973 made the situation worse. There was a rise in food imports to compensate for the agricultural shortfalls which constitute about 20 per cent of Zaire's domestically financed imports. Subsistence farming in the rural areas continues and occupies between 70 per cent and 75 per cent of the population, but low producer prices and transport difficulties have discouraged production of cash crops.

Principal large-scale crops are coffee, tea, cocoa, oil palm, and rubber. Other products include timber, groundnuts, cotton, sugar, maize, fish, meat, bananas, cassava, millet and sorghum. While Zaire could have helped compensate its losses due to low copper prices in 1976 and 1977 by high coffee prices, it is estimated that about half its coffee production left the country fraudulently, losing Zaire around $300 million. Illegal exports of diamonds to the Congo and of ivory to Burundi are also on a massive scale.

The mining industry accounts for over 80 per cent of the country's total exports. Zaire is the world's largest producer of cobalt and industrial diamonds, while copper is its greater source of foreign exchange revenues. Manganese, tin, zinc and silver are among other minerals produced, and some petroleum is extracted from offshore fields. Since 1974 mining production levels have generally been very low.

In the early 1970's high copper prices and almost unlimited international borrowing caused Zaire to throw caution and economy to the wind. Enormous and costly capital-intensive prestige projects such as the ultra-modern Voice of Zaire mass media centre, the World Trade Centre and an oil refinery, were conceived during this period. But in the mid-1970's inflation struck. With rising oil prices, falling copper prices and tightening up of international lending, Zaire was forced to re-examine its priorities. Almost non-existent economic planning, soaring government expenditures, lack of budgetary control, arrears in repayments of foreign debts and rampant graft and corruption finally forced the Government, in 1978, to allow the International Monetary Fund to undertake remedial action. The IMF was invited to establish and implement a stabilisation plan for Zaire. An IMF mission was established in Kinshasa and virtually took over management of the Zairean economy; in return, Zaire was given access to massive credit facilities. Measures were taken to limit Government expenditure, halt corruption and remedy inefficiency in State organisations, but Zaire remains a very bad risk for its Western creditors. Despite favourable terms of lending, both governmental and private loans have had to be repeatedly rescheduled to prevent Zaire being forced to default. Zaire's fundamental problems of heavy budgetary deficits, high inflation and the struggle to keep up with payments on foreign debt plagued the economy in the 1980s.

Wildlife

Zaire has wildlife in great abundance and variety and an effort has been made to preserve it. However, in recent years, poaching, especially of elephants for their ivory, has become so prevalent that it is now feared that if drastic action is not taken soon, this tremendous asset will be beyond recovery.

There are eight different reserves, encompassing about 15 per cent of Zaire's territory. The most well known and easily accessible for tourists is the 8,000 sq km Virunga National Park. This park includes many environmental zones such as active volcanoes in the southern section, like the 11,500 ft Nyragongo which erupted in 1977, vast savannahs, forests, rivers, and Lake Edward. The central part of the park contains the largest concentration of hippopotamus in the world, estimated at about 26,000. There are also buffalo, antelope (including cob, topi, bushbuck, waterbuck and reedbuck), lion, leopard, elephant, monkeys and baboons, wild pigs, jackals and hyaenas.

Zaire has 1,086 species of birds, many of which can be observed in the Virunga National Park and further to the north in the Ituri forest at Mont Hoyo. Included among these birds are the metallic-coloured sunbirds, the industrious if noisy weavers, honey-guides, partridge, storks (including the black, red and yellow saddle-bill) an assortment of eagles and the stately crowned crane.

Mont Hoyo is home to the chimpanzee, to a wide variety of monkeys, including the majestic black and white colobus, and to the very rare and elusive okapi. The Kahuzi-Biega National Park, near the town of Bukavu, was created to protect the mountain gorilla. Excursions for tourists have been organised to observe these gorillas in the wild. Though the trip can prove exhausing, it is well worth the effort. The Garamba National Park, in Haute Zaire, is open from December to June, but is difficult to reach and lodging is rudimentary. It has white rhinoceros and giraffe. The Upemba National Park in Shaba region has zebra, eland, roan and black antelope.

For mountain climbing enthusiasts there are the Ruwenzori mountain range or 'Mountains of the Moon' situated almost on the equator. The 5,120 m high crystalline mountains, the third highest in Africa, are covered with eternal snow at the summit. Guided excursions generally take six days.

On Zaire's eastern border are several of Africa's most important lakes, Tanganyika, Kivu, Edward and Mobutu (formerly Albert). All except for Kivu are rich in fish, as are the rivers which cross the country. Fish include catfish, mbenga and tarpon in the Zaire estuary, and tilapia which are fished commercially in the lakes.

Unorthodox advertising in Lubumbashi

ALAN RAKE

General Information

Government

General Mobutu Sese Seko is President of the Republic, High Commander of the Armed Forces and head of the police. The sole political party, President Mobutu's *Movement Populaire de la Révolution* (MPR) was founded in 1967.

Languages

The official administrative language is French, while Lingala, one of the four major national languages, is the official language of the Zairean Armed Forces. Swahili, Tshiluba and Kikongo are the three other main national languages. Local tribal languages are generally of the Bantu language group.

Religions

Christianity (Catholic, Protestant and Kimbanguist), Islam and traditional African animism.

How to Get There

By air: Air Zaire flies to 15 countries. In Europe: Brussels, Paris, Athens and Rome.
In Africa: Lagos, Nairobi, Libreville, Bangui, Abidjan, Luanda, Lome, Douala, Dakar and Conakry.

Other National Airlines which link up with Kinshasa are: Aeroflot, Air Cameroun, Air Gabon, Alitalia, Ethiopian Airways, Iberian, Lufthansa, Sabena, Swissair, TAP and UTA.

Kinshasa's airport, N'Djili, is 29 kilometers from the centre of the city. Taxis are expensive and fares should be agreed upon in advance.

By road: The rivers Zaire and Oubangui which form the country's western and northern frontiers can be crossed by car-carrying ferries from Brazzaville to Kinshasa, Bangui to Zongo and Bangassou to Ndu. The Brazzaville-Kinshasa ferry provides a very cheap hourly service. When you get to Zaire, however, be prepared for some of the worst road conditions in Africa, especially in the forest areas during the rainy seasons.

There are also roads, in varying states of disrepair, from Juba in Sudan, Fort Portal and Kabele in Uganda, Bujumbura in Burundi, the Copperbelt in Zambia and Kigali in Rwanda. The latter road is well-used and adequate at least as far as Lubumbashi.

By rail: Passenger services on trains from the Angolan port of Lobito through Zaire's mineral-rich Shaba Province were interrupted in 1975 during the Angolan Civil War and have not been opened since.

By sea: Regular 14-day passenger services operate between Zaire's Matadi port (350 km from Kinshasa), and Antwerp, Belgium. This service is run by the Compagnie Maritime Belge (CMB) and the Compagnie Maritime du Zaire (CMZ).

Entry Regulations

All visitors must hold a valid passport and entry visa, which should be applied for from the Zaire diplomatic mission in or nearest to their own country of residence. Visas will only be issued if there is proof of one's intention to leave the country after the visit (eg a return ticket). Transit visas will be issued at the point of entry on presentation of a visa for the destination country. Visitors arriving without a visa may be authorised to stay for 72 hours on surrendering their passport. Passports, visas and vaccination certificates are checked on all internal flights.

Obtaining a Zaire visa, going through customs and immigration, and then travelling within the country once you finally get in, often prove time consuming and nerve wracking. Ample time and adequate patience are thus essential for an enjoyable visit to Zaire.

Customs Regulations

As well as personal effects, 200 cigarettes and an unopened bottle of spirits may be taken into the country free of duty. Customs men keep a sharp watch for precious stones, whether smuggled or not, and for rough ivory or authentic old sculptures.

There is no restriction on the import or export of foreign currency, but it must be declared on entry and the balance on departure. There is a flourishing currency black market, offering exchange rates far above the official level. No local currency may be taken out of the country.

Climate

Zaire is such an enormous country that it is impossible to summarise the climate briefly. The country straddles the equator. In general it is hot and humid, but the Kivu, Shaba and Ituri regions have temperate climates. Roughly speaking, the dry seasons in the north correspond to the rainy seasons in the south. Thus around Kisangani the main dry season is from December to February, followed by a short rainy season in March and May, another short dry season in June and finally a long rainy season in June to November. But around Kinshasa and Lubumbashi the long dry season runs from May to October followed by short rains in November, another dry season in December and January and a long rainy season from February to April. In the eastern mountain area (on the equator) there are only two short dry seasons, in January and July.

On the whole the temperature varies between 20°C and 30°C in the tropical forest and between 15°C and 25°C on the high plateau.

What to wear: Lightweight, loose-fitting clothing is best, though a sweater is necessary for the dry season or if travelling in Kivu or Shaba provinces. An umbrella is convenient during the rainy season. In the city a lightweight suit is required for formal occasions. Take sunglasses and a hat for prolonged exposure to the sun.

Health Precautions

Take precautions against malaria before, during and after your stay. Other hazards to health are dysentery, typhoid, scrub typhus, yellow fever and bilharzia. Tap water should be boiled and filtered before drinking. Medical services are available in city centres and at religious

Bapende initiation dance

SARAH ERRINGTON

missions in the interior, though medicines are sometimes in short supply. If travelling in the interior, take insect repellent, and water purification tablets.

Banks and Currency

Banque du Zaire: BP 2697, blvd. Colonel Tshiatchi au Nord, Kinshasa
Banque Grindlay International au Zaire SZARL: Les Galéries Presidentielles, Place du 27 Octobre, BP 16297, Kinshasa
Banque de Kinshasa SZARL: ave. Tombalbaye, Place du Marché, BP 8033, Kinshasa
Banque de Paris et des Pays-Bas Zaire: bldg. Unibra, ave Col. Ebeya, BP 1600, Kinshasa
Banque du Peuple: blvd. du 30 Juin, BP 400, Kinshasa
Banque Internationale pour l'Afrique au Zaire (BIAZ): ave. de la Douane, BP 8725, Kinshasa
Barclays Bank SZARL – Zaire: 9 ave. de l'Equateur, BP 1299, Kinshasa
Caisse Générale d'Epargne du Zaire (CADEZA): 38 ave. de la Caisse d'Epargne, BP 8147, Kinshasa-Gombe
Citibank (Zaire) Ave Lukusa/Ebeya, BP 9999, Kinshasa
Union Zairoise de Banques SARL: 19 ave. de la Nation, BP 197, Kinshasa
Currency: Zaire divided into 100 Makutas (Exchange rates p.10)

Business Hours

Banks: Monday-Friday 0800-1130
Government Offices: Monday-Friday 0730-1330; Saturday 0730-1200
Offices: Monday-Friday 0730-1200 and 1430-1700; Saturday 0730-1200
Shops: Monday-Saturday 0800-1200 and 1500-1800
Early closing is 1200 on Wednesday

Public Holidays

New Year's Day, 1 January
Martyrs of Independence, 4 January
Labour Day, 1 May
Anniversary of the MPR, 20 May
Zaire Day, 24 June
Independence Day, 30 June
Parent's Day, 1 August
Youth Day, 14 October
Anniversary of the country's name change to Zaire, 27 October
National Army Day, 17 November
Anniversary of Regime, 24 November
Christmas Day, 25 December

Embassies in Kinshasa

Austria: BP 16399, 6 étage, Galéries Presidentielles, tel: 21310
Belgium: Bldg, Le Cinquantenaire, Place du 27 Octobre, BP 899, tel: 24424
Burundi: BP 1483
Cameroon: BP 10998
Canada: BP 8341, l'étage, blvd du 30 Juin, tel: 22706
Central African Republic: BP 7769
Chad: BP 9097
Congo: BP 9516
France: BP 5236, ave de la République du Tchad, tel: 22669
Gabon: BP 9592
Germany FR: BP 8400, 210 ave Lumpungu, tel: 26933
Italy: 8 ave de la Mongola, BP 1000, tel: 22575
Ivory Coast: 68 ave de la Justice, BP 91097
Kenya: BP 9667, 5002 ave Major Ruivet, tel: 30117
Morocco: BP 912
Netherlands: BP 10299, 11 ave Zongo Ntolo, tel: 30638
Nigeria: BP 1700, 141 B blvd du 30 Juin, tel: 31229
Rwanda: BP 967
Spain: BP 8036, Bldg 11 République, ave 30 Juin, tel: 30752
Sudan: BP 7374
Sweden: BP 11096, 17 ave du Port, tel: 23105
Switzerland: BP 8724, ave Lumpungu, tel: 22285
Tanzania: BP 1612, 142 blvd du 30 Juin, tel: 32117

Tunisia: BP 1498, tel: 31632
Uganda: BP 1086
UK: BP 8049, tel: 23483
USA: BP 697, 310 ave des Aviateurs, tel: 25881
Zambia: BP 1144, ave de l'École 54-58, tel: 23038

Transport

By air: Air Zaire links Ndjili Airport (Kinshasa) with about 40 airports in Zaire, including Lubumbashi, Bukavu, Goma, Mouji-Mayi, Kisangani, Bandundu and all the important towns. Service, however, is often irregular. Small planes are available for charter.
River and lake car-carrying ferries: Kinshasa to Kisangani via Mbandaka, generally takes about seven days. Passage should be booked with ONATRA. Getting a ticket can be a problem, as tickets are not sold until the day before the boat arrives. Only luxury and first class are recommended. Kinshasa to Ilebo takes about five days but boats are poorly equipped for tourists. Boat service, when fuel is available, exists between Goma and Bukavu on lake Kivu (five hours).
By road: The roads in Zaire are in general of poor standard outside the main areas of population, except the stretches between Kinshasa and Matadi, Kinshasa and Kikwit, Lubumbashi and Ndola (Zambia), Lubumbashi and Kolwezi (serving the Zairean copperbelt), and Kisangani and Mambasa (eastern Zaire).

Bus services are available in and between main towns but buses are crowded and distances are great. In city centres taxis are usually avaiable and fares are cheap, at about Z15 per trip, because of devaluations of the Zaire.
Car hire: This services is available in Kinshasa on a limited basis. Apply at Autoloc, Avenue des Aviateurs, Kinshasa, tel: 23322, or Hertz, Centre Commercial International du Zaire, tel: 32012.
By rail: The main internal route is from Lubumbashi to Ilebo, with a branch from Kamina to Kalemie (on Lake Tanganyika). Kinshasa is connected by rail to the port at Matadi. Rail travel is not recommended for tourists.

Accommodation and Food

Hotels and restaurants that cater for Europeans are luxurious, but expensive and often heavily booked. It is advisable to make reservations in advance.

There are good restaurants in the main towns, serving both European and Zairean dishes (such as *moambe* chicken cooked in fresh palm oil, with rice and spinach).

Hotels

NAME	ADDRESS	TELEPHONE	TELEX
KINSHASA			
Afrique Hotel	BP 1711	319.02	
Guest House	ave de Flambeau	234.90	
Intercontinental Hotel	BP 9535	318.00	21212
Hotel le Memling	ave de la République	232.60	

[Hotels]		
Hotel Okapi	BP 8697	596.22
MOANDA		
Hotel Mangrove	BP 51	–
BOMA		
Hotel Boma	BP 252	–
Hotel Excelsior	BP 30	–
Hotel Mabuila	Boma	–
MATADI		
Hotel Métropole	BP 49	–
MBANZANGUNU		
Hotel Cosmopolite	BP 57	–
MBANDAKA		
Hotel Ancien	BP 90	–
LUBUMBASHI		
Hotel Karavia	BP 4701	4511
Park Hotel	837 ave du Kasai	3523
BUKAVU		
Hotel Résidence	88 ave Mobutu	2131
Hotel Riviera	Blvd Elisabeth	2326
[Hotels]		
KOLWEZI		
Hotel Impala	BP 209	2421
MBUJI-MAYI		
Hotel Mukeba	22 ave Serpents	–

[Hotels]

KANGA

Hotel Atlanta	700 ave Lumumba	2828
Hotel Musube	ave Commerce	2438
KISANGANI		
Hotel des Chutes	ave Mobutu	3498
Hotel Zaire Palace	ave de l'Eglise	2664

NATIONAL PARKS

VIRUNGA NATIONAL PARK

Hotel des Grands Lac	PO Box 253, Goma	–
Hotel Kariba	Lake Kivu	–
Hotel Kikyou-Butembo	Goma	–
GARAMBA NATIONAL PARK		
Auberge du Mont Hoyo	Bunia	–
Hotel Ngoto	Bunia	–
Hotel Semliki	Bunia	–

Kinshasa

Formerly Leopoldville, until the local name for the area was restored in May 1966, Kinshasa was developed as the centre of commerce and colonial administration. It has a population of two million and is administered as a series of communes, with clearly identifiable smart residential areas, a business centre, and a government centre. It remains, in effect, a divided city with the shops and airline offices on one side and with the Cité, a huge sprawling African township, on the other. Expatriate businessmen and the élite of Zairean Government circles live in the hilly residential area in large detached houses. In the township, groups from various up-country areas live together in cramped conditions.

The city centre has the Boulevard du 30 Juin with luxury shops, banks and airline offices. Mont Ngaliema (formerly Stanley) once had a statue of the explorer, but this was removed in the 'return to authenticity' campaign. The present government has developed an elaborate presidential park with extravagant but attractive formal gardens. This park is now closed to the public for security reasons. The Organisation of African Unity has its own village built on

President Mobutu's orders for the summit meeting in 1967. It has now been opened to the public as a hotel and restaurant, a zoo and a recreation ground, including a swimming pool and tennis courts.

Other sights include the MPR party's town of N'Sele, the open air markets, the University, Kinkole fishing village, Lake Vert, Lake de Ma Vallée, the Black River, the Kinsuka rapids, the National Museum, the Beaux Arts Academy and a scenic walk along the Zaire river.

Restaurants: There are restaurants offering French, Belgian and Zairean cuisine with a wide choice of dishes. Do not be surprised if the service tends to be slow: the result is usually excellent.

The main restaurants in the town are good but expensive. They draw their customers chiefly from businessmen. La Devinière in Binza, the Stirwen on the Boulevard du 30 Juin, the Zoo and la Pergola in town are four among the number of first-rate restaurants. Others in town are the Mandarin (Chinese), Chez Nicola (Italian), Namouna (Tunisian) the New Pub (Oriental), the Plein Vent (fondu), the Chateau and Lolo la Crevette (shrimps). There are also some cafes and snack bars.

Entertainment: Zairean bands are hard to beat; they have a keen local following and move about from bar to bar depending on whether they are well or badly treated by proprietors. Kinshasa is a lively, late-night town and a visit to a nightclub in the Cité is a must.

Nightclubs in Kinshasa include Succès; Un, Deux, Trois; Tshopo, Jambo Jambo; La Rigole; Vatican Club; and Madiata. Casinos include Kin Casino, Olympic, Playboy, Casino National.

Sports: Tennis is very popular and can be played at the Cercle de Kinshasa, Athenée, Elaeis, Familia clubs, OAU and Funa sport centre. Swimming at the OAU and N'Sele Pool. Riding at the Centre Hippique de Kinshasa, l'Etrier. Boating at the Nautic Club de Kinshasa and the Yacht Club.

Shopping and Markets: There are ambitious curio shops in the main streets and a small open-air souvenir market near the railway station on the main boulevard. The central market is large

Kinshasa market scene

MARION KAPLAN

and colourful. Everything is sold there from African wax material to fresh ginger, from woven baskets to magic potions. Prices can be cheap if you have the patience to haggle with the vendors.

Large shops sell goods imported from Europe, but prices are high and it is not a town in which to think casually of buying clothes. Local craftwares on sale include ivory objects, ebony carvings, bracelets, crocodile and snakeskin bags, and semi-precious stones and paintings.

Tourist information: National Office for Tourism, Blvd du 30 Juin (BP 9502), tel: 224.17.

Travel agencies: Agetraf, Avenue Equateur 87, BP 8834, tel: 269.21;
Amiza, Avenue des Aviateurs, BP 7597, tel: 246.02, 230.83;
Immo-Voyages, Blvd du 30 Juin 22A, BP 798, tel: 222.63;
Zaire Tours: Blvd du 30 Juin 11, BP 14795, tel: 222.38;
Zaire Travel Service, Blvd du 30 Juin 11, BP 15812, tel: 232.88.

Lower Zaire, Bandundu, and Equator Regions

These regions are accessible for travellers staying in Kinshasa, though there are hotels in the main towns. The lower Zaire region stretches to the Atlantic at **Moanda,** a relaxing spot with long stretches of lovely, almost deserted beaches. Though the sand is white, the water is coloured a dirty brown from the Zaire river. Fishing is excellent.

Bomba, on the north bank, is also a good place to stay; visit the Mayumbe forest area with its caves, waterfalls and ancient tombs.

Village women

CAMERAPIX

Matadi, on the southern river bank, is Zaire's major port, it is a bustling and colourful town built on terraces along rocky hillsides. There is a ferry for cars over the river.

Other sights in the Lower Zaire region are the Inga hydroelectric scheme, Kisantu botanical gardens and the massive Zongo Falls. A centre for this entire area is the town of Mbanzangungu (formerly Thysville).

In Bandundu province is the low-lying lake that used to bear the name of King Leopold, now called Lake Mai-Ndombe. The pleasant town of Inongo on its shores is accessible by river transport from Kinshasa. It is the best centre for seeing the unrivalled Bayaka and Bapende dancers. In the far south of the region, on the Angolan frontier, are the Tembo and Kasongo-Lunda Falls.

The main town of Equator region is **Mbandaka,** set in the heart of Africa's deepest forests, and accessible only by river transport. About 100 km away is the town of Bikoro on Lake Tumba, with the Eala botanical gardens.

Lubumbashi

Formerly Elisabethville, this is the main town of the country's copperbelt. There are continual blue skies, bougainvilla-lined avenues and an excellent golf course.

Shaba and Kasai Regions

The open, undulating land of Southern Zaire is dotted with lakes such as the Fwa and Munkamba in Kasai and waterfalls such as the Kiobo Falls (60 km high, 250 m wide) on the Lufira river, the Lofoi Falls (340 m high the highest in Africa) north of Lubumbashi, the Johnston Rapids near Kasenga on the Luapala.

An excursion can be made from Lubumbashi to **Kalemie,** on Lake Tanganyika, over either the Kundelungu plateau or the Marungu plateau near lake Mweru. The region between the Lualaba river and Lake Tanganyika is picturesque, especially from the Portes d'Enfer ('Gates of Hell') near Kongola to Kyimbi Falls north of Kalemie, which is a beautifully situated town.

Bukavu

Remote from Kinshasa, Bukavu still has something of the air of an Edwardian watering place, with lakeside views and walks rather than mineral springs to refresh the visitor. Further information from Office National du Tourisme, Avenue President Mobutu, BP 2468, tel: 3001.

Kisangani

Formerly Stanleyville, the town is the headquarters of Upper Zaire Region (ex-Eastern Province), and grew at a point on the river where major waterfalls interrupted navigation. It was a Lumumbist stronghold, and during the years of conflict fairly extensive damage was done, much of which has not been repaired. There is river sailing, and at the Wagenia fisheries a charming fishing community catch the *capitaine du Zaire*, a large tasty fish, in special long baskets placed at the falls. They organise the work and placing of nets through a complex social structure which the village children will happily explain to visitors. The town has a busy central market.

Tourist information: Local tourist information can be obtained from Office National du Tourisme, Avenue de l'Eglise, PO Box 1658, tel: 2648.

ZAMBIA

Zambia is a vast, thinly populated, tree-clad plateau at the heart of Africa, so high that the weather is perfect most of the year round, but especially so during the dry warm sunny days of May to October, the best season to go there.

The main attraction to visitors is without doubt the magnificent Victoria Falls. The Luangwa and Kafue National Parks offer a fascinating variety of animals and birds. Luangwa has the most prolific animal population in Africa. In many parts of the country traditional ceremonies are still very much alive and there are displays of Zambian dancing to be seen, particularly in Livingstone.

Zambia's tourist industry has been hit very hard by the combined effects of its economic recession and the war in Zimbabwe. Despite the ending of the war, serious shortages of basic goods continue, and there has been a significant rise in the incidence of violent crime.

The Land and The People

The Zambezi River marks the western border of the country. It has a broad, fertile flood-plain, where the traditional seasonal movements for agriculture are still adhered to and where canoes and boats are the best means of transport. In the south it becomes the frontier with Zimbabwe from the Victoria Falls to the 274 km long man-made lake of Kariba, formed when the dam was built for hydro-electric power in the 1950's. In the east and north east the country rises to pleasant hills, especially in the Mbala region.

The plateau – about 1,200 m high – is covered by deciduous savannah wood, small trees of no economic value, with occasional outlets of grassy plains or marshland alive with birds. Streams are fairly widespread and villages are sited near them, where the people grow one crop a year during the rainy season (November to April) and, in areas free from tsetse fly, keep cattle. Soils are on the whole sandy, acid and infertile, with pockets of better alluvial types.

In the Copperbelt region and elsewhere are mineral ores, producing copper, zinc and lead. The railway was first built (1906-10) to link the mines and almost all development since then has centred on this line of rail, from the industrial towns like Kitwe to the commercial farms of Southern Province. Altogether 6.8 million people live in this country which is almost the size of France and West Germany combined. The non-African population totals about 60,000 – Europeans, working mainly in mining and industry, Asians, mainly in commerce, and Coloureds (people of mixed race).

The country's motto is 'One Zambia, one nation', reflecting the aspiration to build a non-racial society, divided neither by race, colour nor tribe. There are six main African languages spoken: Bemba, Tonga, Lozi, Lunda, Luvale and Nyanja. While there is no lingua franca, Bemba is used on the Copperbelt, in the Northern and Luapula provinces; Nyanja is common in the Eastern Province and Lusaka. English is the official language and is widely spoken.

Culture

Most traditional Zambian craft is severely practical – undecorated pottery, a variety of spears or ingenious traps. The most interesting products perhaps are elaborate basketwork and carved food-bowls from Western and Eastern Provinces; carefully moulded pipe-ends in the form of animals or mythical

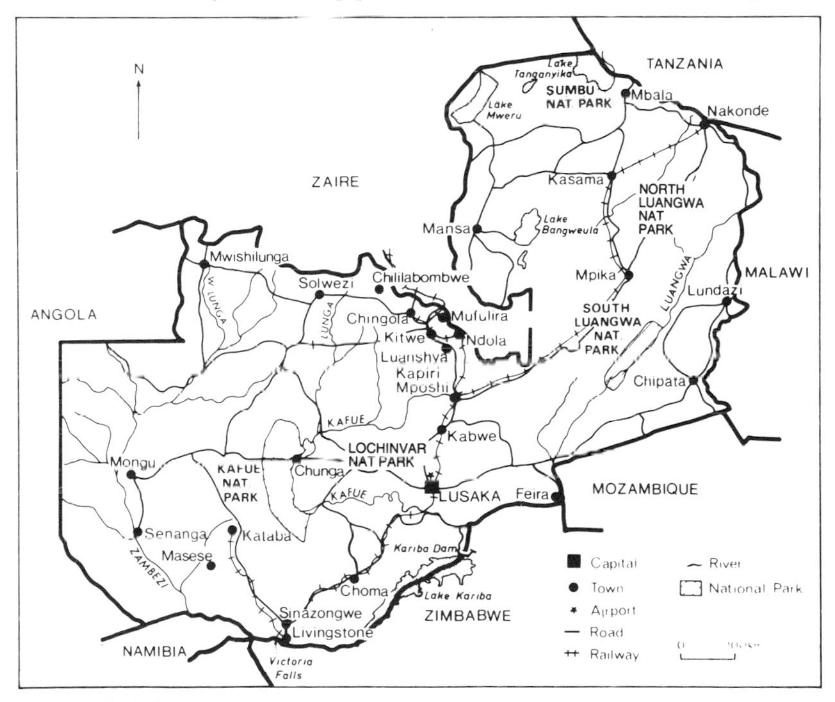

Area: 752,614 sq km
Population: 7.42 million (1989 World Bank)
Capital: Lusaka

creatures from Southern Province; and masks and disguises made of bark and mud, painted ferociously in black, white and red and worn by dancers from North Western Province.

All these may be seen at the Livingstone Museum, along with a comprehensive collection of musical instruments and the tools of the old economy, including copper crosses formerly used as currency and long thin baskets used to drain salt from mud on the Kafue Flats. Most of the crafts are dying out in the villages, but professional craftsmen continue and may be seen at work in the Maramba Cultural Centre at Livingstone. For anyone wanting to buy genuine Zambian curios it is advisable to visit these two places first, as many of the street-sellers' wares may come from East Africa or Zaire.

By contrast traditional dancing is very much alive and appreciated by Zambians in village, township and school. Visitors to the country can see a variety of different dances performed regularly at the Maramba Centre, Livingstone, and the cultural village in Lusaka.

One very colourful ceremony in the west of the country is the *Ku-omboka* during February or March, when the Lozi chief (the *Litunga*) moves all his goods and family, and is paddled by his councillors in striped barges along man-made canals from the main capital of Leaului to another at Limulunga, near Mongu, where they remain for the duration of the flood. A similar, less elaborate move, more accessible to the visitor, is the *Kufulehela* in about July when the royal court moves back again. Other annual ceremonies include the *Shimunenga* of the Ba-Ila people at Maala, on the Kafue Flats, in September or October, and the *Mutomboka* of the Lunda people in Luapula Province on 29 July. For details and information about visiting these ceremonies – contact the Zambia National Tourist Board.

History

Around the 2nd century AD, Zambians began to mine and use iron and to live in villages built on mounds, some of them developing a culture ancestral to the present-day Tonga of Southern Province. The most spectacular archaeological finds come from Ingombe Ilede, a site discovered while digging a bore-hole for the resettlement of the population when Kariba Lake was flooded in 1960-62. Here had been buried several bodies dressed in gold and copper ornaments, near a village which was possibly an outpost of the Zimbabwe empire in the 14th century. These are now in Livingstone Museum.

16th-19th century: From the 16th century small groups of people arrived, some as fugitives, some as conquerors, from the Luba and Lunda empires in Zaire and merged with the earlier population. Most of them set up very small chiefdoms in which the Chief was more a symbolic representative of the people than a figure of authority. However, some large kingdoms did emerge.

Kazembe ruled over the Lunda in Luapula Province, dominating production of the rich copper and salt mines of Katanga, trading with his forebears in Zaire and sporadically with the Portuguese on the East Coast.

Earlier, in Western Province, the Lozi (or Barotse) had organised a highly centralised economic system to exploit the Zambezi food-plain. All the regions sent men to dig canals and build mounds for villages, and all sent their products to the Paramount Chief to be redistributed to other areas.

For some time the Chief refused to sell slaves to traders, partly because he needed people so much in his labour-intensive system.

Zambia suffered greatly during the turbulent 19th century. The Kololo invaded Western Province and the Ngoni Eastern Province. At the same time Portuguese, Arab and Tanzanian slave traders reached Zambia in large numbers bringing guns for sale to those who would help them to collect slaves. So the country was torn by wars and raiding, especially around the fast-growing Bemba kingdom in Northern Province.

The colonial period: In 1890 Cecil Rhodes, who already controlled part of Rhodesia and planned to extend British rule from the Cape to Cairo, sent agents to make a treaty with Lewanika, the Lozi Paramount Chief, agreeing to 'protect' him in exchange of the right to mine in much of western Zambia. Gradually, the whole country was incorporated into the Northern Rhodesia protectorate and a railway linked it to South Africa, but in the north the Belgians in Zaire and the Germans in Tanzania foiled Rhodes' grand design.

The copper mines, which had been worked for centuries with simple iron tools, were mechanised in the 1920's and became the basis of Northern Rhodesia's economy. Whites mostly immigrated to the country at this time and settled along what became known as the 'Copperbelt', a 66-mile long stretch of land 200 miles north of the capital Lusaka. To serve the copper industry a railway line was built running from the border town of Livingstone in the south to the Copperbelt, and into the Katanga Province of what is now Zaire. Mining profits, however, went largely to shareholders in South Africa and Britain.

Independence: From 1953 to 1963 Zambia was federated with Rhodesia and Malawi, a link which in practice meant economic domination by Rhodesia, and which Africans feared would in future mean political domination by white Rhodesians. African nationalist feeling united in opposition to the Federation until finally Britain allowed the two northern territories to break away and become independent separately.

The independence movement was led by Kenneth Kaunda (Zambia's first President) and the United National Independence Party (UNIP). Independence was formally achieved on 24 October 1964.

A year later, the white ruling group in Rhodesia made their Unilateral Declaration of Independence (UDI). Therefore the early years of Zambia's independence were complicated by the need to disengage the country from the economic stranglehold of past links with Rhodesia.

During the 12 year struggle for majority rule in Rhodesia, about half of

Joshua Nkomo's ZAPU guerrilla army was based in Zambia as well as thousands of Zimbabwean refugees. These included over 15,000 school-age children in camps near Lusaka. Zambia's support of the guerrillas led to increasing tensions on the border with Rhodesia culminating in a series of brutal raids by Rhodesian forces into Zambia in 1978-79. These claimed the lives of over 2,000 people.

Zambia supported ZAPU's presence amidst its own growing internal problems. There was resentment among the Zambian people at the cost of the upkeep of the 'freedom fighters' when their own economic difficulties were becoming acute. Under increasing military and economic pressure from the Rhodesian army, Kaunda collaborated with the British Government and President Nyerere of Tanzania, at the Commonwealth Conference in Lusaka in July 1979, setting up the all-party Lancaster House conference in London in September 1979.

The war had effectively destroyed all Zambia's viable external communications with Tanzania, Angola and Botswana, and by November 1979, Zambia was left totally dependent on her railway link through Rhodesia to the south. It was essential that this continue to operate because, due to poor rains, the country was short of 300,000 tons of maize, which had to be imported from South Africa. During the settlement talks, Rhodesia threatened to close the southern rail link unless Kaunda ended his support for ZAPU guerrillas. Under enormous political and economic pressure, Zambia was forced to apply pressure in turn on the Patriotic Front to agree to the British proposals which finally led to Zimbabwean independence in April 1980.

The end of the war, however, and the removal of a heavy burden from the Zambian economy, did not bring the expected improvements in daily life and President Kaunda found himself with an increasingly disaffected population. Shortages of soap, oil, salt, milk and other basic commodities, which had been almost universal during the war, continued. Worker discontent at severe unemployment, high-level corruption and the increasingly high cost of living, resulted in a series of wildcat strikes in various sectors, including education and the railways. Zambia was also hit by an unprecedented wave of armed banditry. Authorities believed that gangsters were buying automatic weapons from former ZAPU guerrillas.

On the eve of the celebrations for the anniversary of Zambian independence in October 1980, a gang of well-armed men engaged security forces in a battle outside Lusaka. The government arrested a large number of Zambians including several prominent businessmen and middle-ranking officers. Zambia celebrated 20 years of independence on 24 October 1984 with Kaunda still firmly in charge.

Economy

Since 1968 State-owned companies have dominated the economy following a series of measures introduced by Dr Kaunda. The country's copper mines were originally developed by two mining houses – Anglo-American Corporation and Roan Selection Trust. In August 1969 the Government took a 51% holding in the two companies. However, despite the extension of State control, the fundamental characteristics of the Zambian economy remain – dependence on copper and supporting industries. Although the Copperbelt towns have boomed, rural incomes have fallen in relation to urban incomes and this has promoted a massive migration to the towns, giving rise to sprawling squatter settlements. The Zambian economy is presently in worse shape than it has ever been and the end of the Zimbabwean war has not terminated its economic problems. Foreign exchange earnings have fallen sharply as a result of the slide in copper prices. Lack of demand in the industrialised world has also made it difficult to sell cobalt, the country's second largest foreign exchange earner.

Efforts to improve agricultural performance have overall been disappointing and Zambia needs to import large quantities of food every year. Traditional farming employs some 600,000 small-holder families cultivating maize, cassava, groundnuts and sorghum and tending cattle. A series of post-independence projects including co-operatives, village regrouping and tractor schemes, have not met with much success. There is a serious shortage of agricultural advisers, essential equipment is lacking and the rural road system is poor. President Kaunda promised an ambitious 10-year food programme to make the country self-sufficient, but food imports were still necessary. The State marketing organisations continue to run inefficiently. As a consequence of low rainfall, the maize crop was poor in both 1979 and 1980, amounting to only half the country's requirements. The foreign currency earned from sales of cobalt and copper have therefore had to be spent on imports of food Zambia could produce itself. The deficit in maize is filled by imports from South Africa.

The government has embarked on a massive reorganisation of Zambia's tourist industry which has fallen behind those of Zimbabwe, Kenya and Malawi since independence in 1964. A Zambia National Tourist Board was set up. Zambia introduced auctions for its currency at the end of 1985, which resulted in a massive *de facto* devaluation followed by another twist in the inflationary spiral. It broke with the International Monetary Fund in May 1987 leading to another wave of readjustment and austerity.

Wildlife

Both the major game parks – Kafue and Luangwa – lie along rivers abounding in hippos and crocodiles, and birds like the fish-eagle (Zambia's emblem) and the crested crane. The plains beside the rivers are thronged with different kinds of buck, from the regal Kudu to the enchanting Thompson's gazelle and the red lechwe, which is unique to Zambia. Luangwa has the Thornicroft giraffe, not found elsewhere. Sumbu National

Park is by Lake Tanganyika.

These three parks contain elephant, rhino, lion and most other species of big game. For the more adventurous, walking safaris and hunting expeditions can be arranged. The Kafue River, Lake Kariba and Lake Tanganyika provide excellent fishing for bream, Nile perch, lake salmon and tiger fish. Altogether there are 18 gazetted National Parks in Zambia.

National Parks

Kafue National Park: The Kafue National Park through and around which runs the Kafue River, is as large as Wales. Game is plentiful, and includes buffalo, zebra, warthog, hippopotamus, hartebeest, lion and innumerable types of antelope, the rarest of which is the red lechwe which is found in no other part of Africa. Over 400 species of birdlife can be seen and the Kafue Flats is a treasure trove for bird lovers and photographers.

Some of the wildlife unique to Kafue National Park has been threatened by a hydroelectric scheme at the southern edge of the Kafue Flats which interferes with the cycle of natural flooding that gives the Flats their characteristic ecology.

There are seven camps open to the public: Ngoma, Nanzhila, Kalala, Chunga, Lufupa, Moshi and Ntemwa. Ngoma is the largest and has a hotel-type lodge with a restaurant, bar and swimming pool. Accommodation consists of double-roomed chalets. Zambia National Tourist Board run the full catering 40 bed Chunga Safari Village. At the other camps food and drink must be provided by the visitors but all necessary equipment, bedding, and maintenance staff, including a cook, are provided.

The whole park is open from June to November; South and Central Kafue National Park are open all year. All bookings must be made through the Zambia National Tourist Board. All-weather roads around Ngoma South, and Chunga Safari Village, Central, have been constructed for game viewing. Zambia Airways operate flights during the season and the Board arranges tours through the park. Entry permits are required.

South Luangwa National Park: Many regard this as one of the finest game parks in Africa. There are six tourist lodges in Luangwa providing comfortable accommodation in chalets. The Tourist Board offers tours at very reasonable prices to Mfuwe, the largest of the lodges and the only one with catering facilities. Visitors are required to provide their own food and drink at the other lodges, although the necessary cooking equipment, bedding and maintenance staff are provided.

One of the features of the South Luangwa National Park is that visitors can walk about among the animals in company with armed guards – whose instructions must be implicitly obeyed. Children under 12 are not allowed on these walking safaris. At dawn it is possible to see elephants crossing the Luangwa River. Game is prolific and elephant, lion, giraffe, zebra, black

MARION KAPLAN

Giraffe in South Luangwa National Park

rhino, Cape buffalo and the antelopes are all to be found.

All bookings must be made through the Tourist Board and visitors are not allowed to enter the Park unless they hold an entry permit.

Sumbu National Park: The Park borders the second largest lake in Africa. One can boat and swim and there are luxury launches for picnic cruises. The fishing is excellent, especially from December to March, for Nile perch, tiger fish, *cundu* (a giant catfish), goliath tiger fish, lake salmon and *kupi.*

Accommodation: There are two lodges, Kasaba Bay Lodge, 30 guests, restaurant, bar; and Nkamba Bay Lodge. Sumbu tourist camp.

Zambia Airways flies to Kasaba Bay and Zambia National Tourist Board provide transfers and game viewing by Land-Rover and boats.

Lochinvar: This is a National Park devoted to the preservation of the red lechwe, but the visitor will also find many different varieties of birds, and zebra, hippo, baboons, and buffalo. The park also has an archaeological site. Accommodation: Game Lodge, 12 guests; bring your own food. Booking is through the Tourist Board.

Nyika: Nyika National Park is a small but attractive area adjoining the park of the same name in Malawi. The altitude is over 2,000 m and the park contains eland, zebra and many kinds of antelope. There is a small non-catering lodge.

Blue Lagoon: Small National Park within convenient reach of Lusaka with plenty of birdlife and the red lechwe. Advance permit required.

Lake Kariba: At present there is no boating or fishing on the lake. There is also a Rest House at Siavonga, and two camping and caravan sites. At Sinazongwe there is a rest camp with three chalets.

General Information

Government

Republic. A one-party state was declared in December 1972 and the United National Independence Party (UNIP) is the sole legal party. Parliament consists of the President and National Assembly comprising 125 elected and ten nominated members. The National Assembly, however, has no power to initiate, modify or veto legislation. The UNIP Central Committee is the most important policy-making body in the country.

Languages

English is the official language. The main African languages are Bemba, Nyanja, Lozi and Tonga.

Religion

Christian, Muslim and traditional religions.

How to Get There

By air: The international airport at Lusaka is served by the following airlines: Zambia Airways, Air Botswana, Air Malawi, British Caledonian, UTA, Air Zaire, Kenya Airways, Air Swazi, DETA, Air Tanzania, Air India, SAS, Aeroflot, LAM-Mozambique and Air Zimbabwe.

Taxi service is available at the International Airport. There is an Airport Departure Tax for international and domestic flights.

By road: Motorists enter Zambia through Kazungula (by ferry) from Botswana; through Victoria Falls, Chirundu and the Kariba dam from Zimbabwe; through Lundazi and Mwami from Malawi, or there is also a road from Chitipa in northern Malawi to Nakonde, usually only passable during the dry season, when there is also a bus service; through Tunduma from Tanzania and through Kasumbalesa or Mokambo from Zaire.

A driver bringing a motor vehicle into Zambia must have a tryptique or carnet de passage issued by a recognised motoring organisation, or a Customs Importation Permit issued at the point of entry under certain conditions. Motorists should contact the Controller of Customs and Excise, Customs Headquarters, PO Box 500, Livingstone, Zambia, for information regarding these conditions.

By rail: The Tazara railway, opened in 1975, gives access to the country from Tanzania. The journey from Kapiri Mposhi, north of Lusaka, to Dar es Salaam takes over 33 hours. The rail link from the south enters Zambia at Livingstone from Zimbabwe. Zambia Railways operate daily trains with overnight sleeper accommodation from Livingstone through Lusaka to Zaire.

Tourist information: Zambia National Tourist Board, **UK:** 163 Piccadilly, London W1V 9DE, Tel: 01-493 0848/1188. Telex: (051) 28956 **USA:** 237 East 52nd St., New York, NY 10155, USA. Tel (212) 7589450 Telex: 620605

Entry Regulations

Visas are not required by holders of valid UK or Commonwealth passports. The same applies to citizens of Romania and Yugoslavia.

Citizens of the United States, France, West Germany, and most other nations of the world, can get a special tourist visa when they enter Zambia if they are visiting the country solely as tourists and provided they satisfy the immigration authorities with regard to character, financial resources and ability to leave Zambia at the end of the visit. Package tour travellers can arrange beforehand to have visas ready on arrival in Zambia. As passport and visa regulations are subject to changes from time to time, intending visitors are advised to consult their travel agents beforehand. Tourist's visas cannot be issued at the Zambian border to any national or resident of the Republic of South Africa. Intending visitors from South Africa should apply directly to the Chief Immigration Officer, PO Box RW 300, Lusaka, allowing from four to six weeks for an application to be processed.

For people who have travelled through the yellow fever endemic zone of Africa (ie between the 15°N and 10°S parallels of latitude) an international certificate of vaccination against yellow fever is required. Similarly, for persons travelling from or via an infected cholera area a certificate of immunity is necessary.

Customs Regulations

Free import is allowed of personal effects (including camping and sports equipment, cameras and binoculars), 200 cigarettes of 250 gm. of tobacco, and one open bottle of an alcoholic beverage. Hunters must obtain a Tourist's Import Permit at point of entry for firearms and ammunition. The permit is valid for six months and must be returned to the Customs Officer at the point of departure from Zambia.

K10.00 Zambian currency may be taken into or out of Zambia, and there are absurdly rigorous searches of travellers' clothing and luggage on departure from Lusaka airport. Any stray *ngwee* have to be donated to the national wildlife fund. Visitors are advised to carry travellers' cheques in small denominations and cash only enough for their current needs.

There is no limit to the amount of foreign currency which can be brought into Zambia, but visitors should obtain a receipt from the customs officer at point of entry as they will be asked to declare the balance on departure. All foreign money should be changed at a bank and receipt kept until the end of the visit. Not more than the equivalent of K20 in foreign exchange may be taken out of Zambia unless a receipt is produced to prove that the amount in excess was brought into the country on that particular visit. There is a very widespread currency black market in Zambia, with some people so desperate for hard currency that they will pay up to four times the official rate. Traveller's cheques can be cashed at banks and most large hotels.

Diner's Club cards are accepted by the Inter-Continental, Ridgeway and Lusaka Hotels; American Express cards by the Inter-Continental, Pamodzi and Lusaka Hotels. Bank credit cards are not yet accepted by shops.

Climate

Although Zambia lies in the tropics, the elevation of the plateau ensures that the climate is seldom unpleasantly hot. The dry winter season from May to September (July: 16°C) is the best time for touring, when the days are sunny but can be cold and windy. The hot months are October and November (24°C) when even the nights are oppressive, though the heat is occasionally relieved by thunderstorms, which become more frequent with the approach of the rainy season in November. Rains usually last a few hours before the freshened countryside returns to sunshine. The wet season continues until early April and then the country is dry for the next seven months.

What to wear: Dress is generally informal. A cardigan or pullover is often needed in the cool early mornings and after sunset, except during the hot months of October and November.

For those who venture into the bush,

khaki clothes, comfortable shoes and a hat are necessary. Long sleeved shirts and trousers are also advisable to protect against insect bites and bush scratches.

Health Precautions

The climate is healthy if reasonable precautions are taken. Lusaka and the Copperbelt towns are practically free from malaria but outside these centres it is endemic and prophylactic drugs should be taken. It is safer to swim only in swimming pools as all water courses and dams are infected with bilharzia, which is a troublesome and debilitating disease. All clothes washed and hung in the open air to dry should be ironed to kill the eggs of the *putsi* fly which it lays on damp clothing. Insect repellent is advised in the game parks and rural areas. There are hospitals and clinics in the main urban areas which are open to outpatients every day, including Sundays and are free of charge.

Banks and Currency

Bank of Zambia, PO Box 30080, Lusaka
Barclays Bank of Zambia Ltd, PO Box 31936, Kafue House, Cairo Rd, Lusaka, tel: 216323
Grindlays Bank International (Zambia) Ltd, Woodgate House, Cairo Rd, PO Box 31955, tel: 217552, Lusaka
Standard Bank (Zambia) Ltd, Standard House, Cairo Rd, PO Box 32238, tel: 218330, Lusaka
Currency: Kwacha divided into 100 ngwee. (See currency table, page 10).

Business Hours

Banks: Monday-Wednesday and Friday 0815-1245; Thursday 0815-1200 and Saturday 0815-1100
Government offices: Monday-Friday 0800-1300 and 1400-1700
Offices: Monday-Friday 0800-1230 and 1400-1630
Shops: Monday-Friday 0800-1700; Saturday 0800-1300

Public Holidays

New Year's Day, 1 January
Youth Day, 10 March
Good Friday, 13 April 1990
Easter Monday, 16 April 1990
Labour Day, 1 May
African Freedom Day, 25 May
Whit Monday, 4 June 1990
Heroes Day, 1 July
Unity Day, 2 July
Zambia Public Holiday, 5 August
Independence Day, 24 October
Christmas Day, 25 December
Public holidays tend to vary, sometimes at short notice, and it is advisable to check them in advance.

Embassies in Lusaka

Belgium: Martin Mwamba Road, PO Box 31204, tel: 252312
Botswana: 2647 Haile Selassie Ave, PO Box 31910, tel: 250804
Canada: North End Branch, Barclays Bank Bldg, Cairo Rd, PO Box 31313
Denmark: 352 Independence Ave, POB 50299, tel: 251634
Egypt: Plot No. 5206, United Nations Avenue, PO Box 32428, tel: 253762
France: Unity House, Corner of Katunjila Rd and Freedom Way, PO Box 30062, tel: 212917
Germany FR: 350 Independence Ave, POB 50120, tel: 217449
Italy: 5th Floor, Woodgate House, Cairo Rd, PO Box 31046, tel: 216703
Kenya: Harambee House, UN Avenue POB 50298, tel: 212531
Malawi: 5th Floor, Woodgate House, Cairo Rd, POB 50425, tel: 213750
Netherlands: 5028 United Nations Ave, POB 31905, tel: 250468
Nigeria: 5th Floor, Findeco House, POB 32598, tel: 212548
Sweden: Kulima Tower, Katunjila Road, POB 30788, tel: 216018
Tanzania: Ujamaa House, UN Avenue, POB 21219, tel: 211422
UK: Stand No. 5210, Independence Ave, POB 50050, tel: 216770

USA: Corner of Independence and United Nations Ave, PO Box 31617, tel: 214911
Zaire: Plot 1124, Parirenyatwa Rd, PO Box 31287, tel: 213343

Transport

By road: Zambia is served by a network of tarred, gravel and earth roads which is being steadily improved. Considerable damage has been caused to Zambia's roads by heavy rains, with some sections of the tar roads under constant repair. Tarmac roads run from the Zimbabwe border to Chirundu, where the Kariba Bridge spans the Zambezi River, and from the Victoria Falls northwards through Lusaka to the Copperbelt towns which are all linked by tarred roads. The Ndola-Kitwe road is, however, one of the worst accident runs in Africa. Take it easy and do not drive on pay-day.

The Great North Road to Tunduma on the Tanzanian border is fully tarred and joins the road systems of Tanzania and Malawi. The tarred highway from Lusaka, the Great East Road, through Chipata links Zambia with Malawi and the main access route to the South Luangwa Valley National Game Reserve.

The Malawians are now tarring the road from the border to Lilongwe, which will make it a comfortable day's drive between the two capitals.

From Mpika a road runs to Mpulungu on Lake Tanganyika, where a steamer operates trips to various places on the lake.

Besides the main arterial roads there are all-weather gravel roads throughout the country, enabling the motorist to visit centres of scenic beauty and game parks, but the rains make January and March the least satisfactory time for motoring as many of the rural roads become impassable.

By air: Zambia Airways (PO Box 30272, Haile Selassie Avenue, Lusaka) domestic service has eight flights weekly between Lusaka and Livingstone and two flights weekly between Lusaka and Kasaba Bay. From the middle of May to the end of October there are three flights weekly to Mfuwe Lodge in the Luangwa Valley which is open all year. Flights operate daily between Lusaka and Ndola, including Sundays. The game-viewing flights from Lusaka may be of interest to the visitor with little time to spare.
By rail: There is one express and one slow train a day in each direction on the line between Livingstone and the Copperbelt. The express trains are quick and comfortable.
By road: The Zambia Travel and Touring Co. Ltd. (PO Box 30017 Lusaka; PO Box 60342 Livingstone) conducts luxury coach tours to the Victoria Falls and Livingstone, Kariba Dam, and Kafue National Park, as well as sightseeing tours of Lusaka.
Car hire: Taxis are plentiful and a number of car hire firms operate in the main centres. Visitors' driving licences are valid for 90 days.
Lusaka: Ridgeway Car Hire Service, PO Box 929, tel: 373968; Motor Holdings (Z) Ltd., PO Box 672, tel: 373181; Streamline Car Hire Ltd., PO Box 3189, tel: 375728. Ndola: Corner Taxi and Car Hire, PO Box 263, tel: 2469; Motor Holdings (Z) Ltd., PO Box 105, tel: 3621.
Kitwe: Motor Holdings (Z) Ltd., PO Box 2795, tel: 2390.

The Zambia Travel and Touring Co. runs a bus and car hire service from Livingstone and Lusaka.

Accommodation and Food

There is international-standard hotel accommodation in Lusaka and the Copperbelt towns.

Reasonably priced Government Rest Houses are available in the following areas:
Central Province: Kabwe (Bwacha Rest

House), Serenje, Mkushi, Mumbwa and Feire.
Southern Province: Livingstone (Maramba Rest House), Namwala, Sinazongwe.
Northern Province: Kasama, Chinsali, Luwingu, Mbala (Mpulungu Rest House), Isoka and Mporokoso.
Western Province: Mongu, Kalabo, Kaoma (formerly called Mankoya), and Sesheke.
North Western Province: Solwezi, Kasempa, Kabompo, Zambezi (formerly called Balovale), and Mwinilunga.
Eastern Province: Chipata (Kapata Rest House), Katete, Petauke, Lundazi (Lundazi Castle and Nyika Rest House), and Kacholola.
Luapula Province: Kawamba, Samfya, Nchelenge, Mwense and Mausa.

Imported food is sometimes in short supply. Although local commodities are usually available, there are periodic shortages of flour, dairy products, beer, cooking oil, etc.

Bream from the Zambezi river, Nile perch, lake salmon and other freshwater fish are excellent.

Tipping: Tipping in hotels and restaurants is illegal and instead a service charge of 10% has been levied.

Royal barge of the Lozi in Ku-omboka ceremony.

Hotels

NAME	ADDRESS	TELEPHONE	TELEX
KABWE			
Mulungushi Motel**	PO Box 80408	224602	
Elephant head Hotel***	PO Box 80410	223121	
KITWE			
Edinburgh Hotel****	PO Box 21800	212188	51220
Nkana Hotel**	PO Box 20664	214166	
LIVINGSTONE			
Mosi-oa-Tunya***** Intercontinental	PO Box 60151	2112	24221
New Fairmount Hotel***	PO Box 60096	2066/68	
North Western Hotel**	PO Box 60069	2255	24266
Rainbow Lodge	NHDC, Lusaka		44130
Zambezi Motel**	PO Box 60700	2887/8	
LUSAKA			
Andrews Motel***	PO Box 30475	216409	40450
Intercontinental Hotel*****	PO Box 32201 Haile Selassie Avenue	212366	41440
Lusaka Hotel***	PO Box 30044	217370	41921
Pamodzi Hotel*****	PO Box 35440	212620	44720
Ridgeway Hotel****	PO Box 30666	218240	42510
MBALA			
Arms Hotel	Mbala, N. Province	3416	
Grasshopper Inn	PO Box 93	291	

▶

[Hotels]

MONGU

Ngulu Hotel**	PO Box 142	221235	
Hotel Lyambai	PO Box 193	221271	

MUFULIRA

Mufulira Hotel	PO Box 727	411477	

NDOLA

Continental Cuisine**	PO Box 71538	3038/3103	
Coppersmith Arms	PO Box 71063	2395	
Savoy Hotel****	PO Box 71800	3771	30020

Safari Lodges

KAFUE NATIONAL PARK

Ngoma Lodge	Eagle Travel PO Box 34530, Century House, Cairo Road, Lusaka	219011/12	45440 40420
Musungwa Safari Lodge	PO Box 20104, Kitwe	215188	51390
Chunga Safari Village	PO Box 31010		44230

LOCHINVAR

Lochinvar Lodge	Eagle Travel PO Box 34530, Century House, Cairo Road, Lusaka	219011/12	45440 40420

SOUTH LUANGWA NATIONAL PARK

Mufuwe National Lodge	Eagle Travel PO Box 34530, Lusaka		45440 40420
Chichele National Lodge	Eagle Travel PO Box 34530, Lusaka		45440 40420
Luamfwa National Lodge	Eagle Travel PO Box 34530, Lusaka		45440 40420 ▶

Chinzombo Safari Camp	Eagle Travel, PO Box 34530, Lusaka		45440 40420
Nsefu Camp	Eagle Travel, PO Box 34530, Lusaka		45440 40420
Chibembe Safari Lodge	Bonar Travel, PO Box 33876, Lusaka	214008	–
SUMBU NATIONAL PARK			
Kasaba Bay Lodge	Eagle Travel PO Box 34530, Century House, Cairo Road, Lusaka	219011/12	45440 40420
Nkamba Bay Lodge	Eagle Travel, PO Box 34530, Lusaka	219011/12	45440 40420
Ndola Bay	T.G. Travel PO Box 20104, Kitwe	215188	51390 ■

Lusaka

Lusaka has been the country's capital since 1935. It has two well defined centres. All the shops, commercial offices, post office, markets, the bus station, etc, are to be found along Cairo Road. Government Offices, Embassies and the big hotels are to be found in the Ridgeway area. Flat-rate taxis (shared) and minibuses operate between the two.

The Zambia National Tourist Board offers a sightseeing tour of the capital which includes the new National Assembly building; the President's residence, State House; the Anglican cathedral; and open-air market; the tobacco auction floor (open from April to August); the curio sellers; a copper boutique, where gemstones are polished, set and sold; and the Geological Survey Museum which has exhibits from the copper industry and local gemstones such as garnets, tourmalines, emeralds, amethysts and malachite.

On a separate tour the visitor can see the Munda Wanga Botanical Gardens and nearby the headquarters of the Zambian Wildlife, Fisheries and National Parks Department of Chilanga. The Tourist Board also offers game-viewing flights.

Restaurants: Besides the restaurants in the hotels the better eating places include the **Fresco Restaurant** and the **Kudu Inn.** Others are the **Woodpecker Inn** and the **Fimbano Night Club.** Prices are high everywhere and menus may be affected by food shortages.

Entertainments: Dancing and floor shows in the main hotels; modern cinemas, including a 'drive-in'; theatre; art gallery; excellent library; sports and sailing facilities at private clubs where temporary membership is usually available to visitors. Casino at the Inter-Continental Hotel.

Shopping and markets: Lusaka has modern shops and supermarkets, and an open air market. African carvings, beadwork, pottery and copperware are readily available. A visit is recommended to Zambia's Gemstones Polishing Works where local gemstones are sold.

Tourist information: The Zambia National Tourist Board, PO Box 30017, Century House, Cairo Road, tel: 217761 Telex: 41780.

The Copperbelt

The seven mining towns of Kitwe, Ndola, Chililabombwe, Chingola, Kalulushi, Mufulira and Luanshya make up the Copperbelt. Luanshya has the country's oldest mine which has the richest ores in Zambia, followed by Mufulira near the Zaire border with the second most extensive underground copper mining installations in the world.

United Bus Company of Zambia run a daily luxury coach service to the Copperbelt and the Zambia National Tourist Board also operates luxury coach tours, but on request only, to the Copperbelt centres, and itinerary includes a visit to the Dag Hammerskjold Memorial. There is also a train service to the Copperbelt. Of interest outside Ndola are the Sunken Lake and Slave Tree. Visits to the copper mines should be arranged in advance from Lusaka; visitors in Ndola should see the Monkey Fountain Zoo.

Entertainments: Casino in the Savoy Hotel; dinner dances in the Edinburgh and Savoy Hotels; private clubs offer temporary membership to visitors, and their facilities include tennis, bowls, swimming pools, and golf (the course at Chingola being particularly good). Near Kitwe is the Mindola Dam with swimming, speedboating and water sports (but boats and equipment cannot be rented at the dam); Kitwe is the major horse racing centre in Zambia.

Livingstone

Established in 1905, Livingstone was the capital of Zambia (Northern Rhodesia) until 1935. The old Government House is now a National Monument. The town is a tourist centre for the Victoria Falls, and there are excellent hotels, rest huts and camping sites and numerous excursions to interest the visitor.

Places of interest
The Victoria Falls have always been considered one of the natural wonders of the world. At the height of the floods, from March to May, more than five million litres of water surge over every second, causing clouds of vapour that can be seen 50 km away.

The recently completed Knife Edge footbridge spanning a narrow ridge of rock between the mainland and an island downstream opposite the Eastern Cataract affords the best view of the Rainbow and Main Falls, the First Gorge and the Boiling Pot. Other main vantage points are the larger Falls Bridge, which is further away, the Boiling Pot, the Power Station and the various gorges. There are two major scenic approaches downriver as far as the Seventh and Songwe Gorges, on one of which is the Lookout Tree, a huge and ancient baobab in which a platform has been built to give an excellent view of the Falls.

The Livingstone Game Park just

Victoria Falls.

ZNTB

outside the town contains over 400 animals which include lion, giraffe, zebra, white rhino, a variety of antelope, warthog, bush pig and gnu. As the park is small the lions are confined to an acre enclosure. In the centre of the park is a fenced area where crocodiles, tortoises, snakes and leguans are housed in pits and cages. There are also aviaries for indigenous birds such as the Zambezi Lovebird, and enclosures for small mammals not normally seen in the main park.

On the Zambezi crocodiles can be seen in the water and a variety of animals and birds on the banks and islands. Elephants and monkeys are plentiful. Further up river, especially as far as Mambova and the Maramba River, there are good places for game fishing.

The Maramba Cultural Centre was established to preserve the arts and crafts of age-old Africa. It contains at least one dwelling typical of each of the main areas of Zambia, where blacksmiths, mask carvers, potters and craftsmen ply their trades as their ancestors did through the centuries. In the centre of the village is an arena where traditional dances are performed, including those of the Makishi dancers in basketweave costumes who used to perform during the Luvala circumcision rites in the North Western Province.

Inside Livingstone itself is Zambia's national museum which records the history of man in Zambia in traditional and anthropological exhibits. The museum is renowned for its collection of Livingstone's possessions and correspondence, including a notebook in which the explorer recorded the date he first set eyes on the Victoria Falls.

A camping site for tents and caravans is situated near the banks of the Zambezi River. Adjacent are the Falls Rest Huts where furnished huts may be rented with or without bedding. The Falls Restaurant overlooks the river and serves both the camping site and Rest Huts with meals and food. Rest Camp, including restaurant catering, PO Box 86, tel: 2981 (ungraded).

Mbala

Mbala is set among lovely hills, and nearby are the Kalambo Falls (240 m high), the nesting place of the maribou stork. At Mpulungu is a harbour for fishing boats on Lake Tanganyika.

Mongu

This town is situated on the upper reaches of the Zambezi in the Western Province. The *Ku-omboka* in March when the Lozi chief moves all his goods and family to Limulunga for the duration of the rains, and the *Kufulehela* in July when they all move back to Lealui are fascinating ceremonies to watch, but unfortunately the date when they take place is unpredictable. The local curio shop displays Lozi basketwork and carvings, and the Zambezi plain is itself a fine sight.

ZIMBABWE

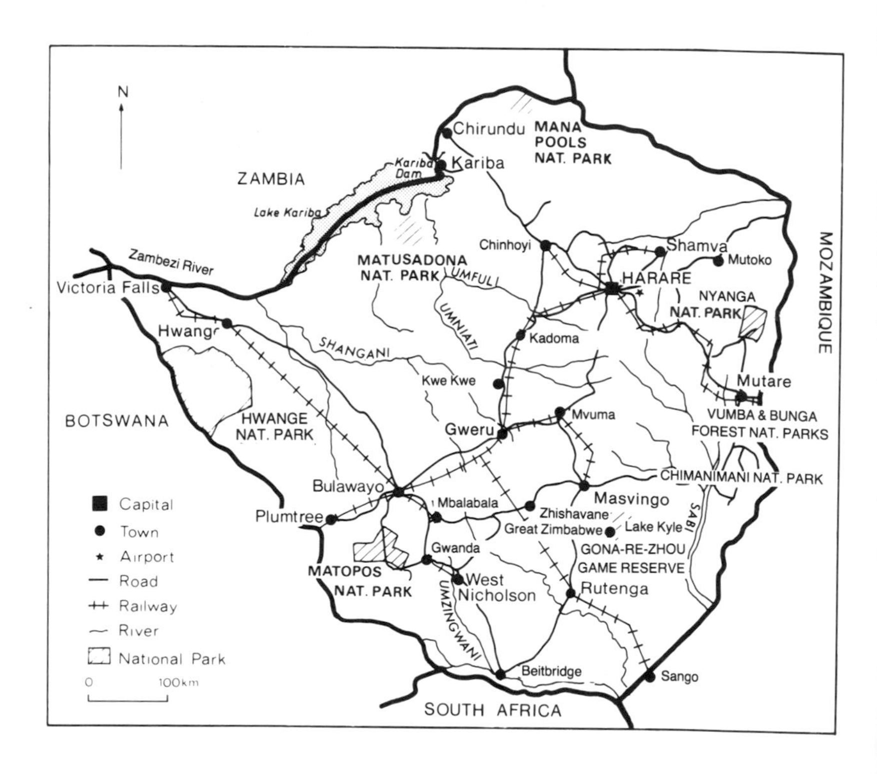

Area: 390,245 sq kms
Population: 9.67 million (1989 World Bank)
Capital: Harare

Zimbabwe, the youngest independent country of Africa, offers visitors a unique combination of some of the world's most spectacular natural and man-made wonders and a superior tourism infrastructure which enables travellers to enjoy the sights in relative comfort. The tourism sector is well organised, and those who land in Harare will find it easy to arrange transport and accommodation for any of a dozen major points of interest as well as many smaller destinations.

The government under Prime Minister Robert Mugabe faces the enormous task of satisfying the aspirations of blacks impatient for immediate and far-reaching changes. The most fundamental issue is the unequal land distribution between blacks and whites. Mugabe has adopted moderate economic and social policies in an attempt to convince white Zimbabweans to remain in the country and offer their skills to the building of a new society.

In six years, some notable economic achievements have been scored, particularly in agriculture: in the fourth harvest after independence (severe drought had taken its toll on the first three), previously landless black Zimbabweans produced on communal lands a bumper maize crop in 1984 that not only fed the nation but made Zimbabwe the ninth-largest maize-exporter in the world. They repeated their success in 1985.

Zimbabwe has some world-famous tourist attractions: the magnificent Victoria Falls, which dwarfs even Niagara; Kariba Dam, an engineering wonder which creates Africa's largest man-made lake; the big game of Hwange National Park; and the mysterious ruins of ancient stone ruins of Great Zimbabwe, near Masvingo. But the country has even more to offer the tourist with time to spare. A drive through the beautiful Eastern Highlands close to the Mozambique border, a visit to the Zambezi flood plains and a tour of the Lowveld region are all highly recommended. As well as escaping the rigorous schedule of the package tour and the often un-African atmosphere of international-style hotels, independent exploration of these areas will allow the visitor to see the real Zimbabwe, as opposed to what the travel brochures offer.

The Land and the People

A land-locked country in south central Africa, Zimbabwe straddles that part of the great African plateau between the Zambezi and Limpopo rivers. The Highveld landscape is studded with massive granite outcrops (*kopjes*). Along the eastern border for some 350 kms is a high mountainous region of great beauty, rising to the highest peak, Inyangani, 2,592 m above the sea.

The area that now constitutes Zimbabwe was inhabited in the first century by stone-age hunter-gatherers related to the 'Bushmen'. Around the 11th century AD Shona-speaking people began to migrate into the area. By 1100 they had established the basis for the civilisation that was to develop into the two great state systems known as the Mwene Mutapa and Rozwi empires. They successfully dominated the area into the 19th century.

The African population, now well over eight million, comprises Mashona peoples – Karanga, Zezuru, Ndau, Manyika and Korekore – and the Ndebele. There are also smaller ethnic groups such as the Tonga of the Zambezi Valley, the Sena, Hlengwe, Venda and Sotho. White settlers began to arrive in significant numbers only in the early 20th century, most of them of European origin, mainly British, Portuguese, Greek and South African. The white population, never much more than 700,000, decreased steadily in the late 1970s as people emigrated at the rate of over 1,000 a month. White emigration has continued since independence despite government attempts to persuade them to stay.

Culture

Urban culture is greatly influenced now by contemporary West European and American culture and education. In the rural areas traditional values and crafts still continue. Fine examples of early rock art of the Bushmen can be seen in the caves found in many of the granite outcrops around the country. The Zimbabwe National Gallery in Harare stages exhibitions of paintings, sculpture and ceramics by local as well as overseas artists. The Queen Victoria Museum in Harare has as its theme the 'Story of Man and Animal in Mashonaland'. Among the exhibits are some very good examples of rock paintings. The National Archives, 6 km from Harare city centre on the Borrowdale Road, has a comprehensive National Reference Library, coins, stamps, maps, audiovisual materials. It also features an expanding Oral History Programme, in which interviews with Zimbabweans in all walks of life are recorded and transcribed, and the Beit Trust Gallery, which has a permanent exhibition showing Zimbabwe's history from earliest times and also many special exhibitions. Admission is free.

The National Museum in Bulawayo houses examples of traditional African crafts, as well as a photographic history of the early pioneer days. There are also displays of the wildlife (including the second-largest mounted elephant in the world) and minerals of the country. Bulawayo and Harare have craft centres where carvings from wood and soapstone, as well as pottery are produced.

History

It was the invasion of the Portuguese in the 16th century that brought about the decline of the Mutapa kingdom and the ascendancy of the Rozwi empire, which maintained its hegemony until the 1830s. A series of invasions from the south by the Ndebele, a breakaway Zulu group led by Mzilikazi, defeated the Rozwi state in the 1830s. Mzilikazi set up his capital in the south-west of the country near Bulawayo.

The first permanent white settlement, the Inyati Mission, was established in 1859 by Robert Moffat. The subsequent discovery of gold in Mashonaland in 1867 led to increased European interest. In 1888 Lobengula, who had succeeded his father Mzilikazi, in 1870, signed the Rudd Concession with representatives of Cecil Rhodes, who formed the British South African Company the following year. In 1890, the 'Pioneer Column' of the BSAC invaded and occupied Mashonaland. In the war that broke out between the Ndebele and the BSAC in 1893, the Ndebele were defeated and forced to forfeit their land. Three years later, they rose again, this time in conjunction with the Shona. It was only with the assistance of British troops that the settlers were able to put down this war of resistance in 1897.

The BSAC instituted its administrative control of the country on the basis of the Royal Charter granted it in 1889 until 1923. In a referendum in 1922, the white settlers voted against joining the Union of South Africa or continuing company rule and in favour of separate status as a largely self-governing colony. Under the constitution which came into force, Britain retained the right of veto on discriminatory and constitutional matters, but in most respects did little to prevent the consolidation of an increasingly racially stratified and segregated society. The Land Apportionment Act of 1930 and the Industrial Conciliation Act of 1934 ensured that the main role of the Africans in the economy was as labour migrants to the European towns, farms and mines.

In the period after the Second World War, moves began to create a Central African federation of Southern and Northern Rhodesia and Nyasaland. If successful it would have combined the large supply of cheap labour in Nyasaland (Malawi) and the vast mineral resources of Northern Rhodesia (Zambia) with the capital and technological know-how of Southern Rhodesia. From its inception in 1953, the Federation faced fierce opposition from both blacks and whites; from the white farmers and workers because of the threat to their privileged economic position; and from the blacks because the increased prosperity from the Federation was unlikely to benefit or change their circumstances in any significant way.

The Land Husbandry Act of 1951, which struck at the roots of both rural and urban African life, acted as a catalyst for mass nationalism. As a result of the Act, many young labour migrants lost their rights to land and security, without any prospect of wages and welfare facilities sufficient to support a permanent existence outside the reserves. It was largely these young men who were active in the revival of the nationalist movement in the late 1950s and early 1960s. Two of the main organisations to emerge were the Zimbabwe African National Union (ZANU) and the Zimbabwe African People's Union (ZAPU).

The Central African Federation was dissolved in 1963, paving the way for the independence of Malawi and Zambia in 1964 on the basis of majority rule. The British government refused to decolonise Southern Rhodesia until some accommodation had been worked out between black and white. It was this issue that brought Ian Smith to power in 1964, and he was given overwhelming support by the whites for a unilateral declaration of independence (UDI) on 11 November 1965.

After UDI, the basic position of the two sides remained unchanged. Britain had publicly ruled out the use of force to quell the rebellion even before UDI and relied upon economic sanctions to produce a negotiated settlement and a realignment of political forces among the whites. Neither factor shook the resolve of Smith and his supporters. Meanwhile, ZANU and ZAPU, which had set up offices in exile in the 1960s, opted for a strategy of armed struggle in 1966.

There were several abortive efforts at resolving the situation. In 1971 Smith and the British government reached an agreement which would have postponed majority rule until the next century. This, however, was dependent on the approval of the black population. Black opposition was mobilised under Bishop Muzorewa and Britain was forced to withdraw from the accord. In 1974, faced with an escalating guerrilla war being mounted by ZANU and ZAPU, Smith released some of the imprisoned nationalists, including Joshua Nkomo, Ndabaningi Sithole and Robert Mugabe, in the hope of arranging negotiations, but these never got off the ground. Mugabe rejoined the guerrillas, replacing Sithole as the leader of ZANU.

In 1976, under increasing pressure from his former South African and American allies to end the war, Smith announced an agreement for majority rule in two years. Mugabe's ZANU and Nkomo's ZAPU formed a Patriotic Front for negotiating purposes, but talks on implementing majority rule broke down. Confronted with a worsening military situation, rising white emigration and a collapsing economy, Smith decided in December 1977 to bring about his own 'internal' solution. Some nationalist leaders, including Muzorewa, agreed to cooperate in elections, under a constitution which would guarantee continued effective white dominance. The elections were held in April 1979 in an atmosphere of intimidation, and Muzorewa became Prime Minister at the head of a cabinet including Ian Smith. The new government failed to win international recognition and the guerrilla war intensified.

In August 1979, a Commonwealth summit meeting in Lusaka called for new all-party talks to be held in London the following month. After some hesitation both the Patriotic Front and the Salisbury government agreed to participate. After intense bargaining all sides at the conference agreed there should be a three-month period of direct British rule, at the end of which elections would be held for a 100-seat House of Assembly. Twenty seats were reserved for whites.

Despite attempts to sabotage the elections, they were successfully held at the end of February 1980, and Robert Mugabe's ZANU-PF party emerged with 57 seats, giving him a clear majority. Nkomo, whose ZAPU-PF party won 20 seats, accepted Mugabe's invitation to join a coalition government, which also included two white cabinet ministers.

The problems facing independent Zimbabwe's first government were immense. Hundreds of thousands of refugees had to be resettled, while 33,000 guerrillas in the assembly points set up by the British during the period of direct rule had to be integrated into the national Zimbabwe army or found gainful employment. Health services in the rural areas had been severely disrupted, and 3,000 rural schools had been closed during the fighting. The national reconstruction programmes to deal with these problems were significantly held up by lack of funds. Foreign aid was slow to arrive, despite Mugabe's decision to pursue pragmatic social and economic policies designed to reassure foreign investors.

The constitution was amended in September 1987 abolishing the 20 seats reserved for whites and making Mugabe an executive president. ZANU and ZAPU finally buried their differences in April 1988 and formed a single party known as ZANU-PF. An Amnesty was extended to the ZAPU guerillas and many came out of the bush and laid down their weapons.

Economy

Aside from South Africa, Zimbabwe has the most broadly based economy of any country in Africa. It has a diversified industrial base, and both its mining and construction industries are technologically advanced. The country is normally self-sufficient in agriculture, although three years of drought made Zimbabwe a net importer of food for the first time in 15 years in the early 1980s. The country returned to self-sufficiency in 1984 and 1985.

After reaching a peak in 1974 with an average growth rate of 6.9% in real terms since UDI in 1965, the economy declined steadily as the war intensified. Before UDI, tobacco, minerals and tourism were the most important earners of foreign exchange. Consumer goods were also exported. The sanctions imposed after UDI forced a considerable restructuring of the economy. Relative economic isolation, coupled with strict import controls to conserve scarce foreign exchange, created a rapid expansion of import substitution manufacturing (more than 100% between 1964 and 1976).

In 1980, whites owned about 90% of the land considered suitable for agriculture, but only about 40% of it was actually being farmed. Only the larger agricultural enterprises, dominated by large transnational agribusinesses – primarily British and South African – were profitable. The African reserves and Tribal Trust Lands, in which 60% of the African population lives, had become increasingly overcrowded and unproductive over the years in the attempt to sustain a population growing at 3.6% per annum. Most African food production was for subsistence. It was estimated that at least 75% of European land was required to settle the excess population from the Tribal Trust Lands.

The government's resettlement efforts, financed in part by the UK, involve two schemes to resettle families from the overcrowded communal areas on 1.1 million hectares of formerly commercial farmland on a willing seller/willing buyer basis. Each family is allocated five hectares of arable land and 5-15 livestock units, but the state retains land ownership and control over cropping. Some large farms are left intact and become producer co-operatives.

The mining sector, which showed expansion in the period following UDI, has continued to grow. The major products of the mining industry are gold, asbestos, nickel, coal, copper, chrome and iron. The mining sector is almost completely controlled by transnational corporations, mainly British and South African, but with an increasing American component. The mining industry is the prime earner of foreign exchange, over 90% of its product being exported.

Wildlife and National Parks

Thousands of square kilometres have been reserved for the conservation of one of the world's largest remaining concentrations of animal life. The best time for game viewing is from July to October. During the rest of the year some reserves are closed.

Hunting is rigorously controlled. Most big-game safaris are registered with the Zimbabwe Tourist Board and are therefore bound to comply with conservation regulations. For more detailed information on hunting operators, write to Guy Percival, PO Box 8052, Causeway, Harare.

Hwange National Park, near Victoria Falls, has some of the largest herds of elephant and buffalo on the continent. Zimbabwe's largest park at 14,600 sq km, it has 107 species of animal, including lion, eland, giraffe, rhino, zebra, sable, antelope, kudu and waterbuck. More than 400 species of bird also live in the park. Most notable of its many watering holes are Nyamandhlovu Pan and Guvalala Pan, near the main camp, where platforms permit visitors to leave their cars and view from an excellent but safe vantage point. The park has 482 km of game-viewing roads. Accommodation is at three camps just inside the park. The main camp, the largest, nearest the Hwange National Airport, is open all year and offers a choice of chalet, cottage or lodge accommodation. Sinametella camp, also open all year, has two-bedroom luxury cottages, each with an uninterrupted view of the animal-filled plain 55 metres below. Robins Camp, only 120 km from Victoria Falls, has two-bed and four-bed chalets and boasts of being the lion capital of the park. Just outside the park are the three-star Hwange Safari Lodge, near the Main Camp and the airport, and the Nantwich Lodges, 8 km west of Robins Camp. Nantwich has three self-contained lodges overlooking a waterhole.

Matusadona National Park lies on the wild southern shore of Lake Kariba and is accessible by a rough road from Karoi or by water from Kariba. Game-viewing on foot is permitted. Tiger-fish and bream can be caught in the lake. No fishing licence is required. (Tashinga camp, 40 km SW from Kariba, accessible by air; Sanyati Gorge camp, 26 km SSW. No supplies provided. Camping equipment can be hired.)

Kyle Recreational Park, near Masvingo (Fort Victoria), is of exceptional beauty. Surrounded by mountains and on the shores of beautiful Lake Kyle, which has an area of 91 sq km, the park provides rest camp accommodation. No supplies are available within the game park. Antelope, giraffe, buffalo and hippo can be seen there, but the park is especially noted for the rarer type of animal – white rhino, oribi, blesbok, Lichtenstein's hartebeeste and nyala. Game-viewing on foot is permitted, and the prize catch for fishermen is black bass. Licences are obtainable from National Parks staff.

Mana Pools National Park occupies over 2,000 sq km of country along the shores of the Zambezi river north-east of Kariba. The large variety of game to be seen includes eland, kudu, hyena, lion, leopard and cheetah, and the bird life is particularly prolific. Viewing on foot is permitted. The best viewing is in October, in the dry season, when animals collect around the "pools" to drink. (The "pools" are really old river channels of the Zambezi.) Good fishing is available. No licence is required, but care should be taken as there are numerous crocodiles in the river. Camping and caravan sites are the only accommodation. Visitors are advised to be well equipped with mosquito nets and insect repellent. Permission to enter the park must be obtained in writing from the Department of National Parks, PO Box 8151, Causeway, Harare. The park is usually open 1 May-31 October, but dates vary according to the rains.

Gona-Re-Zhou lies in the south-east of the country along the Mozambique border. The rare nyala and black rhino may be seen here. Game-viewing on foot is permitted, but fishing is allowed only on the Lundi River. Visitors hope to see Kebakwe, the "Big One" – and elephant with 170cm, 50kg tusks tracked daily with a radio collar. Only four-wheel vehicles are permitted to use roads within the reserve. Accommodation is in camping and caravan sites. Permission to enter the park must be obtained in writing from the Department of National Parks, PO Box 8151, Causeway, Harare.

The parks listed above are the principal ones. There are many other smaller national parks and reserves. Further information on these is available from the Zimbabwe Tourist Board or the Department of National Parks and Wildlife Management.

Even near the towns and cities, wildlife may be found. In the **Matopos National Park,** near Bulawayo, and the **Robert McIlwaine Recreational Park,** near Harare, white rhino, zebra, eland, sable, antelope, wildebeeste, kudu and other species can be seen.

General Information

Government

Robert Mugabe became executive president on 31 December 1987 under new constitutional amendments. He is Head of State and Commander in Chief of the Defence Forces. Under him there is a 40-seat Senate and a 100-seat House of Assembly. The ruling party is ZANU-PF.

Languages

English, Shona and Ndebele.

Religion

Christianity and traditional beliefs.

How to Get There

By air: Harare is served by Air Zimbabwe, Kenya Airways, Ethiopian Airlines, Air Botswana, Air Malawi, Zambia Airways, Royal Swazi, Air Tanzania, LAM of Mozambique, British Airways, TAP of Portugal, Air India, Qantas and South African Airways.

By road: Drivers can enter Zimbabwe from Botswana through Plumtree and Kazungula, from South Africa through Beitbridge, from Mozambique through Mount Selinda Mutare and Nyamapanda, and from Zambia through Chirundu, Kariba and Victoria Falls. Most of these border posts are closed from 18.00 to 06.00 every day.

By rail: Passenger services are available. Trains leave Durban, South Africa, Wednesdays at 18.30 and reach Bulawayo the following Friday at 14.10; the return journey leaves Bulawayo Tuesdays at 11.45 and reaches Durban the following Thursday at 8.15. Daily services link Harare with Bulawayo, Gweru, Kwe, Kwe, Kadoma, Marondera and Mutare. For details contact National Railways of Zimbabwe, PO Box 596, Bulawayo; tel 72211/72311; telegraphic address GEM Harare 70 00 11.

Entry Regulations

All visitors require a valid passport. Visitors from most countries, excluding Britain and the Commonwealth, require also a visa. A visitor must have sufficient funds for maintenance and onward journey. A certificate of vaccination against yellow fever is required if the visitor has passed through an infected area.

Customs Regulations

All goods temporarily imported for a visitor's own use may be allowed entry duty-free. Other goods intended for consumption may be imported up to a value of Z$100 per person. Alcoholic beverages may be imported within this allowance, subject to a limit of five litres per person, of which not more than two litres should be spirits. Not more than Z$20 in local currency may be imported or exported.

Climate

Remarkably temperate conditions prevail all year round, moderated by the country's altitude and its inland position, which keeps the humidity comfortably low. Mean monthly temperatures during October, the hottest month, range from 22°C on the high central plateau to 30°C in the low-lying Zambezi valley. Mid-winter temperatures (July) are around 13°C on the Highveld and 20°C in the Zambezi valley.

What to wear: Light clothing is essential for the summer months. In the winter,

particularly in the evenings, woollens are needed and a warm coat for outdoors. While hotels allow casual dress during the day, men are expected to wear collar, tie and jacket after 6.30pm.

Health Precautions

All water in towns, hotels and swimming pools is perfectly safe for drinking and swimming in, but bilharzia parasites infect many lakes, dams and rivers. Outside the principal urban areas, malaria is also considered an endemic disease, particularly in the lower-lying parts of the country where many of the country's tourist attractions are situated, and prophylactic drugs should be taken during and after visits to these areas.

Banks and Currency

Central Bank: Reserve Bank of Zimbabwe, PO Box 1283, Samora Machel Ave, Harare; it also has a branch at PO Box 399, Selborne Ave at Abercorn St, Bulawayo.
Commercial banks:
Barclays Bank International Ltd, PO Box 1279, Barclays House, First St at Stanley Ave, Harare.
Zimbank Ltd (formerly Rhodesian Banking Corp), PO Box 3198, First St at Speke Ave, Harare.
Grindlays Bank Ltd, PO Box 300, Ottoman House, 59 Samora Machel Ave, Harare.
Standard Bank Ltd, PO Box 373, Second St at Baker Ave, Harare.
Bank of Credit and Commerce, PO Box 3313, 60 Union Ave, Harare.
Currency: The Zimbabwe dollar ("Zim-dollar"); Z$1=100 cents. (See currency table page 10.)

Business Hours

Banks: Monday, Tuesday, Thursday and Friday 0830-1400. Wednesday 0830-1200. Saturday 0830-1100.

Public Holidays

New Year's Day, 1 January
Easter, 13-16 April 1988
Independence Day, 18 April
Armed Forces Day, 19 April
Workers' Day, 1-2 May
Africa Day, 25 May
Heroes' Day, 11-13 August
Christmas Day, 25 December
Boxing Day, 26 December

Embassies in Harare

Australia: PO Box 4541
Belgium: 8 Nigels Lane, Chisipite, Box BW 350
Canada: Monomatapa Hotel, Room 1905
Denmark: 30 Forbes Ave, PO Box 4711
France: 2nd Floor, RAL House, Samora Machel Avenue; PO Box 1378
Germany FR: 14 Samora-Machel Ave, PO Box 2168
Ghana: 11 Downie Ave, Belgravia, PO Box 4445
India: PO Box 4620
Italy: 7 Bartholomew Close, Greendale North, PO Box 1062
Malawi: 42-44 Harare Street
Netherlands: 47 Enterprise Road, Box HG 601, Highlands
Sweden: Pearl Assurance Building, Samora Machel Avenue
Switzerland: Southampton House, 9th Floor, Union Avenue
Tanzania: Ambassador Hotel, Union Avenue, PO Box 4841
UK: Stanley House, Stanley Avenue, PO Box 4490
USA: 78 Enterprise Rd, PO Box HG 81, Highlands
Zambia: Elgin House, Union Avenue

Transport

By air: Air Zimbabwe operates frequent services between all main towns and tourist resorts. Flights are cheap and reliable.
By road: Inter-city and inter-territorial roads are of first-class standards, and all

Hotels

The star classifications below are given by the Zimbabwe Tourist Board
(† = not yet rated)

NAME	ADDRESS	TELEPHONE	TELEX
HARARE			
Ambassador Hotel**	Union Ave, PO Box 872	708121	4164ZW
Courtney Hotel**	Selous Ave, 18th St., PO Box 3150	706411	–
George Hotel**	King George Road, PO Box A93, Avondale	36677	–
Harare Sheraton†	PO Box 3033	729771/ 728728	2621/ 2622ZW
Holiday Inn****	Samora Machel Ave, PO Box 7	795611/ 708655	2076ZW
Jameson Hotel****	Jameson Ave, PO Box 2833	794641	4166ZW
Meikles Hotel*****	Stanley Ave, PO Box 594	707721	4214ZW
Monomatapa Hotel****	54 Park Lane, PO Box 2445	704501	6078ZW
Oasis Motel**	124 Baker Ave, PO Box 1541	704217	2099ZW
Selous Hotel*	Sixth St/Selous Ave	27940/ 27948/9	–
BULAWAYO			
Bulawayo Sun***	10th Ave/Wilson St, PO Box 654	60101	3242ZW
Churchill Arms***			
Grey's Inn	73 Grey St. PO Box 527	60121/2	–
Holiday Inn***	Ascot Centre, PO Box AC88	72464	3341ZW

[Hotels]			
New Royal Hotel	6th/Rhodes St, PO Box 1199	65764/5	–
Selborne Hotel	Selborne Ave, PO Box 219	65741	–
[Hotels]			
GWERU			
Fairmile Hotel***	PO Box 1232	4144	–
Midlands Hotel***	PO Box 276	2581	7666
VUMBA MOUNTAINS			
Leopard Rock Hotel	P Bag V 7441	Mutare 2176-10	–
Mountain Lodge Hotel	Bag V 7464, Mutare	Mutare 2185-20	–
White Horse Inn**	PO Box 3193, Paulington, Mutare	216612	–
VICTORIA FALLS			
Victoria Falls Hotel****	PO Box 10	4203/4/5	3324ZW
Makasa Sun Hotel****	PO Box 90	4275/6/7/8/9	3222ZW
A'Zambezi River Lodge***	PO Box 130	4561	3676ZW
Sprayview Hotel**	PO Box 70	4344	
HWANGE			
Baobab**	PO Box 120	323/493	–
Hwange Safari Lodge***	PO Box DT 5792, Dete	Dete 331/3	3325ZW
KARIBA			
Bumi Hills Safari Lodge***	50km uplake from Kariba, PO Box 41	2353	Via Caribbea Bay

[Hotels]

Caribbea Bay†	PO Box 120	2454/455	4537ZW
Lake View Inn**	PO Box 100	2411/2	4055
Cutty Sark**	PO Box 80	2353	
Spurwing Island Resort	27 km from Kariba, PO Box 101	2466	–
Fothergill Island Camp	20 km from Kariba, P Bag 2081	2253	4316
MUTARE			
Christmas Pass Hotel	5 km from Mutare, PO Box 841	63818	–
City Centre Hotel	Main St, PO Box 3005, Paulington	62441	–
Manica Hotel***	Victory Ave at Third St, PO Box 27	64431	8203
Wise Owl Motel**	Off main Harare/ Mutare Rd, PO Box 588	64643	–
NYANGA			
Montclair Casino***	PO Juliasdale	Juliasdale 231/2/3	4528ZW
Brondesbury Park***	P Bag 8070, Rusape	Juliasdale 242	–
Troutbeck Inn***	PO Troutbeck, Mutare	Nyanga 305	4518ZW
Rhodes Inyanga Hotel*	P Bag 8024 N, Rusape	Nyanga 377	–
MASVINGO			
Flamboyant Motel**	PO Box 225	2005/6	–
Great Zimbabwe Hotel**	P Bag 9082	2274	9741W

tourist centres are linked by tarred roads. Most foreign driving licences are valid for up to 90 days. Driving is on the left. **By rail:** Zimbabwe railways link the main centres with passenger services.

Accommodation and Food

A full range of accommodation is available in the main centres, while at tourist resorts there are hotels or chalets. A comprehensive guide to hotels, rest camps, caravan and camping sites is available from the National Tourist Board. The Department of Tourism rates hotels annually, five being the maximum. In 1985 Zimbabwe had 142 hotels, of which one (Meikles in Harare) had five stars.

Restaurants and hotels provide a wide range of cuisine. Restaurants are generally of a very high standard but do not give the visitor any idea of the kind of food eaten by the majority of the population. The public bars, almost always part of a hotel, do not encourage women, who are expected to drink in the hotel lounges.

Harare

Harare, the capital and largest city, is an attractive, spacious town with modern buildings, wide tree-lined streets and a colourful central flower market. It is divided, like all other towns in Zimbabwe, into the commercial centre with its sprawling white suburbs, and the high density black townships. Although all amenities are multi-racial, the wages of the majority of blacks still effectively exclude them from most establishments in the city.

The effects of the independence war of the 1970s still have not entirely disappeared. The black townships practically doubled their population when people flooded in from the war-torn countryside. With the already acute housing shortage in the townships

Zimbabwe herdsman

these people were forced to become 'squatters' living out in the open. The government's rehabilitation programme has enabled many of these peasants to return to their homes, but the urban unemployment problem remains extremely grave. The August 1982 census held a surprise: the country's third-largest city (after Harare and Bulawayo) was Chitungwiza, with 172,600 inhabitants. It is a low-cost satellite city outside Harare, built on the eve of independence in anticipation of the urban drift that has indeed followed.

Restaurants. Good and often excellent food, at very reasonable prices by international standards, is offered in many Harare restaurants. The following is a selection of good places to eat. Good continental food at L'Escargot. The Cellar La Fontaine and The Bagatelle in Meikles Hotel; Eros Restaurant (Italian); Roger Le Francais (French); Acropolis (Greek, fish specialities); Pino's (expensive but good fish restaurant); The Howff (Scots bias, specialises in steaks, excellent haute cuisine, unexpectedly inexpensive). Less expensive but of a high standard are the Greek Taverna; The Hunting Lodge (traditional English food); Tiffany's and The Sandawama Room (Jameson Hotel); The Bird in the bottle (Ambassador Hotel); Kia Nyama (steaks): Sandawana Room for snacks and light meals (Jameson Hotel); The Oasis (self-service, cheap good food); Bali Hai (Polynesian, in the Monomatapa Hotel).

Entertainments. For daytime visits, the city offers the National Archives Galleries. The Queen Victoria Museum and the National Gallery of Zimbabwe. The works of local artists are frequently exhibited in the Middle Gallery at the Monomatapa Hotel. Harare has a selection of theatres (no longer exclusively for a white audience), cinemas and nightclubs. Dining and dancing to live music at La Fontaine (Meikles Hotel) and at the 12,000 Horseman (Monomatapa Hotel). There are several lively discotheques: Samantha's, Archipelagos, Le Coq d'Or, and less expensive La Boheme and Time and Place.

Sport. Facilities for most sports are available for the visitor. Tennis, squash, riding, swimming and golf (there are a dozen golf courses in Harare alone) are offered. Lake McIlwaine, 35 km west of the city, provides opportunities for fishing for bream and tigerfish and boating, as well as game-viewing. Fishing licences are obtainable from National Parks staff. There is a racecourse and motor-racing circuit.

Shopping: There are numerous curio and local craft shops in the city which sell local soapstone and wooden carvings and sculptures, Zimbabwean copperware and basketware, traditional ceramic pots, skins, ivory jewellery, gemstones and woven wall hangings. Beautifully carved soapstone chess sets are sold by young men who will approach you on street corners. The prices are considerably lower than in the shops, although some bargaining may be necessary. The Harare Weaving Centre produces lovely hand-woven fabrics, as well as woven sheepswool rugs using natural dyes for the designs. Hopefully, Zimbabwe will soon follow Kenya's example and impose a total ban on the sale of animal skins.

Places of interest beyond the immediate city area include the Ewanrigg Botanical Gardens, at their best in the flowering months of July and August, and Lake McIlwaine, with its prolific birdlife, where recreational and camping facilities are provided.

Tourist Information: Department of Tourism, Cecil House, 95 Stanley Ave, PO Box 8052, Harare; tel: 706511.

Bulawayo

With streets wide enough to turn around a full span of oxen, the city centre remains transfixed in its colonial past.

The Eastern Highlands

Although the second largest commercial and industrial centre, the signs of a slumping economy are very apparent in Bulawayo. There are numerous empty shops in the main streets and 'for sale' signs outside houses in the white suburbs.

The black townships, which have benefitted from a more liberal and concerned approach to housing than any other urban area, have not yet reached the desperate state of the Harare townships. Nevertheless, the population has increased by more than a third, and the war made overcrowding worse.

The city offers good accommodation and shopping facilities and houses the National Museum situated in Centenary Park near the city centre. The Mzilikazi Arts and Crafts Centre products local pottery and sculpture. The centre can be visited during the mornings. Items of historical interest are on display at Government House in Stanley Avenue, open daily to visitors. The Zimbabwean Railways Museum houses exhibits dating back to the earliest days of colonial history.

Bulawayo is a good base from which to visit the south-west of the country. Nearby tourist attractions are the Khami Ruins (22 km west) and the Matopos National Park (32 km south). It is believed that the Khami Ruins date from the 17th century and were inhabited by the Rozwi people until about 1830. A small museum displays relics found at the site. The Matopos Hills are rich in historical associations: Cecil Rhodes is buried here and the Matabele fought here in 1896 in the war of resistance. The park is an area of wind-sculptured granite hills with massive balancing rock formations alternating with thickly-wooded valleys. It supports a wide variety of animals including the white rhino and the world's largest concentration of black eagles. Many of the caves in the Park have been decorated with Bushmen paintings.

Mutare

Situated in the eastern highlands only kilometres from the Mozambique border, Mutare became a ghost town during the war. The town lies in a valley surrounded by wooded hills and lays a strong claim to being Zimbabwe's most beautiful town. It offers a choice of modern hotels and camping facilities. Mutare is very close to the tourist attractions of the eastern highlands, and the road to the Vumba mountains begins its scenic climb a few kilometres outside the town.

Gweru

Geographically the most central city in Zimbabwe, Gweru is an important communications and industrial centre. For the black population of Zimbabwe. Gweru is perhaps best known for its prison, where many of the country's nationalist leaders were incarcerated. The town has good shopping and hotel facilities.

Nyanga Mountains

Accessible from Harare or Mutare, this area of the eastern highlands region is one of the most beautiful and provides good hiking and excellent trout fishing. Mt Inyangani is the highest mountain in Zimbabwe. The Nyanga National Park has lodge accommodation. Otherwise there is a wide choice of hotels and camping sites.

Great Zimbabwe

Great Zimbabwe, 30 km from Masvingo, has intrigued archaeologists since their 'discovery' by the settlers in 1898. The ruins comprise a 100 m wide walled enclosure (The Temple), a granite hill supporting extensive building (The Acropolis), and, lying between, an expanse of less spectacular ruins in what is called the Valley of Ruins (which inspired the Dead City in Rider Haggard's *She*). Zimbabwe's walls are made from hand-trimmed granite blocks standing as much as 10 m high and 6 m wide, without the aid of mortar. The Temple is irregularly elliptical in shape. Its exterior wall is more than 250 m in circumference, and for some 70 m runs roughly parallel with an interior wall to form the Parallel Passage. Within these walls stands the Conical Tower. The oldest part of Zimbabwe is the Acropolis Hill, which is thought to have been a special and important religious centre and possibly the burial place of great chiefs. The Temple was probably the royal palace.

The ruins are in a national park of some 1,786 acres and are protected by the Historical Monuments Commission. Near them is a museum which displays many fascinating objects recovered from diggings in the vicinity.

Another attraction near the ruins is a modern reconstruction of a 19th century Karanga village where everything from the huts to the utensils authentically depicts how the Karanga people lived.

Victoria Falls

The 1,700m wide crest of the world-famous Falls is divided into five separate waterfalls: Devil's Cataract, Main Falls (the most impressive stretch), Horseshoe Falls, Rainbow Falls and Eastern Cataract. In mid-April the Zambezi River is swelled by the summer rains, and the Falls are at their most impressive, with water cascading over the brink of the Falls and plunging through eight narrow gorges below.

The Victoria Falls National Park spreads 60 km along the Zimbabwean bank of the Zambezi. It is well populated with Zimbabwe's national animal, the sable antelope, which is relatively rare in other parts of Africa, and with buffalo, kudu, waterbuck, bushbuck, impala and warthog. Elephant and other animals can be seen on the banks of the Zambezi by taking a cruise upstream.

Near the hotels is a replica of a 19th century Matabele village which is open to visitors throughout the week. Craftsmen can be seen making various instruments and curios which are for sale.

Lake Kariba

Lake Kariba was originally built to provide hydro-electric power for the industries of Zimbabwe and Zambia. The lake was completed in 1961 and the Zambezi valley inundated, displacing people of the Batonka tribe as well as thousands of animals. The lakeshore has been rapidly developed to provide sophisticated amenities for tourists. Beyond the developed area of Kariba township (several modern hotels) the lake extends westwards for 281 km. This is largely untouched wilderness with facilities provided by small lakeshore resorts and safari companies. There is a regular car-ferry service between Kariba township and Mlibizi on the western tip of the lake. The voyage takes approximately 19 hours in each direction. Along the southern shore of the lake is the 1,370 sq km Matusadona National Park.

There are two unusual island resorts situated just off the Matusadona lakeshore. Spurwing Island and Fothergill Island. Accommodation is in luxury tents or Batonka-style huts and game-viewing may be enjoyed either on the islands, or by boat along the Matusadona shoreline. Communciations with Kariba may be arranged by launch or float-plane.